Para Pablo y Rocío:
con mucha suerte de
tenerlos como amigos.
cariñosamente, de,
Mónica
12/30/06

Streams of Silver

Streams of Silver

Six Contemporary Women Writers from Argentina

Mónica R. Flori

Lewisburg
Bucknell University Press
London: Associated University Presses

Associated University Presses
440 Forsgate Drive
Cranbury, NJ 08512

Associated University Presses
25 Sicilian Avenue
London WC1A 2QH, England

Associated University Presses
P.O. Box 338, Port Credit
Mississauga, Ontario
Canada L5G 4L8

The paper used in this publication meets the requirements
of the American National Standard for Permanence of Paper
for Printed Library Materials Z39.48–1984.

Library of Congress Cataloging-in-Publication Data

Streams of silver : six contemporary women writers from Argentina /
Mónica R. Flori [compiler and translator].
    p. cm.
Includes bibliographical references and index.
ISBN 0-8387-5283-7 (alk. paper)
    1. Argentine fiction—Women authors—History and criticism.
2. Argentine fiction—20th century—History and criticism. 3. Women
authors, Argentine—20th century—Interviews. I. Flori, Mónica
Roy, 1944–
PQ7633.S77   1995
863—dc20   94-34079
                                                                              CIP

PRINTED IN THE UNITED STATES OF AMERICA

Barrabás llegó a la familia por vía marítima, anotó la niña Clara con su delicada caligrafía. Ya entonces tenía el hábito de escribir las cosas importantes y más tarde, cuando se quedó muda, escribía también las trivialidades, sin sospechar que cincuenta años después, sus cuadernos me servirían para rescatar la memoria del pasado y para sobrevivir a mi propio espanto.

(Barrabás came to the family by way of the sea, wrote the child Clara in her delicate calligraphy. At that time, she already had the habit of writing down important matters, and afterward, when she became mute, she also recorded the trivialities, never suspecting that fifty years later, I would use her notes to reclaim the memory of the past and survive my own horror.)

—Isabel Allende,
La casa de los espíritus

La mujer envuelta en velos era su guía. No era posible perderse. En cierto momento ella suspendería su marcha y las dos se fundirían en un gran abrazo: madre-hija. Y esa fusión habría de significar que había alcanzado la meta. El destino final.

(The woman draped in veils was her guide. It was not possible to get lost. At a given moment she would stop walking and both would fuse in a big embrace: mother-daughter. And that fusion would mean that she had reached the goal. The final destination.)

—Alina Diaconú,
El penúltimo viaje

Contents

Preface

Latin American women writers have a long tradition dating back to Sor Juana Inés de la Cruz in colonial times. Although Latin American women have been writing for centuries, they have not been duly recognized by literary historians, the literary world, or readers, who have not had much access to their writings. Women writers have been the forgotten ones when it comes to being published, reviewed, and awarded prizes.

At the same time, the continent's male writers have been recognized internationally by intellectuals, the media, and the reading public. Since the sixties and seventies, the literary "boom" in Latin America has brought to the forefront writers like Julio Cortázar, Mario Vargas Llosa, Gabriel García Márquez, Juan Rulfo, and Carlos Fuentes. Women writers were not able to break into the literary forefront at a time when Latin American fiction was being recognized around the world. Even graduate students of Latin American literature in the sixties and seventies, when the "boom" was born and developed, were kept in ignorance about the excellent women writers during that time. Their studies reflected a traditional patriarchal view of culture and literature. That situation changed in the eighties, however, when an interest in women's studies signaled new critical paths in the study of literature and deeply affected our concept of Latin American literature and the established literary canon.

In 1980 I traveled to Mexico City. While browsing in bookstores, I made a discovery that would change the direction and focus of my reading, writing, and teaching literature. I picked up fiction by two Mexican women writers, Rosario Castellanos and Elena Poniatowska, which were on display, and discovered the paintings of Frida Kahlo. After my introduction to this outstanding Mexican work, I started looking for fiction by women writers from other Latin American countries. During the eighties my search bore fruit. I was drawn into the fictional world of Marta Traba and Luisa Valenzuela (Argentina), Armonía Somers and Cristina Peri Rossi

(Uruguay), Isabel Allende (Chile), Clarice Lispector (Brazil), and Rosario Ferré (Puerto Rico), among others. I found the literary value of their writings to be as significant as that of their male counterparts, and at the same time, unique. I was dismayed that their recognition was confined to their countries of origin or, at best, to the Spanish-speaking world.

Although critical studies, translation, and distribution abroad were on the rise for male writers, very little criticism had been published on the work of women writers. What had been written was very short, taking the form of a review or article in journals and a chapter in a collection.[1] Even today, there has been no consistent effort to translate their works into English or any other language. A positive sign has been the publication of several literary anthologies dedicated exclusively to women writers and featuring selections of fiction in English translation.[2]

During the eighties, encouraged by the interest the topic was starting to generate and a month-long interdisciplinary seminar on women's studies at Lewis & Clark College sponsored by the National Endowment for the Humanities, I wrote and published articles on women writers while teaching their works in my literature courses. This new orientation of my scholarship and teaching made me aware of the sparse distribution of their work in the United States, with the exception of Isabel Allende's fiction.

Streams of Silver: Six Contemporary Women Writers from Argentina is my response to the dearth of literary studies on Latin American women writers, especially Argentine writers. Though there are many distinguished writers throughout the continent, I decided to focus on the writings by women of just one country so that I could include in-depth studies of their works as well as interviews. Furthermore, by concentrating on one country, I hoped to find a common bond among the selected writers, since they shared similar cultural and sociopolitical backgrounds. I chose Argentina because Buenos Aires is one of the cultural centers of Latin America, a city that has the continent's major presses, publishing houses, and a tradition of female intellectuals like Victoria Ocampo, editor of the respected literary journal *Sur* and the first woman to be admitted to the Argentine Academy of Letters.

The rich cultural environment of Buenos Aires has encouraged the development of writers like the six featured in this volume. Buenos Aires hosts an annual international book fair, which sponsors publications, book exhibits, and sales, and offers panels and other literary events that promote the works of established and young writers. There was also a personal appeal in writing about Argentine writers. I am a native of neighboring Uruguay, and the cultural traditions of that area are part of my own background. And, researching women from the River Plate area, where Buenos Aires and my own city, Montevideo, are located, became in some ways a journey toward myself and my cultural tradition.

Argentina attracted worldwide attention because of the atrocities committed by its military dictatorship from 1976 to 1983 on the Argentine people. These writers feature three important sociopolitical periods in their works: the two Perón eras (1946–55 and 1973–76) and the recent military dictatorship known as the Proceso (1976–83), which created upheavals in the whole of Argentine society, affecting the writers' lives and their work. Although these periods were characterized by dictatorship, repression, and censorship, there is a marked difference between them, apparent in their literary representation. During the Peronist eras, dissidents were faced with persecution that included torture, imprisonment, and exile. But during the Proceso any citizen was subject to the systematic abuse of human rights, and the disappearance of thousands of citizens created an all-encompassing atmosphere of terror. This widespread barbaric repression, which acquired the characteristics of genocide, called for a different response from writers, as we shall see in this book.

It struck me that although Argentine writers, including female writers, were dealing with issues directly related to the sociopolitical climate, there was no concerted effort to find out more about them and their work. In my conversations with the writers and in my essays on their work, I attempt to show the effect of the military repression on their careers and their writing.

As I researched Argentine women writers, I became aware that I would need to be selective if I wanted my volume to be thorough and do justice to the writers represented. I chose six writers whose works have been recognized in Argentina and who, in my opinion, have made a significant contribution to Argentine letters and Latin American literature. Although my original idea had been to focus on younger writers not yet "consecrated" in Argentina, I changed my mind and decided that to have a broader understanding, it was important to choose writers who represented different generations.

Therefore, my volume starts with two mature writers: Alicia Jurado (b. 1922), who started publishing in 1961 and has written six books of fiction, three biographies, and three volumes of memoirs; and Elvira Orphée (b. 1930), who has published nine works of fiction since 1956 and is currently writing a novel. They are followed by two experimental writers who have been prolific in a relatively short period: Alina Diaconú (b. 1945), who published seven novels between 1975 and 1992, and Alicia Steimberg (b. 1933), who has published seven works since 1971. Finally,

I selected Cecilia Absatz (b. 1943) and Reina Roffé (b. 1951), who have each published three novels since 1973, and whose writing is highly skill-ful and promising.

I chose not to include more well-known writers such as Luisa Valenzuela, Griselda Gambaro, and Marta Traba, because they are already known in the United States. Most texts on Latin American women writ-ers feature their work. Luisa Valenzuela and Isabel Allende have entire volumes dedicated to the study of their works.[3] Valenzuela, Gambaro, and Traba are also featured in Evelyn Picon Garfield's work, *Women's Voices from Latin America*. If I had included these writers, my efforts would have duplicated those of other critics. It was foremost in my mind to introduce writers whose voices have not been heard and who were not so well known.

Another reason I chose the writers I did is that the interviews are very important to my project, and that limited my scope to living writers. When I first went to Argentina, my idea was to do a volume of interviews. Later, the project grew to include critical essays as well. I also decided to feature writers who were living in Argentina, and preferably those who had stayed during the Proceso. I also chose writers who dealt with women's or feminist issues and sociopolitical problems in their work. I was careful to include older writers, representative of Argentina during Peronism, as well as the younger generation who lived through the Proceso and reflect this experience in their works. I carefully observed the roles of these writ-ers in the Buenos Aires cultural scene. I found that their work had been recognized by literary prizes and positive reviews by respected critics. Most of the writers I selected participate regularly in the Buenos Aires Interna-tional Book Fair in panel discussions and book presentations. And finally, I talked to local editors, writers, and critics, who suggested some of the authors for my volume.

This volume introduces the English-reading public to the impressive work of six Argentine women writers. It is intended for readers interested in Latin American studies, Hispanic literatures and cultures, women's stud-ies, Argentine studies, humanities, and sociology. Each section opens with a brief biography to acquaint the reader with the accomplishments of the given writer. The biography is followed by a critical essay and an inter-view. The essay discusses the writer's main works, themes, and literary techniques. Since these works are not available in English, I have included my own translations of quotations from them, to give the reader a sam-pling of the writings. I have also shared reviews of the works published in Argentine newspapers and journals, collected during my research. These reviews offer another perspective on the work and indicate how they were received in Argentina at the time of publication. The reaction to the works by Argentine critics seemed invaluable reference material, and I included it whenever it was appropriate.

The interviews were all conducted in Buenos Aires at the writers' homes. I wanted to see them in the environment in which they wrote. I first interviewed each writer in 1987, transcribed and translated the interviews into English, and sent them back to the writers for their approval and comments. In 1989 I returned to Buenos Aires and interviewed them once more to update the information. I found that several had published works of fiction during those two years, so I was able to include comments about their recent work. I returned to Buenos Aires in 1993 and have included studies of the writers' most recent novels (Alina Diaconú's *Los devorados*, 1992, and Alicia Steimberg's *Cuando digo Magdalena*, 1992). At that time I also updated Reina Roffé's interview, since she was residing abroad in 1989 and I was unable to update it then.

I asked all the writers several of the same questions about their lives, writing, and literary influences. I also asked them to comment on the impact of three issues on their work as women writers in contemporary Argentina: (1) how feminism had affected their lives and work, (2) their ideas on female writing and whether their own writing was different from mainstream male writing, and (3) how recent Argentine political developments, meaning dictatorship and censorship, had influenced their personal lives and their writing. The rest of the questions focused on specific works, themes, and styles and their differing points of view on narrative creation and the art of fiction. Each section ends with a bibliography of their works and secondary sources both in English, when available, and in Spanish. All translations of interviews, quotations from the authors' works, and quotations from criticism and reviews are my own.

Acknowledgments

I would like to express my gratitude and indebtedness to Alicia Jurado, Elvira Orphée, Alina Diaconú, Alicia Steimberg, Cecilia Absatz, and Reina Roffé for the time they gave me while I was conducting my research and interviews; for their warmth, graciousness, and, especially, for their friendship. After having worked so closely with each one of them, researching and studying their work and critical material on it, I feel that a special bond will always link me to them.

I also want to offer my appreciation to the Lewis & Clark College Faculty Research Grants, which assisted me with expenses incurred in the preparation of my manuscript, to Maarit Reed for typing the early drafts, and to Rebecca Banyas and Lola Ready for their help with the final drafts.

And finally, my appreciation to my husband, Frank, for his understanding and support during these past years spent researching and writing, as well as traveling to Argentina.

The following publishers and authors have generously given permission to use extended quotations from copyrighted works: From *La cárcel y los hierros*, by Alicia Jurado. Copyright © 1961 by Editorial Goncourt and reverted to Alicia Jurado in 1971. From *En soledad vivía*, by Alicia Jurado. Copyright © 1967 by Editorial Losada. From *Los rostros del engaño*, by Alicia Jurado. Copyright © 1968 by Editorial Losada. From *El cuarto mandamiento*, by Alicia Jurado. Copyright © 1974 by Emecé Editores. From *Los hechiceros de la tribu*, by Alicia Jurado. Copyright © 1980 by Emecé Editores. From *El mundo de la palabra*, by Alicia Jurado. Copyright © 1990 by Emecé Editores. From *Dos veranos*, by Elvira Orphée. Copyright © 1956 by Editorial Sudamericana. From *Uno*, by Elvira Orphée. Copyright © 1961 by Fabril Editora and reverted to Elvira Orphée in 1971. From *Aire tan dulce*, by Elvira Orphée. Copyright © 1966 by Editorial Sudamericana and renewed 1977 by Monte Avila Editores. From

En el fondo, by Elvira Orphée. Copyright © 1969 by Emecé Editores. From *La última conquista de El Angel* by Elvira Orphée. Copyright © 1977 by Monte Avila Editores and renewed 1984 by Javier Vergara Editor. From *Las viejas fantasiosas*, by Elvira Orphée. Copyright © 1981 by Emecé Editores. From *La Señora*, by Alina Diaconú. Copyright © 1975 by Rodolfo Alonso Editor. From *Buenas noches, profesor*, by Alina Diaconú. Copyright © 1978 by Editorial Corregidor. From *Enamorada del muro*, by Alina Diaconú. Copyright © 1981 by Editorial Corregidor. From *Cama de ángeles*, by Alina Diaconú. Copyright © 1983 by Emecé Editores. From *Los ojos azules*, by Alina Diaconú. Copyright © 1986 by Editorial Fraterna. From *El penúltimo viaje*, by Alina Diaconú. Copyright © 1989 by Javier Vergara Editor. From *Los devorados*, by Alina Diaconú. Copyright © 1992 by Editorial Atlántida. From *Músicos y relojeros*, by Alicia Steimberg. Copyright © 1971 by Centro Editor de América Latina. From *La loca 101*, by Alicia Steimberg. Copyright © 1973 by Ediciones De La Flor. From *Su espíritu inocente*, by Alicia Steimberg. Copyright © 1981 by Editorial Pomaire and reverted to Alicia Steimberg in 1991. From *Como todas las mañanas*, by Alicia Steimberg. Copyright © 1983 by Editorial Celtia. From *El árbol del placer*, by Alicia Steimberg. Copyright © 1986 by Editorial Emecé. From *Cuando digo Magdalena*, by Alicia Steimberg. Copyright © 1992 by Editorial Planeta. From *Feiguele y otras mujeres*, by Cecilia Absatz. Copyright © 1976 by Ediciones De La Flor. From *Té con canela*, by Cecilia Absatz. Copyright © 1982 by Editorial Sudamericana. From *Los años pares*, by Cecilia Absatz. Copyright © 1985 by Editorial Legasa and reverted to Cecilia Absatz in 1993. From *Llamado al puf*, by Reina Roffé. Copyright © 1973 by Editorial Pleamar. From *Monte de Venus*, by Reina Roffé. Copyright © 1976 by Editorial Corregidor. From *La rompiente*, by Reina Roffé. Copyright © 1987 by Puntosur Editores and reverted to Reina Roffé in 1987.

I have included in this book revisions of earlier versions of my work published in the following journals:

Chapter 1 contains interview material from "Entrevista a Alicia Jurado," *Hispania* 73 (March 1990): 149–51.

Chapter 2 contains interview material from "Entrevista a Elvira Orphée," *Hispania* 72 (September 1989): 605–7.

Chapter 3 contains interview material from "Entrevista a Alina Diaconú," *Letras femeninas* 15 (1988): 97–103, and "Entrevista a Alina Diaconú," *Alba de América* 9 (July 1991): 381–86. It contains revised material from "Autoritarismo, exilio y recreación feminista en *El penúltimo viaje* de Alina Diaconú," *Alba de América* 10 (July 1992): 183–94; and

"La articulización de lo inexpresable: metaforización del cuerpo femenino en *Los ojos azules* de Alina Diaconú." *Alba de América* 12 (July 1994).

Chapter 4 contains interview material from "Entrevista a Alicia Steimberg," *Chasqui: Revista de literatura latinoamericana* 17 (November 1988): 85–89.

Chapter 5 contains interview material from "Entrevista a Cecilia Absatz," *Chasqui: Revista de literatura latinoamericana* 17 (November 1988): 89–92, and revised material from "Identidad y discurso de la femineidad en *Los años pares* de Cecilia Absatz," *Explicación de textos literarios* 22 (1993–94): 87–97.

Chapter 6 contains interview material from "Entrevista a Reina Roffé," *Alba de América* 6 (July 1988): 423–28.

Streams of Silver

Introduction

Although there were women writers after the independence period (1810–25), such as Mariquita Sánchez (1786–?), who wrote epistolary and autobiographical literature, most women were illiterate when Argentine literature was being born. It was a time when women considered educated were trained exclusively in practical matters of running a household. Since the early nineteenth century, however, there have been women who have overcome these cultural obstacles and written in newspapers and magazines.

During the romantic period in literature, several women writers, such as Eduarda Mansilla (1834–1912), Juana Manso (1819–75), and Rosa Guerra (?–1864), stand out. The most important nineteenth-century woman writer in Argentina was Juana Manuela Gorriti (1818–92), author of numerous works that portrayed the customs, values, and historical events of that era. These women had important social roles, not only as writers but also as teachers, intellectuals, and feminists. It is because of their work that women were allowed to have a greater social role.

The beginning of the twentieth century ushered in more social gains. Most women writers became educators, inspired by President Domingo Faustino Sarmiento's liberal reforms of the previous century and by the work of foreign women intellectuals living in Argentina, such as Peruvian writer Clorinda Matto de Turner. Although it was the modernist era, Ema de la Barra's novel *Stella* (1905), which criticized the education of women in Argentina and was published under a male pseudonym, became popular.[1] About this time, the poetry of Alfonsina Storni (1892–1938) and her ideas about the role of women and women writers in society brought about a major change in women and literature. Her poetry differed from the previous romantic and didactic writing by women. It was marked by a search for identity and social criticism, especially in terms of the silence imposed on women in a male-dominated society. She also stands as the first woman to earn a living from her writing. Storni's concerns about a woman's place in society are also found in the work of Herminia Brumana (1901–54), who offered solutions to problems related to marriage, work, and schooling. A teacher and writer, she emphasized the value of education as a tool for women to overcome their limited positions in society.

In the modern period, new directions in fiction began to dominate. For the purpose of this brief summary, one can divide Argentine modern and contemporary fiction into three periods: 1930 to 1955, 1955 to 1970, and 1970 to the present. The period between 1930 and 1955 was rich in literary figures, and the publishing market in Argentina was expanding. The end of the twenties and beginning of the thirties saw a renewal in world literature, an event that influenced Argentine fiction. At this time the Boedo and Florida literary groups were developing their work. Ultraism superseded naturalism and modernism, which had greatly influenced Argentine literature.[2] The main exponents of ultraism were Roberto Arlt (1900–1942) and Macedonio Fernández (1874–1952), who questioned the Argentine dream of prosperity. Arlt, along with Jorge Luis Borges (1899–1987), developed a literature of social and metaphysical fantasy.

The woman writer most directly connected to the literary groups and the vanguard publications of the period was Norah Lange (1906–72). She incorporated Henry James's point-of-view techniques in her novels, which dealt with women interacting effectively in a male world. She herself frequented traditional male literary circles and was a protégé of Borges. Lange was also known as one of the better writers of autobiography, a traditional genre in Argentine literature. While famous male autobiographers, such as Manuel Belgrano, Juan Bautista Alberdi, and Domingo Faustino Sarmiento, wrote to justify their personal or political trajectories, women writers like Lange focused on evoking the past. That tradition is continued today by one of the writers in this volume, Alicia Jurado.

The fiction that developed between 1930 and 1955 became more psychological and was represented by Eduardo Mallea (b. 1903) and Ernesto Sábato (b. 1911). By this time, women of the upper classes had acquired certain privileges. But more than any other person, it was one aristocratic woman, an intellectual by the name of Victoria Ocampo (1890–1979), who enhanced the situation of other women through education. In 1931 she became founder and editor of the literary journal *Sur*. Through this journal, and through Ocampo's editorial efforts, cultivated Argentines were introduced to world and Argentine literature and culture. The most prestigious Argentine writers contributed—Borges, Mallea, Sábato, and Julio Cortázar. In 1977 she became the first woman to be admitted to the Argentine Academy of Letters. (Alicia Jurado was to follow in 1980.)

Ocampo left a rich legacy of autobiography, as well as her *Testimonials* (1924–79), which include her letters, lectures, and essays. Ocampo was a feminist both in her literary work and political activism. An admirer of Virginia Woolf, she believed that women wrote from a female perspective that was apparent in their particular style. *Sur* managed to inspire a group of women novelists who emerged during the forties: Silvina Ocampo (b. 1906; Victoria's sister, married to Adolfo Bioy Casares), Estela Canto (b. 1920), and Luisa Mercedes Levinson (1914–89). These writers, concerned with language and style, belonged to the upper class and to the *Sur* literary group. They write psychological narratives, and their use of fantasy links them to writers like Borges and Bioy Casares (b. 1915).

After 1955 Argentina experienced a cultural renaissance. New publishing houses and literary prizes sprang forth, which, coupled with new marketing techniques to attract readers and make books more accessible, gave young writers the opportunity to publish and become known. Stylistic concerns were put aside, and the sociopolitical reality occupied the foreground. A new journal, *Contorno* (1953), directed by Ismael and David Viñas, brought together writers who questioned the nature of reality and were inspired by silenced figures like Arlt. These writers took their material from the Argentine historical reality, especially the repression and censorship they felt during Perón's first regime (1946–55).

Like their predecessors, who were greatly influenced by European writers, the writers of the generation of 1955 were influenced by French existentialist figures, like Albert Camus and Jean-Paul Sartre, and *nouveau roman* novelists, like Alain Robbe-Grillet. Nevertheless, they considered American writers like Ernest Hemingway and William Faulkner their mentors. We can perceive two tendencies among these writers—those who felt responsibility toward their social reality and those whose fiction was influenced by psychoanalysis or existentialism. Mainstream writers of this generation include Julio Cortázar (1914–88), Marco Denevi (b. 1922), Antonio Di Benedetto (b. 1922), Bernardo Verbitzky (b. 1907), David Viñas (b. 1929), and Héctor Murena (b. 1923).

This was also a rich period for women writers. Two such writers who started publishing between 1955 and 1965, Alicia Jurado (b. 1922) and Elvira Orphée (b. 1930) are featured in this volume. Others who began to publish in this period include Beatriz Guido (1925–88), María Angélica Bosco (b. 1917), Marta Lynch (1929–86), and Syria Poletti (b. 1919). As social conditions for women changed and publishing became more accessible, women writers proliferated. During Victoria Ocampo's time women writers were mainly from the upper class; now they came from the middle class as well. The characteristics of their writing varies—from political to personal themes, from rural to urban settings. But one trait—neorealism—permeates their work. With the exception of Silvina Ocampo and Levinson and a few others, neorealism characterizes writers of the generation of 1955. Women got the right to vote in 1947, and the late fifties began an era of democracy. This manifested itself in political themes. A change took place in women's writing that paralleled the gains women were making in their public lives. These writers had another important characteristic in common: Although the previous generation believed that women writers wrote from a female perspective, the writers of the fifties discarded this idea and focused on the importance of being a good writer, regardless of gender. Many of their novels use a male narrator or a third-person narration in contrast with the previous generation's first-person female narrators.

Beatriz Guido was the first woman writer to systematically deal with political themes. Her novels are set during the Peronist years and present upper-class characters whose lives and conflicts are intertwined with historical events. Others who have written about the Peronist era in their fiction are Elvira Orphée, Marta Lynch, and, in a more oblique way, Alicia Jurado. During this period some writers produced works that do not fit into the realist framework, such as Olga Orozco (b. 1920) and María Granata (b. 1921). Most of Orphée's material is itself associated more with fantasy.

During the sixties, Julio Cortázar, Gabriel García Márquez, and Carlos Fuentes emerged, creating what became known as the "boom" in Latin American literature, especially fiction. The boom had repercussions in Argentina. Under the influence of Julio Cortázar, experimental styles and language and literary techniques proliferated. Borges continued to influence writers, as he has every generation of contemporary writers. There was a reevaluation of Arlt and his existential expressionism, as well. Several important women writers born between 1930 and 1945 started publishing in 1966: Marta Traba (1930–83), Luisa Valenzuela (b. 1938), Tununa Mercado (b. 1939), and Hebe Uhart (b. 1939). They were interested in the female condition, inspired by the resurgence of feminism in the sixties. They often portrayed the woman writer in their fiction. The works of Traba and Valenzuela also deal with repression, political injustice, and death, and indict societies' dehumanization of Southern Cone populations.

The generation of the seventies was composed of writers born between 1943 and 1950 who started to publish between 1965 and 1973. Their literary genealogy can be traced from "José Hernández to Sarmiento, from Macedonio Fernández to Roberto Arlt, from Borges to David Viñas, from Leopoldo Marechal to Ernesto Sábato, from Cortázar to Haroldo Conti."[3] These writers, however, do not consider themselves part of a literary movement. Rather, they view themselves as individuals who practice their craft in solitude, a view that is probably a result of the persecution of intellectuals in the seventies. Critics have mentioned repeatedly that in addition to being linked by age and common cultural, economic, and socio-historical experiences, these writers also share the theme of marginality in their works. They produced their works during a period of dictatorship and a troubled return to democracy, and felt alienated and on the fringe of society. Marginality also has historical roots in the works of writers like Arlt, Sábato, and Cortázar. These writers present other common themes—Peronism, repression, and decadence—through characters who are constantly searching for their personal identity and a national cultural identity in an unstable and violent society. Social reality left them with this task of reconstructing their fractured private and social identities.

Current mainstream Argentine fiction points in three important directions. One is psychological, represented by Fernando Sánchez Sorondo (b. 1930) and Marcos Aguinis (b. 1935), among others. The second is experimental (Ricardo Piglia, b. 1942); the third is realist, and focuses on the sociohistorical context (Jorge Asís, b. 1946). Women writers seem to go in all three directions. In addition, there is a confluence of the various trends that developed in generations before. The writers combine a concern for the female condition and the psychological; this is especially apparent in fiction dealing with childhood and adolescence and, in some cases, fictionalized autobiography (Diaconú, Steimberg, Absatz, Roffé). The influence of psychoanalysis is also apparent. The psychoanalyst becomes an important character, and analytic techniques become tools in the characters' journeys (Steimberg, Diaconú). Following Cortázar's innovations, which changed Argentine fiction, women writers also experiment with style, language, and narrative techniques.

All these writers lived under a military dictatorship (1976–83) just when they were beginning to publish. This sociopolitical element deeply marks their writing. The effects of repression and censorship are evident in both the content and style of their works. Some chose to conceal their ideas with metaphors (Diaconú, Steimberg, Absatz). Younger writers, like Roffé, chose silence, self-censorship, exile, and the use of a highly fragmented and experimental structure to conceal the real story, as women writers found themselves targets of government censorship.

In the following biographical sketches, critical essays, and conversations, the reader will become acquainted with the work of contemporary writers of the generations of 1955 and 1970. Alicia Jurado and Elvira Orphée (of the generation of 1955) and Alina Diaconú, Alicia Steimberg, Cecilia Absatz, and Reina Roffé (of the generation of 1970) critique, deconstruct, and recreate reality. At the same time, their fiction shows how the creative process can be altered by a violent, patriarchal, and authoritarian society. These writers capture and reflect the political and social conditions to demythologize and reconstruct them through a female vision. They attempt to transcend the obscurity and limitations imposed by mainstream society and literary groups. Their ideology and gender put them at odds with the establishment, and their discourse offers a unique interpretation of reality that earns them a place in the cultural and literary tradition of Argentina and Latin America.

1
Alicia Jurado

Alicia Jurado was born in Buenos Aires, Argentina, on 22 May 1922, and grew up on her family's estate in the province of Buenos Aires. She received a master's degree in natural sciences in 1947 from the University of Buenos Aires, where she also completed doctoral course work in that field.

Jurado received a Guggenheim Fellowship in 1966/1967 and a Fulbright Fellowship in 1976. She was president of the Argentine Pen Club in 1976; in 1980 she became a member of the Argentine Academy of Letters. Her essays and bibliographical reviews have appeared in the literary journal *Sur* and in the literary supplements of two Buenos Aires newspapers, *La Nación* and *La Prensa*.

Jurado's twelve books include biographies, short fiction, novels, and three volumes of memoirs. Her biographical works include *Genio y figura de Jorge Luis Borges*, 1964; *Vida y obra de W. H. Hudson*, 1971, which was awarded the 1971 First Municipal Prize in the essay category; and *El escocés errante: Robert B. Cunninghame Graham*, 1979, which received the 1983 First National Prize in Literature in the essay category. Her novel, *En soledad vivía*, 1967, was awarded the First Municipal Prize in the novel category. She also received the 1975 Alberdi-Sarmiento InterAmerican Prize.

Jurado has traveled extensively in Europe, the United States, Canada, Latin America, Japan, India, Indonesia, and Morocco. At present she is president of the Cultural Commission of the Argentine Association for British Culture, an active member of the Argentine Society of Writers, and a frequent lecturer.

Alicia Jurado. Photograph by Alicia Segal.

ESSAY

Alicia Jurado belongs to a group of writers called "the angry ones," or "the patricidals," who started publishing in the 1950s. Two kinds of writing emerged from this group: (1) testimonial literature denouncing social conditions, in works by Beatriz Guido, Marta Lynch, and David Viñas; and (2) fiction that cannot be classified as social or formalist, in novels by Alicia Jurado, Elvira Orphée, Marco Denevi, and Antonio Di Benedetto. These writers share several common characteristics: (1) a rebellion against the aestheticism of their literary predecessors; (2) an existential focus; (3) an interest in the themes of adolescence, generational strife, and women (female characters trapped in patriarchal, bourgeois matrimony); and (4) a desire to depict the effects of Peronism on Argentine society.

Although Alicia Jurado rebels against the aestheticism of her predecessors, her writing is transitional. Like the writing of her predecessors from the anti-Perón literary establishment, her fiction includes refined settings, characters, and language, reflecting cosmopolitanism, cultural refinement, and the bourgeois world of the Buenos Aires Barrio Norte. Like her mentors Jorge Luis Borges, Victoria Ocampo, and Eduardo Mallea, Jurado was a regular contributor to the prestigious *Sur* literary magazine and a leader of the Argentine Society of Writers. In contrast to contemporaries who write socially and politically engaged literature, Jurado believes that the novel should entertain and teach and keep "the reader in suspense and make him think." It should not be too long. She disapproves of formal experiments.[1] Although her fiction may strike the contemporary reader as traditional in form, it does include modern techniques such as shifting points of view, flashbacks and flash-forwards, and metatexts. Distinguished by its impeccable style and linguistic clarity, Jurado's work reveals a profound love of linguistic refinement, and she avoids vulgar language. Her desire to uphold the purity of the Spanish language is reflected in her protagonists, who criticize other characters who are not as careful in their use of language, or who use dialectal forms, neologisms, and erroneous prepositions, tenses, and grammar.

The author's aestheticism is also reflected in her refined characters and their surroundings, a genteel upper-middle-class atmosphere. Her characters are usually in the kind of comfortable surroundings in which Jurado spent most of her life. Jurado's novels reflect her travels, especially in Europe, and include references to her diverse cultural background. As the alter egos of the writer, characters reminisce about their European experiences, and their conversations and thoughts dwell heavily on art, literature, and philosophy. Their vision of the world is often that of thinkers, poets, artists, and, at times, naturalists. Her characters are traditional: Contained within their own social class, they never come into contact with the masses.

Jurado's novels present an existential focus. Like the work of "the angry ones," Jurado's intent is not just to write a story but to render her vision of the world and her internal reality. The quest to transcend present circumstances in a search for universal values is expressed in universal and timeless issues: love, sexuality, marriage, motherhood, literary creativity, and the search for the Absolute.

Like other women writers of her generation, Jurado focuses on women and their psychological struggle in a changing world.

> It was in this period that a number of Argentine women writers began to write about the frustration, anger, and fatalism of their captive sisters. In the early novels and stories of Silvina Bullrich, Marta Lynch, and María Angélica Bosco, the heroines suffer, endure, and, at times, rebel by taking a lover to help their self-images; seldom do they slam the door to Nora's "doll house."[2]

The protagonists in Jurado's novels are usually, but not exclusively, females whom she endows with many of her own intellectual traits and aspirations. Though they are part of traditional Hispanic society, Jurado's women question the status quo, rebel against taboos that subjugate them, and reject the double standard of female/male sexual behavior. They question social institutions and mores, such as marriage and monogamy. Many feel trapped by marriage and seek a way out by taking lovers, divorcing their husbands, abandoning their families, or following their own intellectual pursuits. In a search for their identity, these women address the erotic and emotional needs unmet in their marriages. Jurado's novels portray this with varying degrees of frankness. Her female characters are often intellectually and culturally superior to her male characters. Although Jurado's female characters lead conventional lives, they rebel against imposed social expectations and roles. As pointed out by Lewald, Jurado belongs to a group of women writers who denounce the limitations of woman's situation.

"The angry ones" share the experience of having lived through the era of Peronism, which developed while they were in their formative years. "The fact that profound forces of social change had been set into motion or at least accelerated in Perón's Argentina: that these forces should manifest themselves in literature through an intense interest in generational strife, adolescence and sex should come as no surprise."[3] Jurado's works, set in the midforties and later when Argentine politics was dominated by Peronism, critically portray a traditional society in transition. The acute social changes and political events shaping the society provide a background for characters who feel these changes only as intrusions in their closed and orderly world. The fictional portrayal of these transformations reflects Jurado's own experiences under Peronism: "[D]uring Perón's dictatorship . . . we had gotten used to living as much as possible on the fringes of the political situation, taking refuge in our private activities and the circle of friends."[4] She focuses on the characters' realization that traditional values are being lost, that the new generation does not live by them anymore. Thus, her novels are somewhat nostalgic. Characters find they no longer fit into modern society, as younger members of their own families do not abide by the old rules. Older characters mourn the past, its traditions and values. On the other hand, Jurado and her enlightened protagonists, nostalgic over the past, are highly critical of the shallowness, hypocrisy, and vanity of their self-contained society. Alienated from their own, they reject the new order imposed by a dictator and the masses supporting him.

La cárcel y los hierros

Jurado's first novel, *La cárcel y los hierros* (The prison and the irons), 1961, takes place in Buenos Aires between 1945 and 1955. A long, first-person flashback to the protagonist's past takes up most of the novel's thirty-one sections. According to Jurado, she chose the first-person narrative "because [she] thought that it was more natural that the minute narration of the protagonist's states of mind should be conveyed by [herself] instead of by a narrator."[5] Luisa's narration covers thirty years, from her early childhood to the present, focusing on the last ten years. During that time she married a man she did not love, had three children, and became trapped in a relationship that grew unbearable:

> Entre él y yo, no existía otro vínculo que el esqueleto de una estructura, como esas casas bombardeadas mantenidas en pie por la armazón de cemento, donde juegan, remotos como siempre, unos niños.

> (Between him and me, no other link existed but the skeleton of a structure, like those bombed-out houses sustained by the cement frame, where some children play, remote as usual.)[6]

However, Luisa discovers true, passionate love with a married man in her circle of acquaintances and has a stormy affair with him. The narration dwells on the protagonist's anguish during the affair, about which one critic remarked:

> For her knowledge of the female soul . . . Alicia Jurado's novel re-
> minds me not of Argentine literature, but of the best era of French
> literature. The description of the impossible love affair between the
> narrator and Diego has the dry, precise, irrefutable lyricism of the best
> passages of *The Princess of Clèves*. Our compatriot has found the exact
> psychological tone that distinguishes Madame De La Fayette. . . .
> The dialogues in *La cárcel y los hierros* are similar in their perfection
> of style, their noble sentiments, and their austerity and discretion.
> Our Madame De La Fayette possesses, also, the most refined feeling
> for nature that one can find in a contemporary novel of the River
> Plate region.[7]

Finally, Luisa resigns herself to giving up Diego and travels on her own to Europe. As prophesied by a psychic friend, it appears that her former lover is waiting for her on the ship. It is ambiguous whether the man is her real lover or a product of her imagination. He is described in general terms: "El hombre estaba de perfil y miraba abstraído el horizonte. Tenía el pelo castaño, lo mismo que los ojos, las manos lindas, la boca firme y un poco triste" (The man was standing at an angle and was watching the horizon absentmindedly. His hair, as well as his eyes, were brown, his hands were nice looking, his mouth was firm and somewhat sad) (188). Narration of the voyage is omitted, but readers can piece it together from the psychic's predictions made throughout the novel. We are left wondering whether the voyage ever really took place or whether it was a projection of the character's emotional state. Technically, this is an effective addition to an otherwise conventional narration.

La cárcel y los hierros was considered autobiographical. Jurado says, however, that while she used many elements from her childhood and adolescence, she portrayed secondary characters as completely opposite to her own parents and husband, so that this story would not be confused with her own life story. One of the most interesting aspects of the novel and a reason it might be considered autobiographical is that it bares the soul of a very refined and cultured woman with emotional, intellectual, and spiritual depth (much like Alicia Jurado herself). The female protagonist stands out from the empty characters who inhabit her world but do not share her cultured background and intellect. Her abandonment of her family to submerge herself in the depths of her passion is convincingly justified by the portrayal of her tedious and unfulfilling marriage and her husband's blatant infidelities. The vibrant and sensitive protagonist vents her feelings and needs, escaping the stultifying marital cage and constraining social demands.

The search for love reveals a second level to the story: the protagonist's quest for rational proof that God exists, something she could not find as an adolescent. As an adult she reads the works of the mystics and other works from the great religions, which inspire her to attempt a mystical union with a deity. Her efforts convince her that God's existence is indubitable, so she revises her former assumptions and embarks on a mystical search for the Absolute. According to Jurado, this novel reflects the metaphysical problems that preoccupied her while she was writing it. She believed then that mysticism would give her access to direct knowledge of an ultimate, spiritual reality transcending matter. She says that she did not realize then that to validate this experience there had to be an external, objective correlation to make the personal experience susceptible to proof.[8] The two levels of the story—the romantic affair and the metaphysical journey—are linked, as the protagonist's obsession with her lover supports her search for the Absolute. This link comes from her belief that true love "se calca sobre el amor místico hacia Dios" (is modeled on mystical love toward God) (18). It is in this way that her quest, and the novel's focus, change to a metaphysical and philosophical search—the mystic's attempt to unite with God. For this reason, she describes her affair as a mystical experience:

> Estoy en un desierto espiritual en el que han perdido su sentido las cosas del pasado y tampoco se perfila claramente la esperanza futura. Es como la noche oscura del alma, de la que hablan los místicos: esa aridez interior que llena el intervalo entre dos deslumbramientos, el último más depurado y perfecto aún que el primero.

> (I'm in a spiritual desert where things from the past have lost their meaning and there is no clearly outlined hope for the future. It's like the dark night of the soul that the mystics talk about: that internal aridity that fills the void between two epiphanies, the last one even more purified and perfect than the first one.) (9)

That she has managed to turn the experience of losing her lover into a liberating one allows her to unveil the mysteries of the human soul and the universe: "La cárcel del cuerpo aprisiona, pero es a un tiempo el instrumento de liberación; sus hierros oprimen, pero sin ellos no encontraríamos la llave" (The body imprisons, but it is at the same time the instrument for liberation; its irons constrain, but without them we would not find the key) (61). We finally understand the allusion to Saint Theresa of Avila's words (in the title and epigraph): "¡Esta cárcel, estos hierros / En que el alma está metida!" (This prison, these irons / Into which the soul is thrust). They express the protagonist's continuous struggle between the spiritual element (the soul) and the physical body (the prison and the irons), which make her prone to obliterate her sense of self (as she did with her lover). She needs to experience spiritual love and attain an understanding of the Absolute because

> desde cualquier parte podría acecharme otro Diego, que no me tentara con la carne sino con el espíritu, y la paciencia de años vería su obra en ruinas. La cárcel cerraría de nuevo sus puertas entreabiertas; los hierros me encadenarían una vez más y yo los amaría.

> (from any place another Diego could lie waiting for [her], who would not tempt [her] with the flesh but with the spirit, and the patience of years would see its work in ruins. The prison would close its half opened doors again; [she] would be chained to the irons once again, and [she] would love them.) (189)

Jurado transforms a psychological novel about a protagonist imprisoned within her gender and class into a tale of freedom. The protagonist transcends her situation through her inner journey into complex philosophical problems. Luisa's newfound freedom has not been attained in vain. Her mystical voyage has transformed her experience of herself and the world: "Detrás de la apariencia se alzaba lo que Es. Y eso, afirmaban los hindúes, era yo" (Behind appearances what Is rose. And that, stated the Hindus, was myself) (53) .

Although the novel deals with esoteric and profound themes, the story maintains its ties with reality by frequent descriptions of actual places in Buenos Aires (Florida Street, Plaza San Martín, the British Tower, Plaza de Mayo), nostalgic locations evoking another era. The changing face of society is inscribed symbolically in the refurbished square (Plaza de Mayo), one of whose side streets bears "el nombre de un coronel desconocido" (the name of an unknown colonel) (181), while the square's name has been changed to that of "un militar oscuro" (an obscure military figure) (181)—an allusion to Plaza de Mayo's becoming "Perón's Plaza" after events on 17 October 1945. A posted sign reminds passersby that "en la nueva Argentina los únicos privilegiados eran los niños" (in the new Argentina the only privileged ones were the children) (182). While the protagonist's personal life is not yet touched directly, these changes will soon transform her world. That the sociopolitical transformation of her society under Peronism is not directly mentioned could be attributed to the prohibition against any critical reference to the regime.

En soledad vivía

En soledad vivía (He lived in solitude), 1967, evolved from Jurado's fascination with Victoria Island, situated in the lake region of southern Argentina near Bariloche. This novel is Jurado's favorite among her own works. It became a pretext, she says, "to describe its beauty and to narrate, by means of the protagonist, my own exaltation before this type of landscape that, for some motive which I don't know how to explain, I always identified with happiness."[9] The novel's twenty chapters, in third-person, describe a love affair amidst the spectacular beauty of the island scenery.

The main character, Andrés, a specialist in agriculture and cattle-breeding, supervises the island, which is part of a national park. He is a sensitive young man who shuts out the world by withdrawing into books and nature. At the start of the novel, he arrives to take up his new post, which he has accepted to get away from an unhappy family situation and a conventional girlfriend. On the island, in contact with the natural world, Andrés experiences a spiritual transformation. After living a year in solitude, Andrés meets Verónica, a married woman with two children, vacationing alone. Although Verónica is cultured and refined, she does not have the spiritual depth that Jurado has given Andrés, who represents the author's concern with spiritual and metaphysical problems. The lovers' passion in the paradisiacal setting is described in terms of a mystical union, reminiscent of *La cárcel y los hierros*. The title *En soledad vivía* refers to a verse from *Cántico espiritual (Spiritual Canticle)* by the Spanish mystic poet St. John of the Cross. According to Jurado, when she visited the island she was preoccupied with mysticism and transferred her state of mind to the male protagonist. Jurado says that he shares her "hope that the confusing states of conscience that nature used to produce in [her] might be insights into a metaphysical reality which might be revealed to [her]."[10] At the end of Verónica's vacation, the lovers part. Verónica returns home, choosing self-sacrifice out of love for her children, giving up any hope of ever seeing her lover again:

> Tiempo de recordar hasta la enajenación, hasta el agotamiento; y también de arrepentirse, acaso, por no haber sido capaz de apurar hasta el fin la copa que le ponían delante, vendiendo su heredad por

el mísero plato de lentejas de algunos pequeños privilegios burgueses, y también vendiéndola por la crédula esperanza de que unos adolescentes serían más felices porque ella bajara para siempre al infierno.

([There would be] time to reminisce until madness and exhaustion took over; and perhaps, also to repent, for not having been able to drink the dregs of the cup placed in front of her, selling out her future for the meager plate of lentils of a few small bourgeois privileges, and also selling out in the credulous hope that a couple of adolescents would be happier if she would descend forever into hell.)[11]

Although the separation is painful, their time together has been a period of growth for both characters. For Andrés the experience is a mystical awakening:

Todo lo que había vivido allí durante un año de asombro, comunión y añoranza, era sólo la espera de Verónica; cuando llegó, justificó su soledad como si se hubiese estado preparando poco a poco para el milagro, en la castidad y la meditación, como un ermitaño que purgaba el pecado de pertenecer al mundo, antes de ser iniciado en los ritos supremos.

(Everything he had experienced there during one year of amazement, communion, and nostalgia was only time spent awaiting Verónica; when she arrived, he justified his solitude as though he had little by little been preparing for the miracle, in chastity and meditation, as a hermit purging the sin of belonging to the world, before being initiated into the supreme rites.) (117)

When Verónica leaves, Andrés understands what he has lost, but he feels ready to face that loss. A year before, in his late twenties and a professional, Andrés was emotionally still an adolescent. After his experience with Verónica, he matures: "Ahora desterrado del bien, tenía la conciencia de su pérdida y también fuerzas para soportarla. Ahora era un hombre" (Now banished from goodness, he was conscious of his loss and he also had the strength to withstand it. Now he was a man) (179). Verónica, although older and more experienced in life than Andrés, discovers that she was capable of experiencing feelings and emotions that had, until then, passed her by.

En soledad vivía expands on *La cárcel y los hierros*. In contrast to the lovers in *La cárcel y los hierros*, the two protagonists, Andrés and Verónica, share a quest for the Absolute. *En soledad vivía* shows that total harmony is attainable in the perfection of human love, reflected in the majestic beauty of the natural world. Here Jurado puts a new slant on the theme of a woman's quest for independence from a failed marriage. In *La cárcel y los hierros* Luisa's infidelity was somewhat justified as a response to her husband's betrayal. In *En soledad vivía,* however, Verónica's husband is not portrayed as a villain but as an everyday person. That Verónica comes to terms with her sexuality and emotions with Andrés evolves from her own needs, not as a result of a previous situation. Jurado portrays women's physiological processes, such as Verónica's pregnancy with Andrés's child and her subsequent abortion. According to Jurado, *En soledad vivía* breaks new ground in its portrayals of eroticism and the vindication of extramarital love. Jurado claims that the erotic is not represented by the descriptions of the female protagonist, but of Andrés. Jurado was surprised that these depictions did not evoke any critical recognition.[12] In fact, Jurado's erotic descriptions are so heavily concealed in refined, poetic language and literary and artistic references that they are scarcely identifiable. Finally, although the ending is traditional—sacrificing the female protagonist's needs for the sake of social harmony—it paves the way for a modern vision of matrimony as a space of confinement and stultification for women, and it opens up a possibility of self-fulfillment for the female protagonist. In this sense *En soledad vivía* stands as a precursor to the questioning of home and bourgeois family undertaken in the more contemporary novels by writers in this volume.

Los rostros del engaño

The title of *Los rostros del engaño* (The faces of deceit), 1968, a collection of twelve short stories, alludes to a poem by Lope de Vega that compares love to deceit. Reviews of the collection unanimously point out the stylistic perfection of these stories:

> Alicia Jurado gives evidence in *Los rostros del engaño* of having reached a literary maturity that borders on perfection. It is difficult not to find delight in the characters she creates with an admirable economy of means. She is not a short-story writer who likes sensational endings: She is classical and conventional in her techniques. But when you read a short story like "The Female Point of View," offering a very original interpretation of Hamlet, or "Closed Orchard," with its formidable woman character, the reader gets the immediate sensation that its writer is a great writer.[13]

The stories, characterized by unfulfilled love, betrayal, separation, and loneliness, deal with the failure and fragility of human bonds among all ages: adolescents, the middle aged, and the elderly. Jurado's accounts are objective and penetrating, but not sentimental. She shows compassion and understanding for her characters, while at the same time dissecting them.

For example, in the first story, "El casamiento" (The wedding), the description of the wedding day alternates and contrasts with flash-forwards, in boldface, narrating the failure of the marriage, its dissolution, and the protagonist's fate of raising her children in poverty. The wedding dress, envied by the bride's girlfriends, symbolizes the protagonist's demise. In scenes depicting the future, remnants of the dress are used as bedspreads and dresses for dolls, and in the end they are incinerated. The story closes as the couple leaves on their honeymoon, but the last sentence evokes the future: "Ana Rosa y Jorge, besándose, partieron hacia la desdicha" (Ana Rosa and Jorge, kissing each other, left headed toward unhappiness).[14]

In "La cama de jacarandá" (The jacaranda bed), one of Jurado's favorites among her own short stories, a woman temporarily moves into her dead aunt's apartment. While sleeping in a priceless colonial jacaranda bed, she has recurring erotic dreams and falls in love with the man in her dreams. They speak English, and she can only invoke him if she sleeps in that particular bed. She sets out to research the history of the bed and the people who slept in it as far back as the eighteenth century. Finally, her search leads her to a package of letters. One of the letters, dated 1807, is written by a man who reveals that his son, a soldier critically wounded in Buenos Aires during the British invasions, was lodged and taken care of by the protagonist's ancestors. Now that she knows the identity of her oneiric lover, the protagonist experiences the affair intensely, to the point that it is difficult for her to distinguish fantasy from reality. Her romance is shattered, however, when the aunt's heirs decide to donate the apartment's furniture, including the bed, to a historical museum. The story ends with the protagonist's suicide. But before she dies, she writes her experience down and leaves all her papers to her friend, Alicia Jurado.

In "El concurso" (The contest) a rather ugly young girl is pushed by her family to enter a beauty contest. She is convinced that if she wins, her boyfriend will marry her. Her pain at losing is compounded by the boyfriend's betrayal; she discovers that not only did he not vote for her, but that he has gone off with her rival. "Las mujeres piadosas" (The pious women) narrates the thoughts of three women—wife, mistress, and daughter—at the wake of a forty-five-year-old man with whom they have all shared their lives. "Huerto cerrado" (Closed orchard) describes a zoology teacher who is mistreated because of her spinsterhood. On her way home every day she crosses darkened streets and parks where, to her disgust, couples are embracing. Once in her room, she breaks down hysterically, unable to bear her empty life. In "Pequeño cuento de Navidad" (A short Christmas story) a family is gathered around an elegant Christmas meal. Their thoughts reveal their discontent, as both adults and youngsters wish that they could be elsewhere sharing this time with their lovers and friends. The story is linked with Jurado's *El cuarto mandamiento*, which works out in detail similar problems among generations of a family.

El cuarto mandamiento

While *El cuarto mandamiento* (The fourth commandment), 1974, deals with some of the themes present in *La cárcel y los hierros* and *En soledad vivía*, its characters are not portrayed with such deep psychological insight. Rather, the focus is on a larger social sector. The novel critically portrays middle-aged women of the urban middle class, their relations with the significant men in their lives, and the generational conflict between middle-aged parents and their adolescent children within a society in transition. In the foreword Jurado states the central theme: the contrast between the hope and tenderness that parents feel toward their young children and the bitter reality they must confront when these children become adolescents. Her intention in writing the work, she says, was to show the parents' point of view.[15]

El cuarto mandamiento tells the interrelated stories of three unsatisfied women, all mothers

> who . . . face their children's selfishness, harshness, and presumption. Each one, within her own family and social environment, ponders and analyzes her own drama, relieves her feelings in passionate arguments, or succumbs to a nostalgia for times that, in her opinion, were better.[16]

The three protagonists represent different aspects of a woman's life: the widow, the married woman, and the divorcée. As we become acquainted with these characters, we are drawn into their lives. Sixteen chapters, narrated in the third person, feature the stories of the mothers and their families. After each chapter, a first-person monologue by an unidentified woman is directed to her baby while it is in her womb. These monologues, titled "Diary of a Young Married Woman," are set apart from the rest of the text by being printed in boldface. The author of the diary is disclosed at the end of the novel, creating suspense, because any one of the three women characters could be the author. (The diary's author, as it turns out, is the widow.) The loving monologue by a young mother contrasts with the other narratives, especially the widow's story, which tells how she is driven by her hateful son to attempt suicide. The more tender and hopeful the words of the diary, written seventeen years earlier, the more tense and unendurable the relationship between mother and child. The conflict between the generations, central to the novel, derives from a clash of values, reflecting social changes:

> ¡Qué mundo, Dios mío! No era, por cierto, aquél en que se había criado ella: ordenado y sereno, de leyes que sin ser severas eran inmodificables, de la familia sentada a la mesa paterna dos veces por día. . . . En cuanto a los hijos, ¿a qué etapa pertenecerían? A juzgar por los modales, el lenguaje, las ropas preferidas y los gustos, sería acaso ofensivo para los hombres de Cro-Magnon . . . compararlos con esos jovencitos.

> (What a world, my God! It was not, for sure, the one in which she had been raised: orderly and serene, with rules that were not harsh but unchangeable, where the family was seated at the paternal table twice a day. . . . As to the children, what era could they belong to? If one judged by their manners, language, favorite clothes, and tastes, it would probably be offensive to the Cro-Magnons . . . to compare them with these youngsters.) (20–21)

The source of this generation gap resides in the changing times and values, as material concerns become more important than the spiritual ones characteristic of the pre-Peronist era, concerns that bonded traditional families and friendships:

> La adoración de los ídolos que antes no se admiraban independientemente del juicio moral y que ahora habían pasado a la categoría de virtudes: el dinero, el poder, el éxito.

> (The adoration of the idols, which were not admired before independently of moral judgment and which had now become [part of] the category of virtues: money, power, and success.) (38)

The reader is reminded that the commandment "Honor Your Father and Mother" has been ignored at the onset of a new era and mentality:

Pero lo peor es que se han olvidado por completo del cuarto mandamiento. Parecería que lo hubieran sustituido por otro: *Desprecia y censura, hiere e insulta a tu padre y a tu madre. Tú eres la nueva generación, y por lo tanto posees la verdad.*

(But the worst is that they have completely forgotten the fourth commandment. It would seem they had replaced it by another one: *Be contemptuous of and criticize, hurt and insult your father and mother. You are the new generation, and therefore, you possess the truth.*) (215; italics are Jurado's)

The story reaches its climax with the attempted suicide of the widow as a result of this clash, and regains its balance with a flash-forward into the characters' futures, especially the settling down of the younger generation. In every case the conflicts are instigated by the younger generation and by the husbands, not by the women.

Jurado masterfully portrays the three female protagonists and their conflicts, expressing their loneliness and alienation. Their dreams for happiness have been shattered as a result of the changes within their families as well as within society, which have brought economic hardship and an altered social structure. The victimization of women stands out in marital relations of dependency. The widow, Sofía, had a perfect marriage, but it becomes obvious that her late husband's overprotectiveness left her defenseless. She has become a silent victim, a target for her son's destructiveness once her husband is not there to shield her from life's problems. We learn that to please her future husband, the married protagonist Susana gave up her studies when she became engaged . She realizes her mistake when he betrays her. She reaches middle age with nothing to show for her life: "Siempre había sido cobarde, y como resultado no tendría un recuerdo deslumbrante para llevarse a la tumba" (She had always been a coward, and as a result she would not have one dazzling memory to take to her tomb) (111). Through Susana, Jurado critiques a social system that stunts women's growth:

[H]abía dejado por el amor la posibilidad de hacer un trabajo interesante que diera sentido a su vida y se había quedado así sin el trabajo y sin el amor, y muy pronto se quedaría también sin la belleza y sin lo que le restaba de juventud, antes de quedarse, como última etapa, sin la vida.

([F]or love she had given up the possibility of an interesting job that would have given meaning to her life, and so she had been left without

a job and without love, and very soon she would be left without
beauty and without what was left of her youth, before being left, as a
last stage, without life.) (112)

The portrayal ends with an acute image of entrapment: "Ahora estaba atrapada,
como un bicho al que le cierran la entrada de su madriguera, y no le quedaba
otro remedio que permanecer en su sitio hasta morir" (Now she was trapped,
like an animal who finds that the entrance to its den has been closed, and it
does not have any other recourse but to stay in its place until it dies) (114).
   Of the protagonists, the most promising is Celina, the divorcée. She
owns a business and supports herself. In the course of the story, she has an
affair with a married man (Susana's husband) simply because she is ready
for the experience. She does not lose her head, however, as in a traditional
romance:

> No quiero necesitarte, porque necesitar a otro es una esclavitud más
> dura que cualquier sometimiento; no quiero que tus ausencias me
> empobrezcan la vida. Esa es la conducta sensata: disfrutar de la felicidad
> que se te concede y no añorarla cuando te falta.

> (I don't want to need you, because to need somebody else is harsher
> slavery than any other submission; I don't want your absences to im-
> poverish my life. That is the sensible behavior: to enjoy the happiness
> that is offered to you and not to miss it when it's over.) (178–79)

Although the pair discover that they have fallen in love, the romance eventually runs its course. While the widow's and the married woman's tales
are replete with images of incarceration and death, the divorcée, in her
independence and fulfillment, shows another path for women, one free
from the constraints of patriarchal dependency.

Los hechiceros de la tribu

Los hechiceros de la tribu (The sorcerers of the tribe), 1980, was the last
novel by Jurado before starting her three-volume memoirs. It focuses on
(1) the writer and the literary world, (2) a theory of the novel, and (3)
Argentine reality under Peronism. The reviewer Luis Pazos has noted,

> As in Manuel Gálvez, Héctor Murena, or Eduardo Mallea, in Alicia
> Jurado sincerity is the raw material of her works, and her only, con-
> stant theme . . . is Argentina. A country, a history, and a lifestyle that
> Alicia Jurado does not describe, but dissects.[17]

The Buenos Aires literary milieu is integrated into the novel by casting a writer, Horacio Quintana, as the protagonist. A married man in his mid-fifties, he leads a personal and professional life that loosely follows Jurado's:

> Pero yo no sé si me podría disfrazar a mí mismo, excepto en las circunstancias exteriores, como mi aspecto físico o mi familia. Lo importante, es decir la profesión de escritor, tengo que contarlo desde mi propia experiencia.

> (But I don't know if I could disguise myself, except for the outer circumstances, like my physical aspect or my family. The important part, that is the writer's profession, I must narrate from my own experience.)[18]

His life, like the author's, is marked by long stays at the country estate he inherited from his mother, travels to Europe (a pretext for describing sites and works of art in the novel), and the trappings of a literary career. He is independently wealthy. That and the unconditional devotion of his wife, Graciela, a practical woman who attends to everyday matters, free him to write. As the novel opens, Horacio is attempting to write a new novel about a happily married couple, inspired by his own marriage. His dilemma: "¿Cómo iba a convertir en novela esa historia en la que nada ocurría?" (How was he going to turn into a novel that story where nothing happened?) (123). He finds the solution in the works of classic writers who placed mastery of craft and style above plot. He starts going through his personal and professional files, a source of material for his novel. The writing of the novel within the novel and the sorting of his old papers provide both the material and the structural framework for the text.

His past life, evoked from files (letters, photos, diaries), and his present life as a writer are inextricably linked to the country's literary establishment. Horacio is unable to completely extricate himself from the many demands to participate in the professional and social functions of this sophisticated, urban, literary world. As Horacio and Graciela attend lectures, book presentations, and other literary events, Jurado gives an ironic, critical portrayal of the Buenos Aires literary institutions (societies of writers, book signings, literary contests, and juries) and writers. Jurado presents a gallery of literary figures (while disclaiming any similarities to real people) who, with the exception of a few serious writers, are mercilessly cataloged by Horacio as upstarts and self-promoters. The text conveys, through Horacio's personal struggle, the experience of committed writers who are used by people to advance their own status within intellectual circles. There are few writers in the novel who can authentically say, "Somos los hechiceros de la tribu" (We are the sorcerers of the tribe) (143), the ones dedicated, according to Stéphane Mallarmé, to "purificar las palabras de la tribu" (purify the tribe's words) (223)—a phrase absentmindedly attributed by Horacio to Paul Valéry. At a certain point, Horacio decides that circumstances in his personal life prevent him from completing his novel, but as Jurado's novel closes, we hear the protagonist typing in his studio. Although the real novel ends, the protagonist's is surging forth. Horacio is one of Mallarmé's true writers:

> Mientras tanto, desde el escritorio se oyó un brusco martilleo, tan seguro de sí que parecía desafiar al mundo. El hechicero evocaba sus fantasmas con dedos impacientes y éstos, dóciles por fin al conjuro, empezaban a materializarse y a cobrar vida.

> (Meanwhile, a brusque pounding could be heard from the office, so sure of itself that it seemed to defy the world. The sorcerer was evoking his ghosts with impatient fingers and finally, compliant to the incantation, they started materializing and coming alive.) (260)

The most significant aspect of *Los hechiceros de la tribu* is not the story of this happily married couple—the plot of the novel and the text within the novel—but the running metatext on the creation of the novel. According to critic Elsa Pucciarelli, the metatext reveals Jurado's deep interest in the craft of fiction:

> Through the characters' allusions, discussions, and conversations about narrative characteristics, devices, functions, and conventions, a theory of the novel is developed in which the ideas already expressed in [Jurado's] criticism reappear, at the same time that these theoretical conventions and mechanisms fall into place.[19]

The critic also points out that Jurado has difficulty presenting her theories while she is applying them, adding that she is following the lead of her precursors—André Gide, Marcel Proust, and Julio Cortázar—in this task. As Jurado comments on the goals of an effective novel, the creation of characters, and issues of style and language, her characters engage in an ongoing discussion about the merits of masterpieces by famous authors such as Jane Austen, Virginia Woolf, and Thomas Mann.

Besides sharing Jurado's aesthetic principles, her alter ego Horacio also shares Jurado's awareness of the social and political reality surrounding an author. Like characters in Jurado's previous novels, Horacio laments the dissolution of a system based on spiritual values, which are being replaced by materialism due to "los acontecimientos afligentes de 1943 en adelante" (the worrisome events from 1943 on) (219). The novel graphically describes the Peróns and the effects of Peronism on the social fabric. Perón and his entourage are depicted as totally corrupt:

[L]a pléyade de gángsters, asesinos, ladrones, chantajistas y delincuentes de toda laya, como la siniestra corte de los milagros lanzada al asalto de la función pública, había existido y ejercido su poder hasta el más remoto rincón de la más lejana provincia. Sentado sobre el sillón de Rivadavia, Sarmiento, Mitre, Roca y Pellegrini se enriquecía un hombre que declaraba no tener más medios de vida que su sueldo de coronel.

([T]he many gangsters, murderers, thieves, racketeers, and delinquents of every sort, like the sinister court of miracles thrust to hold up public function, had existed and exerted its power reaching the most remote corner of the most distant province. On the seat of Rivadavia, Sarmiento, Mitre, Roca, and Pellegrini a man was getting rich who declared that he did not have any means of support other than his colonel's salary.) (219)

Jurado also debunks the myth of Evita Perón, using ironic religious terms to underline her total corruption:

[S]u mujer desangraba el erario público y la cuenta bancaria de los contribuyentes para otorgar dádivas, de las que no debía rendir cuentas al Tesoro, a la interminable romería de suplicantes que desfilaba ante ella. Enjoyada como una imagen milagrosa, distribuía a manos llenas la caridad hecha con el dinero ajeno y recibía en cambio la adoración de sus beneficiados.

([H]is wife bled the public treasury and the contributors' bank account to bestow gifts, which she did not have to report to the Treasury, to the unending pilgrimage of supplicants who paraded in front of her. Bejeweled like a miraculous image, she lavishly distributed the charity bestowed with other people's money and received in exchange the adoration of her beneficiaries.) (219–20)

Also mentioned are the effects of the dictatorship on various aspects of society and its institutions:

El horror, la persecución, la economía desintegrada, la educación interrumpida y transformada en propaganda; las leyes demagógicas

que no podían conducir sino a la inflación y la ruina; la delación, la
amenaza, la obsecuencia y todas las formas de la bajeza que proliferan
cuando no hay más ley que la voluntad de un mandón.

(The horror, the persecution, the disintegrated economy, education
interrupted and transformed into propaganda; the demagogic laws
that could only lead to inflation and ruin; the betrayal, the threat[s],
the obsequiousness and all the forms of vileness proliferating when
the only law is the will of a bossy individual.) (220)

Finally, the reminiscences about this dark period culminate in the descriptions of acts of arson committed by the Peronists, such as the burning
down of the Jockey Club and the old churches in 1955. By having Horacio
sort clippings and photos about this era, Jurado is able to portray a country languishing in political and spiritual poverty and to emphasize the role
of writers in upholding universal spiritual values and preserving the
country's memory. Thus, Jurado upholds the charge traditionally undertaken by Argentine novelists: to assume a leadership role as the nation's
conscience. Although *Los hechiceros de la tribu* was written during the
Proceso, the Proceso is not specifically mentioned. Jurado does manage,
however, to include oblique, critical references to members of the military
in her comments about a writer who has sold out: "Estuvo con todos los
gobiernos, desde la primera presidencia del Innominable hasta el último
gobierno militar, sin olvidarse de ninguno. Fíjese cómo se ha ido derechito
al brigadier" (She was on the side of every government, from the first
presidency of the Unnameable until the last military government, without
leaving any out. Look at how she has gone straight up to the brigadier)
(82).Thus, Jurado depicts Peronist Argentina and the reasons for recurring dictatorships in post-Perón Argentina. Horacio speaks for Jurado:

En cuanto a tus masas, ya verás que, después de todo lo que ha
pasado, siguen y seguirán siendo iguales y caerán en manos de cualquier
otro demagogo que las sepa halagar.

(As to your masses, you will see that, after all that has happened, they
continue and will continue being the same and they will fall into the
hands of any other demagogue who knows how to flatter them.)
(224)

Los hechiceros de la tribu decries Perón's legacy, which has been to empower the masses and to instigate individualism and disunity, making
them prey to political manipulation.

Jurado's novels represent a link to the past and an introduction to the works of the younger writers in this volume. Although her texts are more traditional in content and form, they express many of the same concerns found in the work of the other writers. Argentine political and social reality is treated obliquely, notwithstanding its tremendous effect on the lives of the characters. Jurado, like her predecessors, Teresa de la Parra and María Luisa Bombal, and her contemporaries, Silvina Bullrich and Beatriz Guido, brings to the forefront of her works a denunciation of the subjugated position of women. Jurado's writing is not experimental; her novels display traditional format and linguistic accuracy. Yet they integrate modern techniques regarding point of view and time shifts, traits that are developed in works by contemporary women writers of the next generation.

Conversation with Alicia Jurado

Buenos Aires, 7 April 1987

M.F.: When and how did you start writing?

A.J.: I have been writing as long as I can remember. I studied science and completed the required course work for a doctorate in natural sciences, specializing in biology. My scientific background has been very useful, because the student of science can read material in the humanities, but the opposite is not always true. As soon as I finished school, I was ready to work at the university, but I had to face political obstacles. Those of us who had been active in the student movement during 1945, when the dictatorship persecuted professors, weren't allowed to hold any teaching positions. My botany professor wanted me to be his assistant, but it wasn't possible.

M.F.: Who has inspired you to write?

A.J.: I wasn't inspired by any one person. I've enjoyed writing since I was a small child. When I was older, I met other writers. I've known all the important writers in this country and have close friendships with some of them. I've been friends with [Jorge Luis] Borges for more than thirty years. But that happened later on in life. That wasn't what made me write. I think you are born with a certain predisposition.

M.F.: Why did you choose a literary career instead of a career in the natural sciences?

A.J.: There were several reasons. First, I was politically blacklisted. Then, there was another factor, which wasn't political. When you begin a scientific career, you are delighted because you think all your questions will be answered. You are very interested because you are studying general concepts. Then, when you start to specialize, you also start to lose interest. At least that's what happened to me. Maybe we tend toward the universal and when you start specializing, you start feeling restricted by what [José] Ortega [y Gasset] called "the barbarism of specialization," and you start losing interest. The third reason was that I got married and had children and went through a domestic period, a sort of intermezzo. All those things put together led me away from the natural sciences. And why did I start writing? I had always written; now I started publishing. A friend of mine, Carlos Muniz, had started a small literary magazine that lasted three issues. He asked me to write an article on Borges for the second issue, which was dedicated to him. Somebody took the article to Borges, read it to him, and then introduced me to Borges. That is how I met him in 1954.

M.F.: You mentioned that you have always written. What did you write before this article?

A.J.: As a child I wrote diaries, which weren't exactly diaries because I didn't write every day. I wrote diaries when I was twelve, thirteen, fourteen years old. Then, later, I wrote about books I'd read, about things that happened to me. I've always written travel journals. Whenever I went on a trip, it was my habit to write on a daily basis about what I had done. I still do that. I have lots of travel journals. Those and other notes have been very useful in writing my memoirs, because besides what you remember, the written documents supply you with precise data.

M.F.: How did your friendship with Borges develop after you wrote the article?

A.J.: I was introduced to him as a result of that article and I started seeing him, but only once in a while, in 1954. Then summer came and for me that meant three or four months in the countryside. The following fall, in 1955, which was the year of the revolution, I started seeing Borges more often. During the revolutionary era we became quite close friends and I remember going with him to see the churches that had been set on fire by the Peronists. After the revolution, he was named director of the National Library, and was very enthusiastic about that position. I accompanied him one evening to see the library on México Street. He was starting to lose his sight, and they had forbidden him to read. That's why he wrote the poem, "De los dones" (About gifts), in which he says that he received, at the same time, books and darkness. In the poem he wrote, "I who fantasized about paradise in the shape of a library," and it's ironic that suddenly he's surrounded by books that he is unable to read. We went to México Street and saw the library and he was as happy as a child because he was going to be in charge of it. That took place in September 1955. During his last years we met once a week. I used to go to his place, and we would go out to eat together. Then we'd return and I'd read his favorite English writers out loud in the original. He always went back to them; he didn't want anything new.

M.F.: Who are your favorite writers?

A.J.: Borges is one of them. I also got to work with him and it was an unforgettable experience. I assisted him in writing a book titled *What is Buddhism?* Working with him was a wonderful way to learn about language and clarity of expression. Adolfo Bioy Casares also helped me. When I started publishing, I would send him the originals to read. He was a good critic.

M.F.: Do you consider yourself a member of a literary generation in Argentina?

A.J.: I don't believe in literary generations, I believe in individuals.

M.F.: Besides Borges and Bioy Casares, do you feel an affinity with any other Argentine writers?

A.J.: Yes, Victoria Ocampo. We were friends and I used to go to her home often, but it was always full of people and we didn't have many opportunities for just the two of us to talk. That opportunity finally did come, though, during my Guggenheim Fellowship, when we were both delegates to a woman's congress of the International P.E.N. Club in the United States.

M.F.: What are you reading now?

A.J.: I've just finished Evelyn Waugh's *Brideshead Revisited*, which I first read when I was twenty.

M.F.: Do you read a lot of English literature?

A.J.: Both English and French. I don't read a work because it happens to be in fashion. I'm reading Voltaire's *Dictionnaire philosophique (Philosophical Dictionary)* now and I'm enjoying it immensely. I tend to gravitate more and more toward classical literature. I think that happens when you reach a certain age. I'm not very interested in contemporary literature. In fifty or one hundred years we'll know whether these works are any good. I can't wait that long and so I read what I already know is good.

M.F.: What is the process of writing like for you? Is it easy? Do you have a schedule or routine?

A.J.: You need certain conditions, like peace and quiet, which I don't have, except in the country, where I can write. Here there are interruptions constantly. In that respect, women writers have more problems than male writers, as one of my characters says.

M.F.: Are you referring to *Los hechiceros de la tribu*?

A.J.: Yes, the female character who feels trapped, who says she can't write anything longer than a short story because she has no time. It's a problem for women writers.

M.F.: How do you select a theme?

A.J.: I don't know if I select them; sometimes they show up entirely on their own.

M.F.: Could you give an example?

A.J.: Yes. Here's a circumstance of my life that gave me the background for *En soledad vivía*. I liked southern Argentina so much that I wrote a book that takes place on Victoria Island, on Lake Nahuel Huapi. I went there many times precisely because I wanted to write about that area: to describe the landscape, the trees, the lake, and its effects on me. I had been there at different times of the year and, above all, on that island I'd gone for many walks.

M.F.: What is your favorite genre?

A.J.: I feel comfortable with all of them because they are different. It's hard to write biographies because they are research works, but I like to do it, maybe because of my scientific training.

M.F.: What are you writing now?

A.J.: My memoirs, which I find very entertaining. I have just finished writing the first volume and I intend to write more.

M.F.: Are there definite stages in your work?

A.J.: I don't know. Since I started writing a long time ago, it's possible that there have been some changes in my work. I don't see any great change. What happens is that when you write, you reflect the world around you and it keeps changing.

M.F.: You have received many prizes and are a member of the Argentine Academy of Letters. Can you explain the circumstances surrounding these honors?

A.J.: I have never asked for or sought any recognition. A long time ago, one of the academy members asked me when I was going to join them, and I told him, whenever I was invited. I know that Victoria [Ocampo], who was my predecessor, wanted me to become a member. She was the first woman to join, but was a member for a very short time because she was eighty years old when they invited her.

M.F.: How about the Guggenheim Fellowship?

A.J.: Victoria [Ocampo] suggested I apply. My proposal on [W. H.] Hudson was accepted probably because, like him, I had been a naturalist and I am a writer. Besides, I was very familiar with Argentina and England and the English language. I worked very hard in the United States and in England while holding the fellowship.

M.F.: Did this period spent abroad influence your works?

A.J.: It was extremely important for my writing. In my novels you'll find sections where I describe places in foreign countries. In *Los hechiceros de la tribu*, I include many descriptions of Rome, a city where the male protagonist, a writer, has an affair. My experiences abroad have contributed to the descriptions in my novels, but otherwise I don't think that they have had much influence.

M.F.: Your female characters don't change much, although your works span several decades. They are quite traditional. Does this portrayal reflect your vision of Argentine women?

A.J.: I describe many kinds of women. In *Los hechiceros de la tribu* there's a traditional woman, the protagonist's wife, but there's also the other female character who walks out on her family for another man. She leaves so she can write. Her newfound love gives her the strength to make this decision, but she also knows she must follow her calling.

M.F.: What do you think of the condition of women writers? Do you think there's a distinct female style of writing?

A.J.: I would say no. Through the centuries women, as well as men, have written about what they knew best. Therefore, during the times of Jane Austen, women lived in a very restricted world and they wrote about it as well as any man would have done. Women now have more unrestricted lives, but I don't think there are specific female and male characteristics. There has always been the notion that men are rational, strong, decisive, and that women are shy, cowardly, affectionate, devoted, and so on. I don't believe this. I think each individual is different from others and it's unrelated to gender. There have been women as decisive and courageous as any man, even during historical periods when this wasn't common. There are also men who have all the characteristics attributed to women. That is being discovered now, because, until a short time ago, the stereotypical image was so strong that the reality wasn't perceived. Concerning what they write, there are men who write with a sensitivity that could be attributed to a woman and women who write with a strength that could be attributed to a man. I don't think you can distinguish male or female writing by just reading a text, except in some unusual cases.

M.F.: In *El cuarto mandamiento*, the theme of the frustrated woman appears by alternating a third-person narrator with a diary of the young married woman. Can you comment on that?

A.J.: The "Diary of the Young Married Woman" is somewhat enigmatic because her identity is not revealed until the end of the novel, when the reader finds out that she is the widowed character. I took the diaries from real life. I wrote them when I was expecting my first child. I used the diaries exactly as I had written them.

M.F.: The diary functions as a metatext that establishes both a dialogue and a counterpoint with the primary text. It splits the structure of the work and the role of the character who becomes the narrator as well. Why did you use this technique?

A.J.: The diary's function is to provide a contrast, because, on the one hand, there's the young mother full of hope for this child that she has given birth to and, on the other hand, there's the estranged teenage son and the mother's pain at his hostility.

M.F.: This novel includes a surprise ending as the reader realizes that she's reading the diary of one of the characters. What are the advantages in using this technique?

A.J.: I thought it better not to reveal it until the end. I had always thought of including this diary within a story, as a contrast. A contrast between the hope and tenderness of the young woman and the mature woman's frustration.

M.F.: Why did you summarize the fate of the main characters at the end?

A.J.:, I didn't invent the flash-forward. I remembered a book by Kipling where he tells us about his characters' future lives.

M.F.: Why is it that *La cárcel y los hierros* is open-ended and the love affair on the ship is insinuated to be a fantasy?

A.J.: It can be assumed that it was a real occurrence. At the end of the novel, when she's on the ship, she sees a character whose description fits that of her lover. It's a rather ambiguous ending.

M.F.: Within the ambiguity we can interpret this ending as a fantasy. Why did you include this possibility?

A.J.: It's difficult to know why.

M.F.: Could it be that the protagonist is evading a reality that she's unable to face?

A.J.: She faces reality as much as she is able.

M.F.: Is there a relationship between this ending and mysticism, also prevalent in your works, especially in *La cárcel y los hierros*?

A.J.: During that time mysticism was very important to me. It also influenced *En soledad vivía*. I explain it in detail in my memoirs. I propose the idea that something else might exist, something that isn't determined by a dogma or religion, what Aldous Huxley was searching for in his book *The Perennial Philosophy*: a common denominator for all religions. The search for such a reality occupied a period of my life, but I've given it up because I've come to the conclusion that nothing can be known. I haven't had any experience to the contrary, and even if I had, mystical experiences are subjective.

M.F.: Could you comment on the title of your novel, *La cárcel y los hierros*, which alludes to Saint Theresa?

A.J.: Saint Theresa wrote: "How hard are these banishments / This prison, these irons / Into which the soul is thrust!" She expresses the idea that the soul is imprisoned in the body and is set free by death. I have serious doubts about that.

M.F.: How much is autobiographical in your works, and especially in *La cárcel y los hierros*?

A.J.: There is autobiographical material, but as with all writers, we often modify elements we know. In that novel I worked especially hard to present parents and a husband who were very different from my own. Her career is also different: She studies chemistry. What is quite autobiographical in that novel is the landscape. In my next volumes of memoirs, I'll talk about how each book originated.

M.F.: The protagonist in your novel *Los hechiceros de la tribu* is a male writer. Why did you choose a male alter ego and why is his wife such a conventional woman?

A.J.: Maybe I chose a male writer to get away from myself. The wife is conventional because there are so many women who are.

M.F.: This novel presents social changes stemming from Peronism, like the surge of materialism, ignorance, the loss of traditional values. What was your intention when you included these themes?

A.J.: Peronism and its political persecution and moral corruption brought great changes in our society. The quick industrialization also created new problems.

M.F.: Your novel renders a vivid and critical portrayal of the literary world, especially writers. Notwithstanding the introductory remarks in the volume, did you take characteristics from real persons? Did your critical portrayal bring you problems with your fellow writers?

A.J.: The characters depicted aren't real people. I wanted to describe general cases, not particular persons. I didn't have any problems with other writers.

M.F.: The theme of the writer's craft is usually dealt with in a nonconventional manner. I'm thinking of writers like [Julio] Cortázar, [Juan Carlos] Onetti, and [Manuel] Puig, who dealt with this topic. However, your novel is very conventional in its form. Why did you use this style?

A.J.: Tortuous writing fatigues the reader, and very complex and obscure writing isn't my usual style.

M.F.: Your characters who are writers say that, besides showing an aspect of our universal human experience, style is a very important element in a novel. How would you characterize your style?

A.J.: Style is important in every genre. I would say my style is clear and readable.

M.F.: Your novels include references to world literature, which demand a literary background from your readers.

A.J.: That is something that is involuntary, but I like it when the reader can find references to his other readings in my works.

M.F.: Would you say that your readers belong to the middle or upper-middle class?

A.J.: My readers belong to an educated class. I don't care about their social class, but they should have reached a certain level of education to be able to understand my works.

M.F.: All your titles refer to literary works. Could you explain them?

A.J.: *La cárcel y los hierros* refers to the poem I mentioned by Saint Theresa; *Leguas de polvo y sueños* (Leagues of dust and dreams) is a line from a poem in Borges's *La rosa profunda* (The deep rose); *Los rostros del engaño* alludes to Lope de Vega but it is not an exact quotation. The title *Los hechiceros de la tribu* refers to the writers capable of creating real live human beings with their imaginations.

M.F.: And how about *En soledad vivía*?

A.J.: The title originates from Saint John of the Cross, from the marvelous *Cántico espiritual (Spiritual Canticle)*. It refers to the solitude of the male character who lives on that island like a hermit.

Buenos Aires, 30 October 1989

M.F.: What can you tell me about the memoirs you're writing now?

A.J.: The first volume covers up to when I was thirty years old. The title is *Descubrimiento del mundo* (Discovery of the world), and it's about my formative years. The cover has a picture of me when I was six months old. It starts with my birth and even earlier, because I write about my family and my ancestors in Argentina. By thirty I was married and had children. I learned everything when I was little—science, literature, foreign languages, many things. Then I took my first solo trip to Europe as an adult. That trip was a revelation that has left a permanent imprint on me in terms of the Gothic cathedrals, great paintings, and works of art. The volume ends with that trip to Europe when I was twenty-nine years old. After that came a period of literary production and friendships.

M.F.: Do you have any plans to write other novels?

A.J.: For the time being, I'm writing my memoirs. Until I finish them, I don't think that I'm going to write anything else.

BIBLIOGRAPHY

Primary Sources (listed chronologically)

Jurado, Alicia. *La cárcel y los hierros*. Buenos Aires: Editorial Goncourt, 1961.

———. *Genio y figura de Jorge Luis Borges*. Buenos Aires: Editorial Universitaria de Buenos Aires, 1964.

———. *Leguas de polvo y sueños*. Buenos Aires: Editorial Losada, 1965.

———. *En soledad vivía*. Buenos Aires: Editorial Losada, 1967.

———. *Los rostros del engaño*. Buenos Aires: Editorial Losada, 1968.

———. *Vida y obra de W. H. Hudson*. Buenos Aires: Fondo Nacional de las Artes, 1971.

———. *El cuarto mandamiento*. Buenos Aires: Emecé Editores, 1974.

———. *El escocés errante: Robert B. Cunninghame Graham*. Buenos Aires: Emecé Editores, 1978.

———. *Los hechiceros de la tribu*. Buenos Aires: Emecé Editores, 1980.

———. *Descubrimiento del mundo*. Buenos Aires: Emecé Editores, 1989.

———. *El mundo de la palabra*. Buenos Aires: Emecé Editores, 1990.

———. *Las despedidas*. Buenos Aires: Emecé Editores, 1992.

Critical Articles by Alicia Jurado (listed chronologically)

Jurado, Alicia. "Victoria Ocampo y la condición de la mujer." *Sur* 348 (September-October 1981): 137–42.

———. "Victoria Ocampo, mi predecesora." Membership acceptance speech. *Boletín de la Academia Argentina de Letras* 46 (January-December 1981): 81–95.

———. "La amistad entre Gabriela Mistral y Victoria Ocampo." *Boletín de la Academia Argentina de Letras* 54 (July-December 1989): 523–61.

Jurado, Alicia, et al. "Homenaje a Jorge Luis Borges." *La Nación,* 22 June 1986.

———. "La literatura y sus protagonistas: Homenaje a Jorge Luis Borges." *La Nación,* 24 August 1986.

Short fiction by Alicia Jurado

Jurado, Alicia. "El regreso." *Sur* 248 (September-October 1957): 34–39.

Secondary Sources

Canal Feijóo, Bernardo. "Recepción de la Académica de Número Doña Alicia Jurado." "Discurso del Señor Académico Don Jorge Luis Borges." *Boletín de la Academia Argentina de Letras* 46 (1981): 75–95.

Cruz, Jorge. "Cuentos de la vieja casa." Review of *Leguas de polvo y sueños,* by Alicia Jurado. *La Nación,* 16 May 1965.

"Cuentos entre el amor y la mentira." Review of *Los rostros del engaño,* by Alicia Jurado. *Clarín,* 3 April 1969.

De Miguel, Esther. Review of *Leguas de polvo y sueños,* by Alicia Jurado. *Femirama,* 15 June 1965.

Fares, Gustavo, and Eliana Herman. "Alicia Jurado." In *Escritoras argentinas contemporáneas,* 95–112. New York: Peter Lang, 1993.

Flori, Mónica. "Alicia Jurado." In *Spanish American Authors. The Twentieth Century,* edited by Angel Flores, 449–51. New York: H. W. Wilson Company, 1992.

———. "Entrevista a Alicia Jurado." *Hispania* 73 (March 1990): 149–51.

Gómez Bas, Joaquín. Review of *Los rostros del engaño,* by Alicia Jurado. *Para ti,* 21 April 1969, 68.

Gutiérrez Estrella, Fermín. Review of *La cárcel y los hierros,* by Alicia Jurado. *La Razón,* 21 April 1962.

J. N. "Infierno de padres." Review of *El cuarto mandamiento,* by Alicia Jurado. *La Razón,* 26 October 1974.

Koremblit, Bernardo Ezequiel. "Etica y estética de una vida." Review of *Descubrimiento del mundo,* by Alicia Jurado. *La Prensa,* 14 January 1990.

Magrini, César. "La otra cara de la moneda." Review of *El cuarto mandamiento,* by Alicia Jurado. *El Cronista Comercial,* 11 December 1974.

Mazzei, Angel. "El suave placer de recordar." Review of *Las despedidas,* by Alicia Jurado. *La Nación,* 6 December 1992.

Noel, Martín Alberto. "*El cuarto mandamiento* por Alicia Jurado." Review of *El cuarto mandamiento,* by Alicia Jurado. *La Prensa,* 29 December 1974.

———. "La madurez de una creadora." Review of *El mundo de la palabra*, by Alicia Jurado. *La Nación*, 6 January 1991.

O. D. Review of *Los rostros del engaño,* by Alicia Jurado. *La Capital*, 19 April 1970.

O. P. Review of *Los rostros del engaño,* by Alicia Jurado. *La Prensa*, 11 May 1969.

Pazos, Luis. Review of *Los hechiceros de la tribu*, by Alicia Jurado. *Somos*, 23 January 1981.

Peltzer, Federico. Review of *Los rostros del engaño,* by Alicia Jurado. *La Gaceta*, 18 May 1969.

Pucciarelli, Elsa T. de. "Alicia Jurado. 'Hechicera de la tribu.'" *Sur* 348 (September-October 1981): 41–48.

S. C. C. "Una aventura del alma." Review of *Vida y obra de W. H. Hudson*, by Alicia Jurado. *La Prensa*, 13 February 1972.

Victoria, Marcos. "Novelistas premiados por la Sociedad Argentina de Escritores." Review of *La cárcel y los hierros*, by Alicia Jurado. *El Hogar*, 5 August 1962, 62.

Elvira Orphée. Photograph by Daniel Merle.

2
Elvira Orphée

BIOGRAPHY

Elvira Orphée was born in San Miguel de Tucumán, Argentina, on 29 May 1930. She studied literature at the University of Buenos Aires School of Philosophy and Letters and earned a bachelor's degree. While living in France for eight years in the 1950s, she studied French at the Sorbonne. Orphée lived in Spain (1959), Italy (1960–61), and Venezuela (1970s).

Orphée has published six novels and three collections of short stories. Her first novel, *Uno*, 1961, received honorable mention in a literary contest sponsored by Fabril Publishing Company. *Aire tan dulce*, 1966, received second prize in the novel category from the municipality of Buenos Aires; *En el fondo*, 1969, her fourth novel, received first prize in the novel category.

She has regularly contributed short stories to literary journals and magazines such as *Sur* and *Ficción* (Buenos Aires), *Cuadernos* (Paris), *El Tiempo* (Bogotá), and *Asomante* (Puerto Rico). At present she writes full time and is working on a novel entitled *Basura y luna*.

ESSAY

Elvira Orphée, like Alicia Jurado, belongs to the literary group called "the angry ones," or "the patricidals," whose work was influenced by Peronism and existentialism and, in Orphée's case, by neorealism. The neorealist strain in her fiction is evidenced by a strong current of naturalism that permeates the metaphysical, existential, and sociopsychological issues dominating her characters' existence. Her naturalist vision originates as well in her memories of a sickly and loveless childhood in Tucumán. While her settings evoke the natural beauty of the province, it is a cursed environment

59

for tainted and humiliated characters stigmatized by a fatal flaw. The metaphysical is in the forefront of Orphée's tragic vision, as her characters feel like fallen angels deprived of their connection with the Absolute embodied in the cosmic forces of the universe. They believe that if they succeed in fusing with the natural world, they will recuperate their former state of grace and partake of cosmic splendor. Their metaphysical exclusion results in existential malaise. Orphée's characters are generally social misfits (outcasts, orphans, and criminals) or those who are psychologically dysfunctional (unfeeling, unloved, and humiliated), unsuccessfully seeking to vindicate themselves.

> To affirm themselves or to reconquer their freedom and independence, they rebel, anxious to gain the love or the power that they lack. Irremediably, this search to vindicate the "self" depends on other human beings and, therefore, is destined to fail. Only pure Love and Power, without socio-ethical, temporal, or spatial ties, would fill the vacuum in these characters. They long for the attributes of a god.[1]

To appease their perceived deprivations, Orphée's characters adopt extreme forms of behavior—cruelty, insanity, and murder. They resemble tragic figures of ancient and classical literature as they succumb to blinding passions, insurmountable flaws, and an unrelenting fatal destiny.

Thus, Orphée's fiction, like that of her Mexican contemporary Juan Rulfo, transmits an existential vision characterized by absurdity, fatalism, and purposelessness because of God's absence or indifference. A fictional world containing a nihilist, existential, and metaphysical vision like Orphée's (and Rulfo's) results in a nonjudgmental narration conveyed from a limited point of view. The effect is shocking, as the narration withholds ethical judgment (within the context of an ethical inquiry) while describing serious transgressions against social and ethical morality. To underscore the uncertainty and relativity of Orphée's worldview, omniscience is shunned in favor of first-person narration and narrations from the point of view of her characters. To achieve this effect, Orphée uses a lyrical style, disdaining the aestheticism of her predecessors and concentrating on techniques that convey the psychological effects of events on her protagonists.

> Elliptical dialogue, lyrical introspection, telegraphic rhythm, and analogical rather than chronological linking mark Orphée's prose style. External details and descriptions are so scarce that even the colorful scenery of Tucumán or La Rioja is filtered through memories, rendering them oneiric evocations. Although colloquialisms and the *lunfardo* jargon are present in her prose, Orphée's language generally

preserves its poetic nuance and cadence even in grotesque situations or in deceptively simple passages.[2]

Dos veranos

Elvira Orphée's first novel, *Dos veranos* (Two summers), 1956, bridged "the distance between the traditional world and the characters of the rural Latin American novel, and the Neo-Realist one filled with the personal rebellion and violence of the international contemporary novel."[3]

The novel deals with two summers in the life of an adolescent picaresque protagonist, Sixto Riera. Part 1 is set during his first summer in an uneventful provincial environment. In part 2, set during a summer four years later, the protagonist roams the countryside, ending up in the provincial capital. The introspective part 1 establishes Sixto's strange personality. He is a pitiful creature dominated by self-loathing; he perceives himself as a despicable outcast. As a result, he is consumed by an intense hatred toward the world. In the shorter, faster-paced part 2 the protagonist, carried away by his violence, succumbs to a merciless fate.

As the novel opens, the thirteen-year-old Sixto has been taken in by a prosperous family to do odd jobs at their home and country store. Sixto's reflections explore how his origins and his inferior social position led him to his present servitude, corroborating and heightening his status as an outcast and a victim. He is convinced that this is the result of a (deterministic and fatalistic) cursed heritage: "A alguien de mi familia lo debe de haber picado una víbora. Desde que amanece estoy rabioso . . . y yo heredé la sangre envenenada"[4] (Somebody in my family must have been bitten by a snake. From the moment the sun rises I am furious . . . and I inherited the poisoned blood). His self-definition underscores the importance of his legacy in the shaping of a violent and destructive human being:

> [S]oy Sixto Riera, hijo de padre desconocido, chico abandonado, de raza sospechosa, heredero de una buena carga de pobreza, fealdad y embrutecimiento. Soy Sixto Riera y seguiré siéndolo siempre.
>
> ([I] am Sixto Riera, son of unknown father, abandoned child, of a suspicious race, heir to a hefty burden of poverty, ugliness, and brutality. I am Sixto Riera and I will always continue being that.) (188)

The only memory he has of his biological family is of the time when his older brother was caught stealing, an incident that (prophetically) haunts him:

Imagina los rostros reprobadores que miraron a su hermano, aún de uniforme, pasar preso por las calles del pueblo y se le hace intolerable ese desfile de un solo hombre que provoca la mofa, la curiosidad o el reproche.

(He imagines the disapproving faces that looked at his brother, still in uniform, a prisoner paraded along the village's streets and he cannot bear that one-man parade that provokes mockery, curiosity, or reproach.) (81)

Even though Sixto is treated fairly well in his present situation, he is blinded by his feelings of inadequacy, directing his energies to overcome the contempt he feels for his foster family, schoolmates, and teachers. The protagonist decides to reverse his unfortunate legacy and change his destiny by acquiring power over others. He observes the adult men around him, especially his foster father, and realizes that money is a source of power, as it can buy respect. From that moment on, he dreams of becoming rich and respected, of overcoming his humiliation by defying destiny: "Quiso ser Sixto Riera, el otro, el que desafiaba el obstáculo, el que triunfaba de sus padres, de su raza y su fealdad" (He wanted to be Sixto Riera, the other one, the one who challenged the obstacle, the one who triumphed over his parents, his race, and his ugliness) (188). As he waits for an opportunity to fulfill his dreams, Sixto exerts whatever power he can by manipulating those around him:

Pero Sixto quiere vencer; cuando vence llega al paroxismo del poder porque antes ha llegado al paroxismo del terror, y sólo entonces experimenta algo muy parecido a lo que debe de ser la felicidad: gobernar, obligar, dominar. A sí mismo, a los otros.

(But Sixto wants to vanquish; when he vanquishes he attains the paroxism of power, because earlier he has reached the paroxism of terror, and only then is he able to experience something very similar to what happiness must be like: to rule, to force, to dominate. His own self. Others.) (39)

He avenges past humiliations by dominating others, as manipulation and violence become his weapons. Yet, in the midst of this bleak portrayal of human relations, Sixto has a spark of sympathy for his invalid foster mother, whom he is assigned to care for. She is the only character who escapes his hatred. Once a beautiful woman, she has gradually been crippled by arthritis and lives in seclusion. Her ailment was not treated in time because of her husband's avarice, and she suffers tremendous pain. Sixto feels compassion for her, a soulmate who "sufre como él mismo cuando se siente postergado por feo, por pobre, por tonto" (suffers like he does when he feels that he is being discounted for being ugly, for being poor, for being stupid) (96). Although both characters feel a bond of common suffering, Sixto treats his foster mother brusquely and seeks to humiliate her. She, in turn, is incapable of showing him any love, as communication and affection are beyond the reach of Orphée's haunted creatures. The sight of the woman torments Sixto, who fears her sickness and approaching death. As a result, instead of finding solace, Sixto becomes consumed by his tortured feelings for this character, whose body bears the scars that mark his soul.

The summer atmosphere is similar in quality to the protagonist's fate (allusions to the humid heat, drought, and Tucumán's Zonda wind abound).[5] "Una especie de debilidad pesada invade la noche, la luz de la luna se espesa, pierde sus netos cristales. La misma pesadez húmeda en las manos" (A sort of heavy weakness invades the night, the moonlight thickens, loses its clear crystals. The same humid heaviness on the hands) (38–39). Sixto's desperation contrasts with the poetic and hauntingly beautiful Tucumán settings that torment him (and all Orphée's characters with spiritual and physical scars) for his inadequacies:

> El sol es un insecto de fuego, transparente. Zumba perezosamente, como un moscadón de oro, hasta que sus alas se posan sobre los párpados de Sixto, acariciadoras.
>
> (The sun is an insect of fire, transparent. It buzzes lazily, like a golden blowfly, until its wings alight on Sixto's eyelids, caressingly.) (104)

To Sixto the whole universe seems to be a reflection of God's indifference, so he directs his hatred to God's impassive figure:

> "¿Por qué estarán las cosas tan mal hechas? ¿Habrá algún responsable?" Si lo hubiera, ¡cómo le gustaría martirizarlo, golpearle la cabeza con una piedra hasta que se le derramaran los sesos!
>
> ("Why are things so badly made? I wonder if there is someone who is responsible?" If so, how he would like to martyrize him, to hit his head with a stone until his brains spilled out!) (52)

The violent hatred and sordidness in Sixto's life filters into his fantasies, as he seeks refuge in an imaginary world inhabited by ghosts and his monstrous, make-believe friend, María, whom he makes responsible for his actions.

> Pero la buena María, su amiga, puede volverse feroz, hincharse y saltarle a la cara si se le desobedece. Feroz y repugnante, un bicho monstruoso.

> (But the good María, his friend, can become ferocious, swell, and jump on his face if she is disobeyed. Ferocious and repugnant, a monstruous creature.) (79)

María is the product of a superstitious and fatalistic mind's attempt to communicate with a supernatural reality. Sixto believes that he can do this by commiting evil actions and inflicting pain. His is a rebellion against an indifferent God responsible for Sixto's underdog status and for his subsequent behavior. At the end of part 1, Sixto decides to face his destiny, and he runs away from his foster home.

In part 2, Sixto's destructive violence peaks. According to Diane Birkemoe, "The quickened pace of the second part intensifies the effect of the Neo-Realism already at work in the first, with its flexibility of time sequence, its invisible margin between current and recalled action. . . ."[6] The faster pace is appropriate, for it underscores the many events that take place during Sixto's wanderings. Four years have passed since Sixto ran away. He must have committed a crime (unexplained in the narration), since he has spent these years in a juvenile detention center. While in detention, the seventeen-year-old protagonist has met other young men as evil and violent as he is. Three of them, along with Sixto, run away together. They kill the elderly father of one of the young men and steal his money. After the man is dead, Sixto bashes in his skull with a stone, signifying that this man is the "someone who is responsible" for the evils of the universe. According to Orphée, Sixto is "really killing his own destiny, his fate, or, if you wish, God."[7] Subsequently, he roams the countryside raping women. He perceives sexual relations as "algo claramente inmundo, un imperativo tan sucio como el de la defecación" (something clearly repulsive, an imperative as dirty as defecating) (55). The protagonist establishes a brutal relationship with women because he is incapable of feeling love (or any other emotional bond) with a human being. By abusing women, he fulfills his need to exert power through humiliation and suffering. Finally, Sixto becomes a victim of his own actions. In a brawl with a stranger, he is recognized as one of the murderers and is imprisoned. The fatalistic denouement, including the description of Sixto's being caught and dragged off to jail, is reminiscent of that of his older brother, the image that Sixto has tried to run away from. Thus, Sixto Riera has fulfilled his destiny, pushed by his destructive self-loathing, by the indifference of the world around him, and by the impossibility of attaining transcendence in an absurd world.

Uno

Uno (One), 1961, takes place in Buenos Aires in the fifties. It is a study of how political events—the first Perón era—deeply change the lives of approximately a dozen characters (representing a broad social spectrum). The characters, introduced in the opening scene, are attending Perón's address at the Labor Day rally at the Plaza de Mayo on 1 May 1954. The novel follows the characters' comings and goings for one year, closing at the same location on 16 June 1955, toward the end of Perón's regime. We see that the destruction resulting from a revolt against Perón affects most of the characters.

Thus, the novel focuses exclusively on Peronism and its effects on Argentine society. There is no other plot and no main protagonist. Orphée's *Uno* signifies that Argentina is in its present predicament because it is full of "unos": egotistical individuals dedicated to the sole pursuit of their personal, immediate goals. The characters are linked by a general feeling of malaise; many are on the fringes of society; all are deeply alienated. The story follows several characters from the lower class (factory workers and Peronist thugs, like Royarte, Luna, Falcón, and Selva Flores, a domestic servant who is Royarte's mistress); middle class (Margarita Cámpores, a secretary, and Néstor Achával, a tango singer turned police informer); and the oligarchy (landowners and professionals, like Agustín and Pedro Bláinez, Martín and Teresa Cabal, Justa Bláinez [Agustín's wife and Martín's mistress], and an enigmatic Swiss woman, Annie Derbaar, who has a fling with the tango singer). The characters, notwithstanding their different classes, are all interconnected by a personal or professional relationship, a conversation, or a brief encounter. This technique creates the feeling of a complete and realistic society. All these characters could be the "one" alluded to in the title, as they blend into the capital city's life and the melées at the Plaza de Mayo. Their essence is expressed by "Uno," the title of a popular tango:

> El tango era la patria que los estaba esperando. Desde esa patria los acechaban la pampa, la madreselva y el puñal que cortó el corazón y las trenzas. Los acechaba Uno, el hombre sin confianzas, disfrazado

de Uno para no sentir vergüenza de contarse en yo. Se vertía en el
tango, estaba en la pista. Uno, que no puede hablar de su afectividad
enferma y desencadenada, aparecía bajo alguna de esas pétreas
fisonomías indias, celosas de su secreto. Por todos los ángulos del
local se podía ver a Uno, reconstruir su historia.

(The tango was the fatherland awaiting them. In that fatherland the
pampa, the honeysuckle, and the dagger, which cut the heart and the
braid, were lurking. "Uno" was lurking, the distrustful man, disguised as "Uno," too ashamed to disclose himself as "I." He fused
with the tango, he was on the dance floor. "Uno," who can't talk of
his sick and runaway emotions, appeared underneath one of those
Indian stone faces, zealously guarding their secret. You could see
"Uno" everywhere in the place, [you could] recreate his story.)[8]

To María Luisa Bastos, "Uno" is "a sort of x-ray of the paradoxical
personality of the Argentine people."[9] To Birkemoe, "Uno" is more indefinite: "In many of the characters the lack of a real identity, partially
caused by the stifling atmosphere of the regime, is revealed in their use of
the term 'uno,' or sometimes 'nosotros' in an indefinite sense, rather than
to make a personal statement."[10] Thus, Orphée's characters represent a
slice of life. Each one is "everyman." As their lives are touched by the
effects of Perón and his policies, they become representative of the plight
of the Argentines during that era. According to Bradley Class, "The novel's
plot can be best described as a hodgepodge of identity quests and power
plays, which converge in the abortive coup of 16 June, symbolizing the
inevitable outcome of a society powerless to pull itself together."[11]

     In contrast to most novels about the Peronato, which include only de-
scriptions of the consequences of Perón's actions, Orphée's portrays Perón's
mannerisms, emphasizing his influence on every aspect of daily life and his
responsibility for events: "Es el líder. Está en el balcón moviendo los brazos.
'Compañeros', y una pausa (It is the leader. He is on the balcony moving his
arms. "Comrades," and a pause) (16). Orphée then focuses on the conversations of the characters who have converged on the square as they express
their perceptions of Argentina's leader, making it clear that Perón has affected all of them. Upper- and middle-class characters provide a portrayal of
Perón as a ridiculous creature who nevertheless aspires to greatness:

Ya en los retratos me parecía ridículo, pero ahora, con esos bracitos
cortos, el saludo que parece se lo hubieran pegado con cola, y las
frases en que se hace aplaudir, su ridículo me avergüenza como si
fuera mío.

(And he already seemed ridiculous to me in the portraits, but now, with those short little arms, his greeting that seems to have been stuck to him with glue, and the sentences he utters to get applause, his ridiculousness shames me as if it were my own.) (16)

Ahora es un sacerdote, ya no sólo un hombre de estado. Un gran sabio, un gran santo. Quiere erigirse en norma de vida.

(Now he is a priest, not anymore just a statesman. A great wise man, a great saint. He wants to set himself up as a norm for life.) (18)

—Sí, prostituyendo medio país.

(Yes, prostituting half the country.) (18)

Next, Orphée manipulates our concept of the classes, portraying the lower class as the masses who are mesmerized by their leader, in contrast to the articulate upper and middle class:

En la turba el cambio es por momentos más evidente: se mueve hipnotizada por la promesa de diversión, pregusta la orgía. De pronto, como conjuradas, aparecen en algunas manos cacerolas viejas; el ritmo de sus golpes resucita tambores de brujo.

(In the mob the change is more evident by the moment: It moves hypnotized by the promise of entertainment, foretasting the orgy. Suddenly, as though conjured, old pots appear in some hands; the rhythm of its pounding resurrects witch drums.) (19)

This contrasting view of the different social classes is developed throughout the novel. Although Orphée is objective in showing that corruption and brutality prevail at all social levels, her characters are divided into the traditional Argentine dichotomy between civilization and barbarism. The lives of upper-class characters flounder in existential problems. These characters—like Martín Cabal, so wrapped up in his personal anguish that he sees others as "fantasmas mortecinos que hablaban con voces apagadas y hacían gestos demorados" (fading ghosts who talked with muffled voices and made lingering gestures) (251)—are more likely to be accepted by the contemporary reader, who can empathize with them. In contrast, portrayals of lower-class characters always emphasize their bestial traits:

La cara de Royarte, morena, de pómulos poderosos, ajena al razona-miento, con el vello de terciopelo de las arañas, pasaba por las estaciones. Uno del andén la veía quizá tenebrosa, otro fugazmente criminal, un tercero con negras alimañas en lugar de ojos.

(Royarte's face, dark, with powerful cheeks, alien to reasoning, with the velvet hairiness of spiders, passed by the stations. From the platform somebody saw it maybe as sinister, another one as fleetingly criminal, a third one with black vermin instead of eyes.) (64)

Su cabeza, entre el humo, se alejaba espectacularmente de lo humano, como varias otras allí.

(His head, among the smoke, distanced itself spectacularly from the human, like many others there.) (67)

The oligarchy and the middle class can voice their opposition to Perón in their conversations, while lower-class characters express their unquestioning support by violently destroying any opposition. A considerable part of the novel portrays the infighting of union workers at a textile factory, culminating in a brutal scene in which the Peronist mob beats up Luna, one of the workers who wants the Peronists to adopt more conciliatory positions in their struggles for rights. Perón supporters are also members of an extreme right, special paramilitary force, the Alianza Libertadora Nacionalista (Nationalist Liberation Alliance), which was active during the fifties.[12] In this capacity they secretly perform the regime's dirty work: kidnapping and torturing people. The episodes depicting these activities are present in *Uno*, but become the central focus of *La última conquista de El Angel* (El Angel's last conquest). Characters use torture as a deranged path toward divinity; it is therefore described in religious language:

> El fraternal encuentro de los policías de la Sección Especial no se producía al aire libre sino bajo techo. Se juntaban para comulgar en la alegría que trae la sangre, como iniciados en la espera de la divinidad.
>
> (The fraternal get-together of the policemen of the Special Section did not usually take place in the open air, but under cover. They got together to share communion in the happiness that blood brings, like initiates awaiting divinity.) (174)

Thus, torture acquires a metaphysical dimension, and "such sociopolitical subjects as Peronism and political torture in Argentina are manipulated by a psychological introspection that focuses on perennial questions that eclipse the limited, historical context. Individual characters embody the immortal forces of good and evil and life and death with a feverish lucidity."[13]

The conflict between civilization and barbarism transcends the public sphere and reaches into the private lives of the characters, as evidenced in the confrontation between Justa Bláinez and her domestic servant, Selva Flores (the head torturer's mistress). Justa (Fair) strikes Selva Flores (Jungle Flowers) in self-defense and then fires her upon learning that Selva and Royarte (Selva's lover) have abused her children. Since workers, including domestics, were protected by the Peronist agency Trabajo y Previsión (Labor and Security), Justa is forced to account for her actions. Justa and Selva Flores's confrontation represents civilization versus barbarism. The barbaric element of society (Selva and Royarte), representative of the Peronato, is a violent force attempting to destroy civilized life (Justa Bláinez's world). Balance is reestablished, however, as it becomes clear that the workers were blinded by devotion to their leader, the real force behind the violence. The brutality is an indictment of the regime, not of the lower classes. This becomes apparent as Orphée points out the corruption of the upper classes as well: Factory lawyers and managers profit by maneuvering and stalling union negotiations. As Birkemoe points out, Orphée's "pejorative treatment of the working class accrued the novel a scathing review. . . . This social level is made to appear despicable for the bestial behavior of its representatives in the novel—evidently a distorted and exaggerated portrait—but the other classes are no more worthy of respect, no more capable of enlisting the reader's sympathy."[14]

As the novel ends, the Pink Government House is laid siege to by dissident military factions joined by activists (Pedro Bláinez), most of whom become passive victims (Margarita Cámpores) or unwilling heroes (Martín Cabal). The massacre and destruction, which sucks the characters in, does not destroy the leader: "La bomba cayó sobre la casa de gobierno y no encontró al que buscaba. El que buscaba estaba en otro sitio, protegido" (The bomb fell on the house of government and did not find the one it was looking for. The one it was looking for was in another place, protected) (255). The ending expresses Orphée's message: The "unos," the divided and egocentric citizens, are incapable of a concerted effort to free themselves from the leader's oppression and disastrous policies.

The novel alternates conversations and episodes without explicit introductions. Nevertheless, transitions are swift. The dialogues reflect the characters' personalities and social levels, and the descriptions consistently repeat motifs and patterns. There is no character development. Only Margarita Cámpores, a secretary who studies physics, is distinctly presented. Although her sequences are narrated in first-person monologues, giving us a deeper view of her mind, this technique does not make her a more prominent character. By rapidly alternating the stories of the many characters, Orphée achieves her goal of presenting them as fleeting presences manipulated by historical events. Their destinies are sealed by fate, a characteristic of Orphée's fictional world.

Orphée has written a contemporary novel that interprets the feelings of Peronists and anti-Peronists. Characters are caught up in events that force them to become torturers, martyrs, or heroes, depending on their personalities and circumstances. All of them become victims of the blind violence and chaos attributed to Perón and his followers.

Aire tan dulce

Aire tan dulce (How sweet the air), 1966, is Orphée's longest and probably most complex novel. Gwendolyn Díaz sees *Aire tan dulce* as illustrating Joanna Russ's concept that lyrical prose is characteristic of women's fiction.[15] According to her, lyrical prose is a particular style developed by women writers who organize narrative elements around an emotional center and use associations, rather than chronology and causality, as links. This is clearly the organizing principle in the forty-seven chapters of *Aire tan dulce*. The narration is developed from the perspectives of the three protagonists—Félix Gauna, Atala Pons, and her grandmother, Fausta, called Mimaya. Although they narrate in alternating monologues, the speaker is not identified, so the reader must determine who is narrating.

The exterior world is alluded to only as a backdrop. The narration follows an order corresponding to introspection, mnemonic associations, and the psychological effects of actions and events. Throughout the first six chapters, Félix Gauna is the protagonist, but from the seventh chapter on, it becomes increasingly clear that Atala is the most important character, and Félix recedes into a secondary position. The central plot begins as a love story in a provincial city and becomes a tale of hatred and revenge. Félix Gauna is a young man with an inferiority complex reminiscent of Sixto Riera. He comes to hate and harm everyone around him, especially those who love him. He thinks he has been cursed by fate manifest in his place of birth:

> Pero desafío al que quiera encontrar la infancia al pie del Aconquija. La dulzura del azúcar antes de ser dulzura deja arroyos podridos en la orilla de los caminos, huellas cenagosas y la infancia.

> (But I defy whoever wants to find childhood at the foot of the Aconquija. Sugar's sweetness before becoming sweet leaves putrid streams at the side of the roads, swampy trails and childhood.)[16]

Félix also blames the family he has been born to, especially his father, whom he hates because he is humble and shy. Félix holds his father responsible for his own marginal social condition: "Vuelve ahora para joderme con el recuerdo de mi inferioridad. Inferior a mis compañeros por causa de él. Inferior a él porque soy su hijo" (He returns now to piss me off with the reminder of my inferiority. I'm inferior to my schoolmates because of him. I'm inferior to him because I'm his son) (68). Malicious pranks get him expelled from school, and, as a result, he faces a hopeless future. His inferiority complex spurs him to destroy his parents, his sister, and his close friends. The main target of his hatred is Atalita Pons, a young woman he has known since childhood, who has carried on a love-hate relationship with him. She is the victim of an illness that has made her an outcast in provincial society. Hers is a life of pain and resentment. Félix and Atala resemble each other. They are both outcasts suffering from a lack of love in their families; both are consumed by hatred, and their only goal in life is to gain power by manipulating and inflicting pain on others.

Mimaya is the third important character who narrates parts of the story. She is the only one who loves Atala, her favorite granddaughter. Atala rejects Mimaya's love because it constrains her. Mimaya's monologues focus on her past, especially on her two marriages, which she considers the source of her discontent and failure. She used to be daring like Atala, but when she married, she conformed to provincial society. The rebellion she sees in Atala is a continuation of her own impulses, which she feels she has denied.

As the story develops, the characters become victims of their situations and their rage. Félix lives only for revenge, which he imposes on his loved ones. He saves the biggest revenge for Atala:

> Cuando se pisa un bicho, ¿quién se preocupa? A lo sumo se puede desear que el bicho se muera con dolor, sufriendo, sabiendo que moría así porque era malvado. Atala es un bicho.

> (When one steps on vermin, who cares? At best, you can hope it will die in pain, suffering, knowing that it died that way because it was evil. Atala is vermin). (360)

Atala also weaves her own tragic destiny as she becomes involved in drugs and prostitution. She is shot at a carnival by one of her lovers whom she supplied with drugs. It is an ironic, final comment on Félix's failures: He misses his major goal—to become "The Great Assassin" by killing Atala.

The second half of the novel features eleven sections printed in italics and titled "Tiempo extraño" (Strange time). These sections appear between regular chapters narrated by Atala. Time and events become even more erratic, as explained by the following references: "*Los años siguen un desorden. Yo lo respetaré*" (*The years follow a disorder, I'll respect it*) (254); "*Los años están confusos. Como si no fueran más para adelante. Corre el tiempo, sale de la conciencia, sale de mí con la densidad del humo. Mi tiempo está extraño*" (*The years are confused. As though they did not advance anymore. Time runs, exits my conscience, exits me with the density of smoke. My time is strange*) (268). (Italics are Orphée's.) In these sections Atala expresses her pent-up emotions, especially her love for her deceased mother and grandmother to whom she never showed her real feelings. As Orphée indicates in the "Conversation with Elvira Orphée," this takes place during Atala's agonizing death. Díaz interprets it as delirium at the moment of death, after Atala has been shot. The three-minute death scene takes up several chapters of the novel, as she chaotically recalls her life. Her reminiscences are intertwined with hallucinations of what could have been and what she had hoped to get from life.[17]

Characters are persistently placed in negative situations filled with threats and fear, an atmosphere that alters traditional behavior.[18] Consequently, the three main characters deny the existence of God as traditionally conceived. Their god is a monster, a cruel and avenging figure. Nevertheless, they want to decipher eternity, and see themselves as fallen angels who, through evil and hatred, will reclaim eternity. Félix Luna tells his life story by means of a fairy tale, which culminates in his escape as he runs after a snow queen. She locks him in a palace and has him form all kinds of words with pieces of ice in geometrical shapes. His failure is recorded even in his fantasies, as the only shape he cannot form is the word "Eternity." As for the other protagonists, Atala is cast as Mimaya's hope to regain an eternity that she has lost:

> Caigo y caigo en un extraño vacío, desprendida a hachazos de la eternidad. ¿Pero es que no hay un punto para aferrarme? ¡Sí, lo hay! Atala. En ella habitan lo delirante, lo criminal, lo fantasmagórico, todo eso a lo que falsamente renuncié.

> (I fall and fall into a strange emptiness, separated by ax blows from eternity. Isn't there a point to hang from? Yes, there is! Atala. She is inhabited by delirium, criminality, the phantasmagoric, all that which I falsely gave up.) (277)

Eduardo Moctezuma interprets Atala as a new fallen angel, and the novel as a negation of the Western theological tradition recovering a hellish space.[19] As with Sixto Riera in *Dos veranos*, Orphée denies these characters any possibility of redemption. They are victims of fatalism, circumstances, and tragic personal flaws.

En el fondo

Orphée's fourth novel, *En el fondo* (Down deep inside), 1969, is reminiscent of *Dos veranos* in its setting, introspective mood, and structure. Like *Dos veranos*, it is divided into two parts, but instead of a temporal division into two summers, the parts are spatial: "Cold Country" and "Hot Country."

In part 1, the protagonist is living in the "Cold Country" (France) where her paralytic mother, now deceased, was born. Her home is the "Hot Country" (obviously Tucumán). She is in the "Cold Country" because her mother wanted her to live there and "grow wings." Throughout her first-person narration, she reminisces about and idealizes her sickly childhood in that torrid landscape filled with the supernatural and the unknown. While reminiscing, she seems to become part of nature (like Sixto Riera in *Dos veranos*):

> [C]aos de montañas tumbadas sobre estrellas, una explosión de mercurio en nuestro viejo fondo de mar. Las ráfagas de luna azotan la cara. La luna es un fulgor fallecido y aullante, un fantasma que alumbra a otros fantasmas reemplazables. Nosotros.

> [(C]haos of mountains knocked over atop stars, an explosion of mercury on our old sea bottom. Flashes of moonlight whip the face. The moon is a dead and howling gleam, a ghost lighting up other replaceable ghosts. Ourselves.)[20]

The quest for interaction with nature through games, rituals, and magic is an attempt to make up for the lack of love in her childhood. She blends landscapes and feelings:

> Carecen de lógica y quizá del amor mismo. Tal vez la culpa no sea de ellos. Están rodeados de pura geología. Montañas dinosaurios, restos de cataclismos, cicatriz cósmica donde el bálsamo gente no fue aplicado. Un mundo nada más que de paisajes no es un mundo de amor.

(They lack logic and maybe even love. Maybe it's not their fault. They are surrounded by pure geology. Dinosaur mountains, remains of cataclysms, cosmic scars where the people ointment wasn't applied. A world of just landscapes is not a world of love.) (83)

The protagonist's nostalgia evokes a lost paradise, which Picon Garfield calls a "primordial atmosphere," involving not only external aspects, like the landscape and natural elements, but also the characters' passions, which define them, piercing through them and endowing them with a cosmic force.[21]

In part 2, "Hot Country," the protagonist has married Manuel and returns home with him and her beloved blue-eyed cat, P. T. T. As they are driving down the road toward her house, the title of the novel is explained: "Tan en el fondo parecía la casa que me asustó. Era un fondo como para abajo o en lo profundo" (The house seemed to be totally at the far back, which scared me. It was far back pointing somewhat toward the bottom or deep down) (41). She asks her husband: "¿Qué nos esperará allá en el fondo?" (I wonder what is awaiting us there down deep inside?). He answers, "Una chiquilina que dejaste hace años" (A young girl you left years ago) (41). "Down deep inside" in her childhood house the protagonist will recover her past.

But she is disappointed. Her dreams do not match the reality of her home and family life. She also realizes that she does not love Manuel anymore, that he is changing in her mind. While she is at the cemetery where her mother is buried, she has a vision of herself and a man who has the same blue eyes as P. T. T. and whom she has supposedly already encountered in the "Cold Country" by the sea. When she finally meets him again, she is disappointed: "Quizá el amor entre hombres y mujeres sea el peor. Quizá ni sea necesario. Quizá el mejor sea el amor por una planta o por un animal" (Maybe love between a man and a woman is the worst kind. Maybe it's not even necessary. Maybe the best is love for a plant or an animal) (143). The only love she can imagine is of a cosmic nature, as both become part of a mineral landscape for eternity: "Deberíamos ser dos estatuas de yacentes, con el cuerpo recto, volviendo la cabeza para mirarse, sin complicidad, sólo con geometría y con eternidad" (We should be two recumbent statues, with our bodies stretched out, turning our heads to look at each other, without complicity, with only geometry and with eternity) (161). When the imaginary man leaves her, the protagonist loses her will to live and seeks a cosmic union with her beloved and the earth:

A mí se me murió el hombre de los ojos azules y alguien más que era yo. Debo estar inmóvil, volverme a la piedra de la que me desgajé hace mil años. Entonces, hace millones de años, por no sé qué cataclismo, me salí de la piedra o la piedra se salió de mí.

(The blue-eyed man died and somebody else who was I. I should be immobile, return to the stone from which I broke off a thousand years ago. Then, a million years ago, due to I don't know what cataclysm, I broke off a stone or the stone broke off from me.) (165–66)

These are almost the same words used by Mimaya in *Aire tan dulce* to convey the desire of a distraught protagonist who escapes into madness after losing her loved one. *En el fondo*'s protagonist believes there is only one way to overcome her present situation and reestablish equilibrium:

[S]he considers a cosmic encounter with her loved one and she prays to the god of prehistoric nature to restore to her the harmony of the geometric form and the eternity of the heavenly bodies, after the celestial collision that would produce, *this time*, a love lacking passion and the timing of two planets petrified in neighboring orbits communicating with each other. Thus, there would be a resurrection because she would participate in the creation of the universe.[22]

As the novel closes, the protagonist, who has been in the hospital, returns to her childhood world where she seeks refuge and, through imaginary conversations with her mother and reenacted childhood games, a return to her origins. In the final image, she walks into her childhood house—backwards (alluding to a childhood game and a reclaiming of her past). She is going down deep inside herself, reclaiming the "Hot Country," her roots, the place where she was deprived of love: "Yo entraré siempre de espaldas. En el fondo, soy como ellos, soy de aquí" (I will always enter walking backwards. Deep down inside, I'm like them, I'm from here) (175).

When the protagonist becomes sick (as did her mother before her) and madness takes hold of her, she thinks this is a sign that God does not love them anymore. Sickness recurs in Orphée's novels, confining female characters to houses and rooms. Male characters react to what they feel is a manifestation of God's indifference or lack of love toward them by committing violent acts that destroy their lives. Their female counterparts reach the same metaphysical conclusions, but direct their destructive behavior toward themselves instead of others. While Orphée's male protagonists create havoc in the world around them, her female protagonists (with the exception of Atala) remove themselves from reality (literally and figuratively) to become the embodiment of the diseased human condition.

La última conquista de El Angel

The eleven stories in *La última conquista de El Angel* (El Angel's last conquest), 1977, can be read individually or as one story (they were published in 1984 as a novel.) The stories are linked by the protagonist/ narrator, the main characters, and the theme of political torture. This thematic focus was inspired by real activities of two officially unrecognized organizations that functioned as extensions of repressive police forces: the fifties' Nationalist Liberation Alliance (featured in *Uno*) and the Argentine Anti-Communist Alliance (AAA). The AAA was already operating during the early 1970s, in the years preceding the "dirty war" when some of the stories were written. The temporal framework, which places the stories within Argentine sociohistorical reality, has been noted by María Luisa Bastos:

> The first seven stories unmistakably develop during the peak of the Peronist era, toward 1953 or 1954; the eighth marks Perón's fall, which coincides with Winkel's transition to madness. . . . The three last ones cover with exaggerated haste the stages from 1955 until the guerrilla activities started toward the end of the sixties.[23]

Orphée disclaims attempts to link the stories to reality, although in the "Conversation with Elvira Orphée" she explains that she wrote about torture "out of hatred for actions against forsaken human beings."[24] She says that the subject matter "was born in [her] like a nauseous feeling, an impotence, a frenetic abhorrence of arrogant macho dominance, until one day a little book fell into [her] hands . . . in which a man, Santiago Nudelman, a member of the Chamber of Deputies, wrote about torture in his time, some twenty-four years ago."[25]

Orphée reconciles her apparently contradictory statements by avowing that she was able to deal with the topic when she realized that "[her] novel wasn't about exposing a reality in itself . . . but, rather, about why a man becomes a torturer."[26] Therefore, Orphée departs from real events, blurring and concealing them, as her goal is to portray universal issues. *La última conquista de El Angel* deals with power (the central theme of *Dos veranos* and *Aire tan dulce*) extended to the limit; her flawed protagonists wield absolute power. Orphée chooses to place this situation within a political context "to explore the position of the torturer."[27] Her endeavor examines universal metaphysical and ethical issues: (1) Why does a man become a torturer? (2) What is the nature of evil? (3) What is God's role regarding human suffering? (4) What is the individual's place and purpose (if any) in the universal scheme?[28]

Only the stories' surface plots focus on the secret activities of the Buenos Aires Police "Special Section"—the abduction, torture and disappearance of suspects—and events taking place in the "yellow," or "mystery," torture chamber. The real story is not found in the blurred sociodocumentary, but in the unnamed protagonist's first-person narration of a bildungsroman of abjection, describing "how by means of the inflicted, witnessed, and, above all, *narrated* torture, the narrator becomes the successor and reflection of his admired boss, Winkel."[29] The stories have a similar structure: a detective story with a mystery to be solved.[30] The solution (a confession) is sought by torturing the victims with specific "ceremonies" devised by Winkel (the protagonist's "secret king"),

> sin apartarse de ningún requisito, siguiendo cada paso de la ceremonia. . . . Cada paso debe cumplirse, cada regla debe seguirse, cada gesto está establecido de antemano. . . . La ceremonia estaba fijada de una vez para siempre. Me acuerdo todavía de cómo me sacudieron las palabras que Winkel dijo en nuestro primer encuentro: La noche se ha acabado, se acabó la ceremonia.

> (without deviating from any requirement, following every step of the ceremony. . . . Every step must be carried out, every rule must be followed, every gesture is established in advance. . . . The ceremony was set once and for all. I still remember how I was shaken by Winkel's words on our first meeting: The evening has ended, the ceremony has ended.) (110)

Orphée focuses on the psychological dimension, while the narrator chronicles the horrors perpetrated by himself and his comrades in abjection. What makes the stories so effective is Orphée's choice of a torturer—the narrator—eliciting "an intuitive understanding of a person capable of torture," making readers his accomplices, as "[their] consciousness cannot again choose ignorance with innocence."[31] The readers' sympathies for the narrator develop as the story of the protagonist's life is voiced over the narration of the Special Section's grisly actions, from his début at the Section, when he was in his early twenties, until he is middle aged. This time frame expands because of the protagonist's thoughts and memories that reveal incidents in his childhood. His childhood recollections center on devastating earthquakes, which he recalls during the torture sessions: "Yo dentro miraba La Rioja lejana que ardía de frío en la noche de junio. Bajo las estrellas heladas la tierra de La Rioja estaba presintiendo el temblor" (Inside I looked at distant La Rioja that was ablaze with cold in the June night. Under the icy stars the land of La Rioja had a presentiment of the tremor) (15). Winkel bears the stigma of provincial origins as well. Like the protagonist, he has been affected by the natural world, as his father died when struck by lightning. The protagonist realizes these bonds and describes his boss accordingly: "Winkel, envoltura de hielo seco que le ardía dentro" (Winkel, bundle of dry ice that burned inside him) (20).

In the fourth story, "Nada" (Nothing), the protagonist explains the devastating effect that the natural cataclysms had on him, providing a clue as to why he has become a torturer:

> El fundió los cuerpos con la piedra en íntima papilla y me proveyó de horror ya para siempre. Lo que él me ha dado yo lo pongo en la Sección porque es lo único que tengo mío.

> (It fused the bodies with the stone in an intimate pap and provided me with horror forever. What it has given me I put into the Section because it is the only thing that belongs to me.) (43)

Both the protagonist and Winkel have experienced powerlessness and loss as a result of natural disasters, and by inflicting pain on their victims, they have "turned the tables" and become the cosmic force that tried to destroy them in the past. They justify their belief that the only thing they can do in life is to torture by embracing it like a crusade: "[T]he torturer acts like a priest exorcising a devil."[32] Their labor becomes a transcendental quest; they do not torture to obtain confessions, but out of a

> necesidad de que algo extraordinario nos contestara por qué.

> (need that something extraordinary would answer [them] why.) (111)

> ¿Por qué qué? Vaya a saber. Por qué él era él, por qué estábamos haciendo eso. Una cosa de brujos, qué sé yo.

> (Why what? Who knows. Why he was he, why were we doing that. A labor of witches, what do I know.) (111)

Theirs is a metaphysical journey with religious overtones to reestablish their omnipotence:

Lo que llaman la tortura pertenece a un orden sobrenatural, como el cielo o el infierno.

(What they call torture belongs to a supernatural order, like heaven or hell.) (9)

Sección Especial igual a Dios. No hay diferencias entre nosotros y Dios en este sector de la vida. . . . El interrogatorio es un arte y nosotros sus artistas.

(Special Section equals God. There are no differences between us and God in this sector of life. . . . Interrogation is an art form and we are its artists.) (63)

The protagonist and Winkel perceive themselves as instruments of an indifferent natural world or a distant deity. Consequently, they act in an emotional and moral vacuum. In "Ceremonia" (Ceremony), the first story, the protagonist at first empathizes with the prisoner, but then stifles his feelings, as he learns to dehumanize the prisoners. In the process, the victims become "un fardo" (a bundle), "esa porquería" (that piece of shit), "otro estudiantito" (another little student), "ese porcino" (that pig), "lo que había en el piso" (what was lying on the floor), "el tipo" (the guy), or "el pibe" (the young guy). The prisoners are stripped of their humanity and reduced to exterior and physical descriptions, so that the narrator and the readers suspend any emotions that the situation might conjure up.[33] The protagonist and Winkel's emotional emptiness is linked to their sexual impotence and fear of intimacy, which they attempt to conceal by directing their torture to their victims' sexual organs: "La piel chisporroteaba en los testículos" (The skin crackled on the testicles) (70); "Le aplicaría los santos óleos de la aguja en todos los huecos que tuviera, y si no tenía bastantes, se los crearía (I would apply the needle's holy ointments on all the hollow spaces that she might have, and if she didn't have enough, I would create them for her) (140). The physical brutality is accompanied by derogatory comments, another way the protagonists deflect their fear of feelings, especially those that female subjects might stir in them: "Las hembras de la tortura pueden ser hermosas, pero eso ¿a quién le importa?" (The tortured bitches can be beautiful, but who cares about that?) (110).

The sixth story, "Tormenta, tormento" (Storm, torment—a pun on *atormenta* [he torments], *atormento* [I torment]), significantly placed in the central part of the volume, depicts a revealing ceremony devised by Winkel when the Special Section has reached the delirious heights of impunity. Winkel introduces a new twist in this torture session by making Argentina's patron Virgin of Luján a participant. The voltage applied to the victim is indicated by a fluorescent image of the Virgin, which is turned on and off in synchronization with the electric shocks ravaging the prisoner's body, in a bloody scene of macabre and blasphemous sexual overtones:

> [L]os ocho dedos del jefe abiertos justo delante de la reina del cielo, como recorridos también por sangre fluorescente.

> ([T]he boss's eight fingers opened exactly in front of the queen of heaven, as though fluorescent blood were flowing through them as well.) (62)

> El baile de las luces se puso todavía más rápido. . . . Nos agarró a todos la convulsión.

> (The dance of lights became even faster. . . . We all caught the convulsion.) (69)

Winkel's blood (sperm?) appears to flow through the religious image, mingling with that of the tortured victim and spreading to the other torturers, and it becomes apparent that his creative effort is leading him toward a new threshold where insanity awaits him.

The open expression of emotions and sexuality is combated by Winkel and the protagonist, who deny their feelings by molding their environment, comrades, and victims so that everything is totally under their control. The torturers perceive their activities in terms of a battle against disease (terminology used in various sociopolical contexts, including Perón and the military's discourse during the Proceso):

> Es un combate por la salud y el orden. . . . ¿Quién dije que era el enfermo? Son ellos, claro, los que entran aquí, los crueles. Están agujereados de enfermedad y vienen para que nosotros los curemos.

> (It is a combat for health and order. . . . Whom did I say was the diseased? It is them, of course, those who enter here, the cruel ones. They are full of holes from disease and they come to us to be healed.) (91–92)

This struggle between torturers and victims, represented by the forces of health and sanity against disease, provides the torturers with self-justification. Their behavior stems "from a messianic and manichean conception of the struggle between good and evil, which takes place in the torturer[s'] mind."[34] The metaphysical dichotomy contained in the health-versus-disease metaphor acquires significance in the torture chamber, where the torturer perceives himself as "the Hero whose quest was to purge, to cleanse, to slay, to restore health and Natural Order."[35] In reality, the opposite takes place, as the victims arrive in good physical shape and are dismembered in a ritualistic ceremony. The positing of the conflict by means of opposing dualities (victim/victimizer, health/disease, good/evil) starts to crumble in the seventh story, "Qué artista ha perdido el mundo" (What an artist the world has lost), when Winkel begins to identify with his victims, recognizing that they represent an aspect of himself that he is trying to obliterate:

[Y] para dormir uno estaba obligado a convencerse de que los tipos eran una porquería, que lo que querían era hacernos mierda a todos, pero que aun así quedaba como una llamita que lamía los sesos y no dejaba parejo el sueño, tanto que si uno llegaba a soñar hasta oía una voz entonando "ni malo ni traidor, igualito a vos, igualito a vos, lo que le tocó puede tocarte."

([A]nd to sleep it was necessary to become convinced that the guys were shit, that what they wanted was to make shit out of all of us, but even so something like a small flame remained licking the brains and disturbing sleep, so that in the case that one might be able to dream one would even hear a voice singing "not mean nor traitor, the same as you, the same as you, what befell him can befall you.") (89)

As Fernando Reati points out, "Inside the self of the torturer his Other, the opposer, insinuates itself, and this unresolved contradiction ends up by leading the Special Section's boss to madness."[36] In fact, Winkel's madness surges from within, from the stifled aspect of himself:

¿Dónde había perdido Winkel a Winkel? ¿Hasta qué recodo se le había trepado el otro, el intruso espantoso.

(Where had Winkel lost Winkel? Until what turn had the other climbed on top of him, the horrible stranger?) (82)

Winkel ya no podía contener al otro, al distinto que se le salía en palabras y ademanes y que ya había desalojado casi del todo al verdadero.

(Winkel could not stop the other one anymore, the different one who came out in words and gestures and who had almost totally evicted the real one.) (91)

As a result, a "diseased" Winkel becomes deranged, turning into the victimized Other committed to an insane asylum, where he receives electric shocks. After Winkel's demise, which symbolically coincides with the end of Perón's regime, the Special Section is dismantled and the protagonist drifts, working awhile for the regular police. Fourteen or fifteen years go by, a period compressed in the three last stories. It is the end of the sixties, and the fortyish protagonist has become acutely disillusioned and disempowered. Things gradually change, however, as there is evidence of guerrilla activity, and bombs are set off in various parts of the city. As a result, the Special Section and torture are reinstated.

The last story, "La última conquista de El Angel," from which the volume takes its title, presents a revitalized protagonist, who feels that he can finally achieve his lifelong dream to become Winkel and return the Section to its former "splendor":

Yo tenía la situación que ocupaba él, Winkel, mi jefe iluminado, cuando empecé. El oficio era el mismo, pero como neblinosamente cambiado.
. . . Iba a mostrarles yo a hacer las cosas como se debe.

(I had the job that he, Winkel, my illuminated boss, had when I started. The profession was the same, but as though vaguely changed.
. . . I was going to show them how to do things right.) (134)

The story deals with a police informer, a double agent and pimp called El Angel because of his good looks, which he uses to attract and humiliate women. When he dies suddenly, the police think it is suicide, but the protagonist suspects treachery when he meets one of El Angel's women, his "last conquest." Judith (an allusion to the biblical character who decapitated in his sleep the commander besieging her town) is a nineteen-year-old revolutionary who taunts and arouses the protagonist. Feeling threatened by Judith and by the stories of El Angel's virility, which haunt him even after the informer's violent death, the protagonist transfers his sexual desires to his dirty work. The stories have come full circle, as this is the only occasion, after his first experience with torture in "Ceremonia," the opening story, that the protagonist responds emotionally to a (prospective) victim. Critic Bell Gale Chevigny comments: "As Winkel before him, the narrator is menaced by an intrusion from within, by a repressed self seeking to vanquish the self he has made as torturer." Therefore, he persecutes her relentlessly to "abolish forever, what this couple might stir in him,"[37] and to revive the prime of his power attained in Winkel's "mystery chamber":

> Esta mujer niquelada sería mi nueva oportunidad. Yo cambiaba el curso del tiempo, era boomerang hacia la juventud. ¿En qué momento se me había perdido el destino? No importaba. Lo volvería a encontrar.

> (This nickel-plated woman would give me another chance. I was changing the course of time, boomeranging toward youth. At what point had I lost my way? It didn't matter. I would find it again.) (139)

The protagonist's interpretation of events (withheld until the end of the story and uncorroborated by evidence) is that the revolutionaries caught El Angel double-crossing them, put a gun in his hand, and had Judith pull the trigger. As a consequence, Judith is hauled into the torture chamber by the narrator, who has prepared a "matrimonio consagrado por el horror" (a wedding consecrated by horror) (140). It is clear that the protagonist considers his handling of the case and staging of the "ceremony" a feat comparable to Winkel's in "Tormenta, tormento." Both events signal the highlight of their respective careers and power; however, they also indicate that Winkel and the protagonist have become possessed by a degree of destructive violence and evil leading to derangement.

The "ceremony" becomes the climax of the story. Judith is literally made to ride the angel of death; she is blindfolded and tied to El Angel's partly naked corpse while electric shocks are applied to her body: "Primero el cuerpo sobre el de ella, atado a ella. Luego descargas en su vagina y en el sexo del hombre, sincrónicas" (First the body atop hers, tied to her. Then discharges in her vagina and on the man's penis, synchronized) (141). The protagonist's use of the electric *picana*, eliciting convulsions in a necrophilic reenactment of Judith and El Angel's previous lovemaking, denotes that the *picana* has become a phallus changing his impotence to omnipotence.[38] The spectacle perpetrated by the protagonist is a result of his repressing whatever feelings Judith stirred in him. He has finally reached his goal: becoming "'the angel of death' the messenger of a deformed god made in the image of the man of the Special Section."[39]

The brutal course of events forces a reconsideration of the meaning of the story's title. "Ultima" can refer to the protagonist's latest conquest as well as to his last one, but the latter is more meaningful, since it is the protagonist's last chance to consolidate his full power while he is still in his prime and while the timing is right. There is another nuance: By becoming like Winkel, the protagonist's last conquest marks his inescapable transition to madness.

Orphée's volume masterfully presents the effects of a social and political situation involving a totalitarian state, revolutionary movements, victimizers, and victims, without dealing with specific times and events. She manages to render a psychological study of human beings who are a product of these circumstances, while holding up a mirror where readers see their own guilty reflections as they are turned into accomplices and witness the events firsthand. Readers must come to terms with these characters, who reveal themselves as human beings as well as torturers. Issues raised by Orphée make readers who choose to ignore atrocities accountable to their own consciences. And finally, readers are confronted with the incarnation of evil, with cruel and avenging self-styled deities, and with the nihilism of the two central characters. The work culminates a cycle. Previous characters, like Sixto Riera, Félix Gauna, and Atala Pons, appear in these stories in their final transformation, achieving power in modern Argentina's dirty wars.

Las viejas fantasiosas

Orphée describes *Las viejas fantasiosas* (The fanciful old ladies), 1981, as

> a collection of short stories that take place in small towns. They are neither fantasy nor pure reality. One critic called them "intrareality," that is, an inner reality that imposes itself upon the one who lives it. Every small village in Latin America knows about the facts and events that enter a realm beyond reality in the imagination of people deprived of external life. That is how they nullify the boredom of an existence where tomorrow is the same as today and succeed in making the monotonous sand clock of time flower with malice, abomination, or enchantment.[40]

The small town atmosphere is captured in the story bearing the same title as the volume and shows Orphée's ability to build a fantasy world from a mundane situation. The story narrates life in a provincial boardinghouse run by an old lady who loved to entertain. The unusual element is that she loved to adorn herself and her house to play out her personal fantasies. As the story opens, she has died. Her two favorite boarders, young civil servants who work for the post office, keep the house. She has also passed on to them her yearnings for a life where fantasy prevails.

In response to an advertisement selling unusual furniture, the two young boarders travel to a dreamlike house where three old women, who remind them of their former landlady, keep them captive for several weeks. Every night they are given a potion that stimulates nightmares and disorientation. At the house they encounter strange, mute animals resulting from cross-breeding, and beautiful, though unusual-looking, young women. The protagonists think that the young women are the offspring of the three old ladies and men who, like them, answered advertisements. Realizing that they have been chosen to take part in the ladies' odd experiments, they escape, returning to their boardinghouse. Their return, marked by hallucinating madness (frequent in Orphée's stories), unleashes the descent of monsters on the town in a twist reminiscent of the original expulsion from Eden, as it bears the traditional connotations of punishment and banishment for the "fallen angels." Thus, as fantasy takes over, the characters attempt to escape the confinement of provincial life and attain "intrareality."

Orphée's works partake of the best of Latin American literature. The suffering characters cast in stifling atmospheres and succumbing to evil forces are reminiscent of Juan Rulfo's fictional world. Jorge Luis Borges's and Julio Cortázar's quests for a metaphysical and fantastic reality also appear in her fiction as her characters reach out to their cosmogonic origins. Several contemporary Argentine writers incorporate political themes, as does Orphée in *Uno, La última conquista de El Angel,* and *Basura y luna,* the novel she is currently writing.[41] Orphée's oblique treatment of political themes in *La última conquista de El Angel* foreshadows the techniques developed by the four writers studied in the subsequent chapters of this volume. Orphée developed an original strategy to blur the links between the subject matter in her stories and the sociopolitical reality. Following Orphée's lead, writers trying to evade external censorship as well as self-censorship resort to these nonmimetic, metaphorical, and allegorical forms of representing political violence.

Conversation with Elvira Orphée

Buenos Aires, 18 April 1987

M.F.: Tell me about your life, about the events and people that you consider important.

E.O.: That would take a long time, the time it takes to write a book. Besides, I'm basically a loner. Even though I admire some people very much, I don't like to spend long hours with any of them. I don't believe, either, and it's to my detriment, that they would have influenced me from a literary standpoint, even if I had tried. They would not have been able to touch me like the works of some Japanese writers did, like Ishikawa Takuboku, Tanizaki Junichiro, and Agutagawa Ryonosuke, who has written an admirable work titled *The Gears*. It's a novella about the daily events of a man who travels by train, but from the start these trivial events become a road toward tragedy.

M.F.: And among the Latin American writers, whom do you admire?

E.O.: I would never be able to write like [Juan] Rulfo, although he touches me deeply, because I can't leave out the intellectual element. In his books the characters seem to act in response to impulses, sensations, and intuitions that are distant from intellectual thought. While answering your previous question, when I said that I wouldn't be able to spend long hours with admirable people, I must have been thinking of Rulfo. With him, any dialogue was painful.

M.F.: However, you create an atmosphere in your works that is reminiscent of Rulfo's *Pedro Páramo*.

E.O.: Yes, I like Rulfo very much, but I find it impossible to achieve his simplicity, so, even if I had tried to write like Rulfo, it would have been impossible for me.

M.F.: Do you admire any Argentine writers?

E.O.: Borges, naturally. But, my admiration developed in stages. During my youth, I was attracted to his formal perfection. As time went by, I understood that he wrote metaphysical works. And I suspect metaphysics is what I'm mainly looking for in literature.

M.F.: What are you reading now?

E.O.: A bit of everything: Maupassant alternating with Isaac Bashevis Singer, Elsa Morante, and Javier Torre. Torre is a young Argentine writer who, in his second book, reveals qualities that better-known writers of his generation don't possess. My voracity for worlds of fantasy also includes best sellers, which, although devoid of literary qualities, use suspense effectively. I don't have any discipline when it comes to reading and writing.

M.F.: Do you have a writing routine?

E.O.: I am not the kind of person who sits down and writes twenty pages a day. Italo Calvino once told me that when he settled down to write, he would take advantage of any pretext to get up from his chair. It's the same for me. And, getting away from the sheet of paper is just as anguishing. You feel fearful about whether you'll be able to continue. And when you've finally finished a text, you despair about the time you lost procrastinating.

M.F.: How do you select a theme?

E.O.: The theme is usually the easiest part. The problem is deciding how to narrate it. According to an anecdote by the French writer Colette, a young man who wanted to become a writer told her he was planning to write a grandiose work, but was lacking only a theme. Colette answered more or less as follows: "Don't worry about that, I'll give you one: a man and a woman in love."

M.F.: How did you start writing?

E.O.: I started writing because I was lonely. As a child, I was frequently sick, so I read and fantasized a lot during long periods spent in bed. When I was eleven years old, I wrote some awful poems, and when I was fourteen, I started writing a long novel with a protagonist called Roland and lots of woods. It was probably a combination of Robin Hood and Roland, the French knight. Besides, my family is of French descent, one of my cousins is called Roland, and, at the same time, I was living in Tucumán, a place full of trees.

M.F.: Does Tucumán have much influence in your works?

E.O.: Its influence is like the lingering scent of perfume on someone's clothing. Tucumán gave me its ghosts. For me a ghost is a ray of moonlight over a blooming orange tree in an inner courtyard. The houses in the provinces generally had three courtyards, and the third one is a very mysterious yard filled with trees. My grandfather's courtyard had fig, guava, and lime trees. In any case, what is important is not the physical presence of the house, but the moon-filled atmosphere. It generally produces fear because the streets in the provinces are usually deserted by early evening. I remember passing by a convent's iron grates and suddenly seeing the moon reflected on them and feeling frightened. I think what was happening was that I was perceiving divinity. That sensation in Tucumán touched me deeply. That combination of aromas, feelings, and sensations became the Absolute and transfixed me.

M.F.: Would you say your work is autobiographical?

E.O.: Like any other writer. An oblique, transformed, made-up autobiography.

M.F.: Which women writers do you like?

E.O.: Colette, undoubtedly, because she offers a very valid combination of intelligence and intuition.

M.F.: And among Argentine women writers, do you have any favorites?

E.O.: Alejandra Pizarnik, a poet who committed suicide; Olga Orozco, also a poet, who wrote a book of short fiction as well, *La oscuridad es otro sol* (Darkness is another sun); Silvina Ocampo, when she isn't writing for her grandchildren; and Sara Gallardo and her book, *El país del humo* (Land of smoke), among others.

M.F.: Are you a feminist?

E.O.: Yes, I am.

M.F.: How is feminism present in your work?

E.O.: It isn't, in the sense that I'm not a militant feminist.

M.F.: Do you think your works could be considered feminist literature?

E.O.: Maybe some books. Definitely *Aire tan dulce* and *Dos veranos*. Feminism isn't so obvious in *Uno* and *La última conquista de El Angel*.

M.F.: Why do you consider *Aire tan dulce* and *Dos veranos* feminist novels?

E.O.: The valid protagonists, those who have a very defined personality, are women. The men are fillers.

M.F.: Also in *Aire tan dulce*?

E.O.: Yes. Félix Gauna is mediocre, he isn't great in any respect. He doesn't show any lyricism, poetry, or action. He doesn't even have a definite evilness.

M.F.: But in *Dos veranos*, Sixto Riera is the main character. Why is it a feminist novel?

E.O.: Because Sixto Riera is also pushed by circumstances, as well as a lack of initiative characteristic of the provinces. He thinks he's going to own a white silk sofa someday, just effortlessly, not because there is something in his actions that makes him get the white silk sofa. So he sets out to bash in an old man's head with a stone. In contrast, the female protagonist shows more courage about facing life. It is also a feminist novel because men are seen from the point of view of a woman.

M.F.: The character who plays the role of the lady of the house is always lying down on her bed, sick. She is a very traditional woman.

E.O.: Yes, but she's the woman who loved him like a son and defended him in spite of everything. Although she's traditional, she's ready to do anything for him.

M.F.: Were you in Argentina during the "dirty war"?

E.O.: I was in Venezuela and occasionally spent some time in Buenos Aires.

M.F.: Did you leave because of political reasons?

E.O.: No, but whenever I came back from abroad, I would suffer terribly because of what was going on. At first, like many people, I didn't know what was happening, but in the later years we found out.

M.F.: Was your work influenced during those years by the Argentine political situation?

E.O.: No, I don't write testimonial literature.

M.F.: Are there stages in your work?

E.O.: The word "stages" brings to mind something that is definitely closed. I would say that in every life there's a pattern of growth comparable to that of a tree. It's like branches that send out shoots at different times on different parts of the trunk, but they're all the same length.

M.F.: Your characters are described subjectively rather than objectively; there aren't any physical descriptions. Why do you use this technique?

E.O.: Direct descriptions turn me off. Homer never described Helen. He just made us aware of the magnitude of her beauty by a comment made by the elders of Troy, when they saw her on the wall and said that now they understood why they were fighting a war.

M.F.: What importance do dreams and fantasy have in you works?

E.O.: They are very important. My dreams have a literary quality. I even dream phrases, but without a setting or characters.

M.F.: If we compare your collections of short stories, *Su demonio preferido*, *Las viejas fantasiosas*, and *La última conquista de El Angel*, there is great diversity in the themes, setting, and plots. Why is there this diversity?

E.O.: Because of the diversity of the human spirit. *La última conquista de El Angel* became a novel in its last edition just by placing chapters, as there was a central theme running through the volume. It's really a novel. The themes and techniques used in the stories in *Su demonio preferido* and *Las viejas fantasiosas* are different. Perhaps I was in a more intellectual phase in *Su demonio preferido*.

M.F.: Why is there a change in direction in the narration of *Aire tan dulce*? Félix Gauna is the central character who is then placed in a secondary position.

E.O.: There is no change, it's simply not linear. And if we take into consideration the date it was published, I'm a precursor. Félix Gauna was never intended to be the central character. Atalita is the main character. Or, we could say there are three protagonists: Atala, her grandmother, and Félix.

M.F.: Did you intend to give one of them a more prominent role?

E.O.: I wanted to contrast two kinds of human beings—the prosaic character who is ready to take advantage of others, and a lyric and spiritual one, represented by Atala and her grandmother.

M.F.: Why did you end the novel like you did?

E.O.: Why can't I? It was impossible for me to let somebody get old losing their love and thirst for the Absolute.

M.F.: What does the yearning for the Absolute mean in your novels?

E.O.: It's a metaphysical point of reference, to remind us that we aren't just beings restricted to the present. Even though reality might destroy us, I can't help thinking that fate intervenes in our lives.

M.F.: What was your goal in using contradictions within the different narrations?

E.O.: I suppose what you call "different narrations" are the dialogues the characters carry on with themselves and others. Their mental dialogues recount events and why they're happening.

M.F.: Why did you use such complex techniques, like different points of view and time shifts, to integrate narrations? It makes the reading difficult.

E.O.: The different points of view stem from the fact that there are three characters who narrate. As for the time shifts, there's only one and it distinguishes life from the agony of death. The chapters titled "Strange Time" refer to the time of death, and are clearly distinguished by their typographical presentation in the second edition of *Aire tan dulce*, published by Monte Avila in Caracas. The first one, published by Sudamericana in Buenos Aires, and it's my fault, did not include the typographical distinction, nor were the chapters divided in a clear fashion.[42]

M.F.: Why do you depict society and your characters as depraved, marginal, and irredeemable?

E.O.: That's your opinion. For me Atala and her grandmother represent redemption. They are rebellious and angelical.

M.F.: Some critics say at her death, Atala is a fallen angel who will inhabit an infernal space. Is this true?

E.O.: I don't see it that way. I don't think she'll inhabit an infernal space because her hatred has found its target. So she dies, maybe in peace.

M.F.: A critic says, "The novel places the characters in an atmosphere where there is an inversion of the traditional codes because persistently negative situations are evoked. This is related to the perception of the Absolute. The three main characters deny the existence of a traditional God. Their God is a monster, a cruel and avenging figure."[43]

E.O.: All that is true.

M.F.: The same critic says, that the characters are perceived as fallen angels who reclaim eternity through evil and hatred, who will live through eternity hating and practicing evil.[44]

E.O.: Yes, in Atala's case, she experiences through her hatred unreciprocated love. Felix's hatred is not justified; it's a response to the circumstances of his life; it's the hatred of a resentful person. Her hatred comes from deep down, stemming from her sickness. She has joined a struggle against a God, whom she perceives as unfair. He's struggling against a society that has denied him the level of wealth he aspires to. He's not terribly poor, but simply a mediocre being.

M.F.: What is the meaning of the title, *Aire tan dulce*?

E.O.: A whole chapter titled "Aire tan dulce" explains it: "En esta ciudad de aire tan dulce sólo debería haber hombres que viviesen cada día como si fuera el último y las mujeres de esos hombres. Aquí sólo debería haber hombres que vivieran jugándose la vida" (This city where the air is so sweet should be inhabited only by men who live each day as though it were their last, and by the wives of these men. Only men who live putting their lives at risk should live here). During the month of September, Tucumán is pure orange flowers. Its streets are bordered by orange trees in bloom. When summer comes, it's the jasmines and magnolias that perfume the air. This should coincide with a certain magnificence in life, the kind I suspect exists in beings who in the peak of their vitality defy it—for instance, bullfighters and mystics. But in reality, that sweet air characterizing some towns in the provinces only coincides with meanness.

M.F.: Under what circumstances and when did you write *La última conquista de El Angel*, published in 1977?

E.O.: I had written it long before that, in Venezuela.

M.F.: Did you have any problems publishing it?

E.O.: I don't think they even noticed it in Argentina, even though I, with total innocence not to be confused with courage, sent it to the state comptroller of a radio station. He probably didn't read it. The Venezuelan publishers read it and feared for me.

M.F.: Why did you choose torture as the central theme of this work?

E.O.: I've already said it on other occasions: out of hatred for actions against forsaken human beings.

M.F.: Was your inspiration based on the Argentina experience?

E.O.: No. These were imaginary occurrences that coincided with reality.

M.F.: What are you writing now?

E.O.: I'm writing a novel that does not satisfy me completely, because I've discovered that I prefer to create an exasperated atmosphere in fiction, like the one in *Aire tan dulce*.

M.F.: What is the title and theme of your novel?

E.O.: I prefer not to tell you for reasons I'll explain privately, but not for publication. I can only tell you that it deals with two lives, from childhood to the end, set in the Perón era. But as I don't want to write testimonial fiction (although everything that is written is testimonial, including Kafka's testimony of humanity), the historical circumstances appear only as flashes: "All the clocks stopped at eight p.m. Then Eva said, 'The trains already had a reason to arrive late. And now?'"[45]

Buenos Aires, 30 October 1989

M.F.: What have you been writing recently?

E.O.: A novel that takes place during the Proceso. It's called *La muerte y los desencuentros* (Death and missed encounters), which should have come out last June. And I've written an erotic novel, which I've just finished and sent to the publishers.

M.F.: What is its title?

E.O.: *Amada Lesbia* (Beloved Lesbia). But it's unrelated to lesbianism. It's simply about a poet who calls his beloved "Lesbia."

M.F.: And what is the novel about?

E.O.: It's a love story and also an erotic novel, besides being a historical novel. It contains both history and eroticism.

M.F.: Is it about contemporary history?

E.O.: I don't want to say. It scares me because it takes so long to get novels published here, and, in the meantime, somebody might snatch my story. I'll just say I've combined history and eroticism.

M.F.: Who is going to publish it?

E.O.: I don't know. I sent it to Tusquets.

M.F.: Can you tell me what *La muerte y los desencuentros* is about?

E.O.: Yes, it's about a family in a small provincial town with five teenagers. The kids don't have anything in common with other kids their age because their experiences have been totally different. They don't follow norms. They stand like a wall between two groups, as though they were going to be the target for the bullets shot by both groups. They represent the anarchy of the province, the state, and the country. But while these (province, state, and country) are ruled by strict norms, they don't follow any. Nobody has taught them any norms. The missed encounters are the reason they never find anybody with whom they can form a group together. There's always the missed encounter between the siblings, between them and the parents, between them and the town, including the ghosts of these two different groups who can't communicate even when they want to.

M.F.: Is it an allegory about the Proceso?

E.O.: It's not an allegory; it's the story of a missed encounter.

M.F.: Is the military dictatorship present in the novel as background?

E.O.: It's like a background present through allusion. It enters like a mystery. What has happened to so and so? What has happened to this other person? Why do they hate us? And at the end everything is defined, from what has happened to these characters to the inscriptions on the cemetery tombstones.

M.F.: Is politics the main focus of the novel?

E.O.: I'm never exclusively political. The political is present, as is the human dimension. Because if it were only political, I'd be taking sides or looking for a dialectical balance. I place these teenagers in the middle. They don't take sides and there's the human dimension of the missed encounter.

M.F.: What is the relationship between this work and your previous ones? Does it open a new cycle?

E.O.: I don't think so. It seems difficult to me, for a writer to open a new cycle without keeping something from the previous one.

M.F.: Do you deal with some of the themes of previous novels?

E.O.: No, just the teenagers.

M.F.: Who is going to publish it?

E.O.: Fraterna Publishers.

M.F.: Two years ago you were working on a novel that takes place during the Perón era. Have you finished it?

E.O.: I'm still working on it.

M.F.: Do you have a title?

E.O.: It's called *Basura y luna* (Garbage and moon).

M.F.: You mentioned in our previous conversation that it is about two lives from childhood to death. What else can you tell me about it?

E.O.: It's a novel that is getting longer and longer because there's always something new to add.

M.F.: Is it related to your other novels at all?

E.O.: Its characters are also teenagers. Teenagers are present in almost all my works because it's a stage when we take in so many experiences that life seems like an endless source.

M.F.: Is the focus on the teenagers any different?

E.O.: It hasn't changed in the sense that they are always full of surprises, somewhat like children. They see things that adults don't see anymore. It's a vision that doesn't demand explanations. *La muerte y los desencuentros* deals quite a bit with the unexplainable.

M.F.: What projects are you planning?

E.O.: I plan to write and write, but I'd like to become much sharper stylistically. I don't want to write any more lyrical and long sentences; instead I'd like to perfect a short and hard one, but not in the style of Hemingway. I'd like to write a sentence that expresses something.

M.F.: Many of your novels deal with a historical period. Are there any other historical eras you intend to explore in your future works?

E.O.: I don't know that yet.

BIBLIOGRAPHY

Primary Sources (listed chronologically)

Orphée, Elvira. *Dos veranos*. Buenos Aires: Editorial Sudamericana, 1956.
————. *Uno*. Buenos Aires: Fabril Editora, 1961.
————. *Aire tan dulce*. 1st ed. Buenos Aires: Editorial Sudamericana, 1966. 2d ed. Caracas: Monte Avila, 1977.
————. *En el fondo*. Buenos Aires: Emecé Editores, 1969.
————. *Su demonio preferido*. Buenos Aires: Emecé Editores, 1973.
————. *Las viejas fantasiosas*. Buenos Aires: Emecé Editores, 1981.
————. *La última conquista de El Angel*. 1st ed. Caracas: Monte Avila Editores, 1977; 2d ed. Buenos Aires: Editorial Vergara, 1984.
————. *La muerte y los desencuentros*. Buenos Aires: Editorial Fraterna, 1989.
————. *Ciego de cielo*. Buenos Aires: Emecé Editores, 1991.

Short Fiction by Elvira Orphée (listed chronologically)

Orphée, Elvira. "Las casas." *Sur* 198 (May-June 1950): 44–51.
————. "La calle Mate de Luna." *Sur* 262 (January-February 1960): 43–50.
————. "La pequeña Ning." *Sur* 306 (May-June 1967): 39–44.
————. "¡Ay, Enrique!" *La Opinión*, 27 November 1977.
————. "Nunca la compasión." In *Rencontres. Encuentros: Ecrivains et artistes de l'Argentine et du Québec/Escritores y artistas de la Argentina y Quebec*, edited by Gilles Pellerin and Oscar Hermes Villordo, 209–16. Québec: Les Editions Sans Nom, 1989.

Critical Articles by Elvira Orphée

Orphée, Elvira. "La realidad y las normas del cuento." *La Nación*, 27 July 1985.

Works Available in Translation (listed chronologically)

Orphée, Elvira. *El Angel's Last Conquest*. Translated by Magda Bogin. New York: Ballantine, 1986.
————. "Angel's Last Conquest." Translated by Evelyn Picon Garfield. In *Women's Fiction from Latin America: Selections from Twelve Contemporary Authors*, edited by Evelyn Picon Garfield, 162–77. Detroit: Wayne State University Press, 1988.

———. "The Silken Whale." Translated by Evelyn Picon Garfield. In *Women's Fiction from Latin America: Selections from Twelve Contemporary Authors*, edited by Evelyn Picon Garfield, 178–86. Detroit: Wayne State University Press, 1988.

———. "The Beguiling Ladies." Translated by Christopher Leland. In *Landscapes of a New Land: Short Fiction by Latin American Women*, edited by Marjorie Agosín, 173–81. New York: White Pine Press, 1989.

———. "Do Not Mistake Eternities." Translated by Oscar Montero. In *Women's Writing in Latin America*, edited by Sara Castro-Klarén, Sylvia Molloy, and Beatriz Sarlo, 180–81. Boulder, Colo.: Westview Press, 1991.

———. "Silences." Translated by Oscar Montero. In *Women's Writing in Latin America*, edited by Sara Castro-Klarén, Sylvia Molloy, and Beatriz Sarlo, 178–79. Boulder, Colo.: Westview Press, 1991.

———. "Voices That Grew Old." Translated by Oscar Montero. In *Women's Writing in Latin America*, edited by Sara Castro-Klarén, Sylvia Molloy, and Beatriz Sarlo, 181–85. Boulder, Colo.: Westview Press, 1991.

———. "An eternal fear." Translated by Janice Molloy. In *Secret Weavers: Stories of the Fantastic by Women of Argentina and Chile*, edited by Marjorie Agosín, 93–99. New York: White Pine Press, 1992.

———. "How the Little Crocodiles Cry." Translated by Janice Molloy. In *Secret Weavers: Stories of the Fantastic by Women of Argentina and Chile*, edited by Marjorie Agosín, 104–7. New York: White Pine Press, 1992.

———. "I will return, Mommy." Translated by Janice Molloy. In *Secret Weavers: Stories of the Fantastic by Women of Argentina and Chile*, edited by Marjorie Agosín, 100–103. New York: White Pine Press, 1992.

Secondary Sources

A. C. Review of *Uno*, by Elvira Orphée. *Ficción* 32 (8 July 1961): 78–82.

Alvarez Sosa, Arturo. Review of *Su demonio preferido*, by Elvira Orphée. *La Gaceta*, 8 July 1973.

Bastos, María Luisa. "Conversación con Elvira Orphée." *Zona franca* 3 (July-August 1977): 26–27.

———. "Elvira Orphée: *Uno*." Review of *Uno*, by Elvira Orphée. *Sur* 272 (September-October 1961): 107.

———. "Tortura y discurso autoritario: *La última conquista de El Angel*, de Elvira Orphée." In *The Contemporary Latin American Short Story*, edited by Rose S. Minc, 112–19. New York: Senda Nueva de Ediciones, 1979.

Birkemoe, Diane S. "Elvira Orphée." In "Contemporary Women Novelists in Argentina (1945–67)," 258–312. Ph.D. diss., University of Illinois, 1968.

Chacel, Rosa. "Un libro ciertamente nuevo." Review of *Dos veranos*, by Elvira Orphée. *Sur* 245 (March-April 1957): 11–17.

Chevigny, Bell Gale. "Ambushing the Will to Ignorance: Elvira Orphée's *La última conquista de El Angel* and Marta Traba's *Conversación al sur*." In *El Cono Sur: dinámica y dimensiones de su literatura*, edited by Rose S. Minc, 98–104. Upper Montclair, N.J.: Montclair State College, 1985.

Class, Bradley M. "Fictional Treatment of Politics by Argentine Female Novelists." Ph.D. diss., University of New Mexico, 1974.

Correa, María Angélica. Review of *Uno*, by Elvira Orphée. *Señales* 131 (Summer 1961): 29–30

Crespo, Julio. Review of *Aire tan dulce*, by Elvira Orphée. *Sur* 307 (July-August 1967): 47–49.

Díaz, Gwendolyn. "Escritura y palabra: *Aire tan dulce*, de Elvira Orphée." *Revista iberoamericana* 51 (July-December 1985): 641–48.

Duvojne Ortíz, Alicia. "Diálogo con Elvira Orphée: Los demonios de lo cotidiano." *La Opinión*, 27 November 1977, 10–11.

E. D. Review of *Dos veranos*, by Elvira Orphée. *Ficción* 4 (1956): 192–94.

Fares, Gustavo, and Eliana Hermann. "Elvira Orphée." In *Escritoras argentinas contemporáneas*, 137–52. New York: Peter Lang, 1993.

Flori, Mónica. "Entrevista a Elvira Orphée." *Hispania* 72 (September 1989): 605–7.

García Pinto, Magdalena. "Elvira Orphée." Translated from the Spanish by Trudy Balch and Magdalena García Pinto. In *Women Writers of Latin America: Intimate Stories*, 145–61. Austin: University of Texas Press, 1991.

Gómez Paz, Julieta. Review of *Aire tan dulce*, by Elvira Orphée. *La Prensa*, 13 September 1967.

Justo, Luis. "Elvira Orphée y sus novelas." *Sur* 315 (November-December 1968): 88–89.

Lagmanovich, David. Review of *Uno*, by Elvira Orphée. *La Gaceta*, 11 June 1961.

Loubet, Jorgelina. "Tres miradas en trascendencia." *Boletín de la Academia Argentina de Letras* 51 (July-December 1986): 343–58.

Moctezuma, Edgardo. "Para mirar tan lejos antes de entrar: Los usos del poder en *Aire tan dulce*, de Elvira Orphée." *Revista iberoamericana* 45 (October-December 1983): 929–42.

Pérez, Ramón Alberto. Review of *Su demonio preferido*, by Elvira Orphée. *La Gaceta*, 8 July 1973.

Picon Garfield, Evelyn. "'Desprendida a hachazos de la eternidad': lo primordial en la obra de Elvira Orphée." *Journal of Latin American Lore* 5 (1979): 3–23.

———. "Elvira Orphée." In *Women's Voices from Latin America: Interviews with Six Contemporary Authors*, 97–113. Detroit: Wayne State University Press, 1987.

Reati, Fernando. On *La última conquista de El Angel*. In *Nombrar lo innombrable: violencia política y novela argentina, 1975–1985*, 102–8. Buenos Aires: Editorial Legasa, 1992.

Alina Diaconú. Photograph by Eduardo Grunberg.

3
Alina Diaconú

BIOGRAPHY

Alina Diaconú was born in Bucharest, Rumania, in 1945 and emigrated to Buenos Aires, Argentina, with her family in 1959. She obtained a bachelor's degree from Mallinckrodt College in Buenos Aires in 1962. After studying communications and stage decorating at the University Del Salvador in Buenos Aires, she graduated in 1969 with a degree in public relations. She lived in Paris from 1968 to 1970.

Diaconú has developed a career in journalism. From 1979 to 1980 she published a biweekly column for the magazine, *Gente*. Between 1979 and 1982 she regularly contributed short stories and articles to the cultural magazine, *Vigencia*, published by the University of Belgrano in Buenos Aires. She has been a columnist for the prestigious Buenos Aires newspapers *La Nación* and *Clarín* since 1979 and 1981, respectively.

Diaconú has been honored with many literary prizes and awards— among them, the 1979 Argentine Society of Writers' Honor Band for her novel, *Buenas noches, profesor.* Her "Imaginary Interview with Borges" received special mention in the journalism category of the Coca-Cola Prize in the Arts and Sciences for 1980. Her novel, *Enamorada del muro,* was also given a special mention in the 1979/1982 National Prize contest. In 1985 she obtained a Fulbright Fellowship to attend the International Writing Program at the University of Iowa. Diaconú received a special mention in the 1986 short-story competition sponsored by the Center for Spanish American Studies. In 1989 *El penúltimo viaje* was awarded the Silver Meridian trophy for the best novel of the year.

At present, after having published her seventh novel, she continues writing fiction and contributing to *La Nación* and *Clarín*; the Tucumán newspaper, *La Gaceta*; and the magazine *Cultura* and the Argentine edition of *Vuelta sudamericana,* edited by Octavio Paz. She also coordinates cultural events for several foundations in Buenos Aires.

Essay

"Literature of ambiguity. Literature of disquietedness. These are the salient, substantive characteristics of Alina Diaconú's works—*La Señora*
[The Lady], 1975; *Buenas noches, profesor* [Good night, Professor], 1978;
Enamorada del muro [Morning glory], 1981; *Cama de ángeles* [Bed of
angels], 1983; *Los ojos azules* [Blue eyes], 1986." Thus reads the introduction to a review of her novel, *Los ojos azules*, which ends a cycle in the
writer's fictional world described as "narrative which undoubtedly de-
serves an important place within contemporary Argentine literature."[1]
Critic Elías Miguel Muñoz points out the importance of Alina Diaconú's
fiction in contemporary Latin American and Argentine narrative:

> I am not surprised by the fact that the Spanish-American woman is
> the one who writes the best books today, that her writing—best
> exemplified by that of Isabel Allende, Elena Poniatowska, Ángeles
> Mastretta, Ethel Krauze, Rosario Ferré, Ana Lydia Vega, *Alina
> Diaconú*, Lucía Guerra—is a parody and a critique of the official
> worldview, and while ridiculing the male character, rewrites the rules
> established by the enshrined boomers.[2]

As Muñoz points out, Alina Diaconú's fiction differs from that of the
boomers, in both content and form. Diaconú portrays antiheroic male,
female, and androgynous characters in all stages of life. Despite their diversity, these characters share certain traits. They are fallen heroes or antiheroes, who have failed in life or have set themselves up to fail. Diaconú
said in an interview: "Me importan los que se sienten solos en este mundo,
los que sobrellevan un gran fracaso, los que han tenido grandes ilusiones
y las han perdido" (I am interested in those who feel alone in this world,
those who carry the burden of great failure, those who have had great
expectations and lost them).[3] As a consequence, her characters display
traits that make them different from other human beings in either a real
or symbolic sense. Because of these differences they are outcasts from the
mainstream of society and feel their uniqueness and marginality as a stigma.
They often confine themselves in enclosed spaces: a room, a house, an
apartment, or an island—metaphors expressing the confinement felt by
an alienated mind marked by loneliness, isolation, despair, and madness.

Alina Diaconú's narratives are fraught with ambiguity at all levels.
They contain a distorted and fragmented narration and narrator, creating
a metatext, which, in many cases, acts as counterpoint to the main text,
offering several versions of a story, surprise, twisted endings, and the

blending of times. All these aspects are filtered through a fallible narrator who may be both male and female. The narrator's views, distorted by solitude and/or madness, appear in endless monologues and dialogues of various narrative voices.

Characters and themes alluding to a marginal reality (conveyed by distorted and ambiguous narratives) are characteristic of the writing that developed in response to the repressive conditions of the Proceso.[4] Dissident writers, like Diaconú, created an allegorical fiction that disguised its subversive intent by using metaphor and intertextuality. Her discursive strategies affect point of view and narrative voice as well as traditional structure, time, and space to elicit an antitext—in opposition to the hegemonic, authoritarian discourse. It is writing that emerges from suppression and silence: marginal writing. Its goal is to render a voice to those who have been denied one. Critic Francine Masiello describes this writing, developed to circumvent censorship and repression imposed by the regime:

> Desgarrados entre el centro y la periferia, entre el discurso dominante y la posibilidad de algo distinto, los escritores y artistas argentinos cultivaron pues el espacio marginal, que ofrece una alternativa a la centralizadora inmovilidad del régimen . . . lo marginal transforma la oposición binaria de dominadores y oprimidos, con el propósito de fragmentar cualquier discurso unificado que pueda apoyar al estado autoritario o aislar irremediablemente al otro.

> (Torn apart between the center and the periphery, between the dominant discourse and the possibility of something different, Argentine writers and artists cultivated the marginal space, which offers an alternative to the centralizing immobility of the regime . . . marginality transforms the binary opposition of dominators and oppressed, with the purpose of fragmenting any unified discourse that may support the authoritarian state or isolate the other irremediably.)[5]

La Señora

Her first novel, *La Señora* (The Lady), 1975, resorts to fragmented discourse to recover a marginal and suppressed vision of reality. Although a work dear to its author, *La Señora* was hardly noticed by the critics when it was first published. Its theme, the destruction of a traditional, bourgeois, repressive family, is a metaphor for subverting the regime's hypocritical explanation of its actions. In military discourse repression was justified under the guise of being a defense of Western Christian values embodied in the family. Yet families were being systematically destroyed by the most violent means imaginable. The regime appropriated the paradigm of the family, stressing its patriarchal and authoritarian aspects. Writers who responded incorporated strategies used by vanguard feminist novelists to subvert the traditional authoritarian representation of the family, in which the father occupied a privileged place within the home:

> [L]a novela feminista de vanguardia inicia un cuestionamiento de la genealogía como índice de la identidad personal; con ella se repudia la figura paternal como eje de los procesos de significación social.

> ([T]he vanguard feminist novel initiates a questioning of genealogy as the guiding principle of personal identity; with it the paternal figure is repudiated as center of the processes of social significance.)[6]

This concept extends to the home, which traditionally represents "a desirable place, a revered space, a miniature reflection of the providence of power."[7] In *La Señora* home becomes the madhouse where the protagonist ends up being committed. Such a symbolic fate awaits dissenters. It also represents a subversive vision of the multiple transformations that the house/country suffered under the regime. In the context of Argentina in the seventies, Diaconú chooses to voice her dissent by focusing on the institutions of the patriarchal family and home. They metaphorically represent the opening of a space for contention. This is aptly expressed in *La Señora*, the story of the disintegration of a family due to the mother's rebellion; the mother, the protagonist, flees to search for a repressed identity and develop her creative capabilities. The members of this traditional upper-middle-class family bear generic names—"The Lady" (capitalized), "The master," "The daughter," "The son," and "The young man" (the daughter's boyfriend)—indicating they represent the institutionalized bourgeois family that lacks identity yet fulfills traditional roles. It is a dysfunctional family, symbolic of Diaconú's concept of traditional patriarchal institutions and their effects on human beings.

The conflict is presented from the viewpoint of the thirty-eight-year-old protagonist, who is initially defined by her role as wife and mother. An alienated housewife, confined to an upper-middle-class golden cage of a household, experiences a midlife crisis when she realizes the sterility of her life. She feels estranged from her family and perceives herself as "un huevo roto, en desuso, una cáscara, para tirar a la basura, un espacio vaciado en Uds." (a broken egg, no longer in use, a shell to throw into the garbage, a space emptied in you).[8] As she looks at her reflection in the mirror, an inner voice tells her:

Pero, Señora, acaso su vida no es obsoleta? y su marido y sus hijos y sus mucamos con guantes blancos y sus cuadros y sus botellas de Armagnac y su colección de marfiles, cuando Ud. bien lo sabe, el mundo no es esto, Ud. Señora no existe, ni nada de lo que la rodea existe.

(But Madam, isn't your life obsolete? And your husband and your children and your white-gloved butlers and your paintings and your bottles of Armagnac and your ivory collection, when you know very well that this isn't the world, you, Madam, don't exist, nor does anything surrounding you exist.) (12)

La Señora tries to escape the truth by creating fantasized, alternative narrations of her life, which she thinks will give her freedom and develop her authentic self. These narratives fragment the apparent plot, the story of an alienated bourgeois woman, to create new plots (her own) subverting the narrative space and hegemonic discourse. In these new plots she tries to break away from her confinement—first, by taking a lover (her daughter's boyfriend, who later commits suicide), and then by becoming a prostitute. But her double life, whether real or imaginary, results from a deranged mind. She becomes obsessed with her daughter, who becomes the embodiment of the guilt conjured up by her delusions. Her anguish culminates in an attempt to kill her daughter. As a consequence, she is committed to an insane asylum.

The traditional plot of the dutiful wife and mother uncovers a new script "written" by the protagonist, who at first imagines her daughter seducing her boyfriend. She intertwines this fantasy with her own past sexual history. In her fantasy, her daughter becomes a seductress, acting out the mother's wish-fulfilling imaginary rebellion. Thus, the protagonist rewrites her past life, altering the script of a chaste and failed relationship in which she gave up her youth to marry her husband in exchange for security. Taking her daughter's place, she becomes the boyfriend's (imaginary?) mistress to alter her past, as well as to evade her present situation. By fantasizing an adulterous relationship, she seeks to attack the institution of the bourgeois family and take away her husband's power. After the boyfriend drowns accidentally (commits suicide?), both mother and daughter undergo nervous breakdowns. The mother seeks to distance herself from her daughter and her family, thus rejecting the role imposed upon her by society. She spends her time in nightclubs as an aspiring prostitute, parodically rewriting the role of confined housewife and attempting to express the repressed self by creating a new life story independent from her past. Her efforts to save both of them from patriarchal society fail, as her hallucinations turn her daughter into her own guilty conscience. The daughter, she imagines, represents the voice of society and its values, which the mother is attempting to flee. She tries to kill her: "La agarró del cuello y empezó a apretar. Luego se detuvo un segundo y mirándola con sus ojos desorbitados, le dijo: 'andate, no quiero matarte a vos también'" (She grabbed her by the neck and started to press. Then she stopped for a second and looking at her wide-eyed, she said to her: "Go away, I don't want to kill you too") (134). She is referring to the boyfriend's death, which represents the impossibility of recreating her past life according to her wishes. It also means that her daughter will not be able to marry the man she loves and might follow in her mother's footsteps. Her failure symbolizes her daughter's failure to reinvent her own life script.

When the protagonist's attempts to contest society fail, she must retreat, creating her own space within the realm of madness. This space is her only alternative. She must remove herself from the patriarchal, authoritarian world. This strong image of a woman retreating into madness is a metaphor for the fate of those who dare to rebel and dissent in a repressive society:

> La vio sentarse luego en el piso y golpearse la cabeza. Su largo pelo enredado, su boca crispada y pequeñas babas que le salían de la boca. . . . Una hora más tarde, la internaban a la Señora.

> (She saw her sitting down on the floor and hitting her head. Her long hair tangled up, her mouth drawn, and short spittle coming out of her mouth. . . . An hour later, they committed the Lady.) (134)

That a female protagonist embodies this vision points to madness as a dual symbol, used both traditionally in the apparent plot and also as a liberating motif in the embedded story. It is the usual punishment bestowed on female characters who transgress (an interpretation favored by critics who see this traditional ending as proof of the softening of the subversive intent of the novel):

> En sus primeras tres novelas ya está presente el gesto cuestionador y subversivo, aunque hay una cierta "domesticación" de los finales de estas obras que obliga a un re-planteo de lo leído. Resulta de este modo, que el esfuerzo manifiesto en el mismo hacerse de la escritura de esos textos, se ve acallado por la convención de adecuamiento con que acaban las novelas. "La Señora" se atreve a romper con los lugares comunes que la encasillan y a la vez confirman, pero su búsqueda transgresora sólo la lleva a un manicomio. Si se lee desde la tranquilidad del "orden impuesto y establecido" por los sistemas vigentes, es

necesaria la señora encerrada en el manicomio para re-establecer la "normalidad."

(In her three first novels the questioning and subversive gesture is already present, although there is a certain "domestication" of the endings of these works which forces a reevaluation of the reading. The result of it is that the effort manifest in the development of the writing of these texts is muffled by the conventional ending of the novels. "The Lady" dares to break with the commonplace, which both pigeonholes and confirms her, but her transgressive search only takes her to the insane asylum. If it is read from the reassuring "imposed and established order" of the existing systems, it is necessary to lock the woman in an insane asylum to reestablish "normality.")[9]

But another reading of the ending signals a subversive intent. Diaconú utilizes madness to free and empower the protagonist, placing her in a space that is inaccessible to others. In conjunction with the protagonist's fantasy, this ending symbolizes her newly gained freedom and the acquisition of a space where she can create and reinterpret reality. The ending is a social commentary on her society and the role of the dissident who is driven to madness in order to survive and find a space from which a creative voice can emerge.

The Lady's gestures of despair and the flight of a female protagonist who shatters the golden cage of patriarchy to rewrite her life script in fragmented discourse are symbolic of dissident writing. Diaconú has aptly rendered a critical vision of her time: the image of this mad female protagonist is a subtle metaphor of any individual trapped by repression.

Buenas noches, profesor

Diaconú's second novel, *Buenas noches, profesor* (Good night, Professor), 1978, further develops these themes and techniques. It is the story of a fifty-five-year-old high school literature teacher who falls in love with a young student. Critic María Adela Renard has identified a mythic element in this story:

With *Buenas noches, profesor*, her novel published in 1978, she deals with the ancient Sophocles myth—the love of an older man for an adolescent—showing her acute knowledge of male psychology.[10]

As the narrative opens, the protagonist is home with a severe case of influenza. While convalescing, the professor appraises his past, feeling disgust for what he perceives to be a failed existence. This self-image seems to be the crux of the story. His childless marriage is totally predictable and uneventful, a routine domesticity providing security and stability. His professional dreams have failed and he is doomed to the unrewarding task of teaching literature to uninterested students. At one time he thought he could give meaning to his life by writing an essay on Don Quixote (his choice of literary character is no coincidence), but he has never attempted to publish the manuscript. Its yellowed pages, lying on his desk, are a constant reminder of his frozen existence. During his absence from school, a male colleague and the professor's best student, a beautiful young girl, inquire about him. The protagonist magnifies their concern for him to the point that it changes his lonesome and barren existence. As a result, the professor decides to lead a new, revitalized life. He encourages his wife to teach outside the home; he submits his manuscript to a publisher. At school, he develops a friendship with his colleague and courts the student, hoping that a love affair will develop.

We follow these episodes with great interest, until it becomes clear, toward the end of the novel, that we have been tricked: We have accepted as the "authentic" text that which is only one of several possible versions imagined by the alienated mind of the sick protagonist:

> Finalmente todo es real y todo es mentira y cada vez que uno quiere buscar las fronteras se encuentra en un desierto donde el horizonte se aleja a medida que uno cree acercarse.

> (Finally everything is real and everything is a lie and each time we want to find the borders we find ourselves in a desert where the horizon gets farther and farther away while we think we are getting closer.)[11]

We learn that the professor has not left his room for twenty days, that his wife has been dead for years, and that the events of the story are actually only wishful fantasies. His delusions stem not only from the fever but from the shock of his wife's death, which he has never accepted. Neither has he accepted his mother's death. He has been overtaken by madness, confusion, and isolation. This novel questions the very nature of fiction and, above all, confronts us with existential problems of universal dimensions. At the same time, it develops the themes of madness and alienation within narrations that negate each other. As in *La Señora*, the schizophrenic character symbolizes an entire society caught in a dual reality: an official regime espousing traditional values yet contradicting them by its actions. This is a metaphor for a society in which it is impossible to openly formulate the "real" story. Prevalent political conditions require that the story be expressed ambivalently.

The schizoid personality that develops as a consequence is expressed not only in a narrator who retreats from reality to live in a fantasy world but also in a narration that originates in a male identity, transgressing the authorial gender identity. Such a gender-balanced narration undermines a single-voiced authorial discourse.[12] By utilizing a ventriloquial voice, Diaconú weakens the authority of the narrator. The different narrative voices negate or contradict each another. This becomes especially evident in the last chapter, "Ultima instancia" (Last request), consisting of a dialogue between the character's sane part and his deluded self, where we learn the truth about the hallucinations and how they have slanted the reading of the story. With this narrative device the author emphasizes the importance of integrating various voices instead of presenting a unified discourse. By bringing together different points of view in a dialogical context, the text acquires socially symbolic dimensions insofar as it places marginalized and repressed voices in the limelight.

Enamorada del muro

Enamorada del muro (Morning glory), 1981, has been categorized by critics as the third novel in a trilogy, which completes a cycle in Diaconú's writing.[13] The novel is divided neatly into seven chapters, each covering one day in the life of Bruma, an eighteen-year-old upper-middle-class young woman. This format gives the false appearance of a diary, an ironic device, as the protagonist lacks the aptitude even to keep a journal. The protagonist wanders along the streets of Buenos Aires at the beginning of spring. She rejects the adult world of her parents, who do not understand her unproductive life without commitment or responsibility. A lifeless individual, she cruises aimlessly through an absurd and meaningless environment:

> Los minutos se ponen a flotar sin dimensión ni peso alguno, el tiempo es un gran cielo nublado, en él como sobre un telón de teatro se dibujan y se desdibujan personajes mecánicos, muñecos articulados, expresiones grotescas, paisajes sin relieve, todo es una gran convención, un gran guignol, nada es verdad ni creíble, Bruma misma es un fantasma dramático, así sentada en el escalón color barro, la cabeza unida a su cuerpo por una jugarreta accidental . . . como si Dios hubiese hecho un transplante apoteótico de miembros y de almas, y

he aquí a esta pobre criatura fragmentada y fragmentaria, una cabeza llena de mechones nocturnos, pensando pensamientos que no incluyen nada de lo que ella, toda ella es.

(The minutes start floating without any dimension or weight, time is a huge cloudy sky; on it, like on a theater screen, mechanical characters, jointed dolls, grotesque expressions, landscapes without borders, appear and disappear; everything is a scam, a Punch-and-Judy show, nothing is true or credible, Bruma herself is a dramatic ghost, seated as she is on a mud-colored step, her head attached to her body as if by accident . . . as though God had made an apotheosized transplant of joints and souls, and here is the result, a poor fragmented and fragmentary creature, a head full of nocturnal curls, thinking thoughts that don't include anything at all of what she, her complete self, is.)[14]

She seeks a relationship, any relationship, with an individual or a group that is "different" and that will assume responsibility for her, absorbing her personality in a way that will render her still more of an automaton. In this pursuit she becomes attached to a dubious character called King Kong, a homosexual, drug-addicted young man. While deluding herself with dreams of marriage to him, she joins a sect and becomes involved in very strange goings-on at their meetings. One of its young members commits suicide, an event that Bruma erases from her memory. The story captures the conflicts of adolescence while it critically portrays a class of people who lead mechanical, empty lives. They seek solace in meaningless relationships and rituals, resulting in isolation, a lack of love, and suicide.

At this point in Diaconú's literary career *Enamorada del muro* stands out: It marks the beginning of her focus on the female body, to be more fully developed in *Los ojos azules*. Loathing and alienation from reality are inscribed in the female protagonist's body. Throughout *Enamorada del muro*, Bruma escapes reality by gorging on ice cream until she gets sick and faints, usually achieving a high similar to that of a person on drugs:

[Q]ue aquellos viajes—mejores que los de marihuana, mucho más fantásticos y más excitantes—nacían de algo tan inofensivo como un helado.

([T]hat those journeys—better than those of marijuana, more fantastic and more exciting—were born of something so harmless as an ice cream.) (80)

Con uno o dos no ocurría nada, recién despúes del tercero se iniciaba el preludio del viaje, ese suave vértigo, ese aturdimiento manso, apacible, que se tornaba benigno y total y que llevaba los colores de los sabores, hoy el rosado, mañana el que uno quisiese elegir.

(Nothing happened with one or two, only after the third one the prelude to the journey would begin, that soft vertigo, that mild, gentle daze, which became benign and total and which had the colors of the flavors, today pink, tomorrow whatever color one might want to choose.) (80–81)

Inscribing an escape from reality to the protagonist's physiology and linking it to the abuse of food signal a feeling of abjection. According to Julia Kristeva, abjection results from internalizing horror and abuse in our bodies by means of a conduct of excess. Abjection denies our reality. The protagonist perceives herself as a negation, a nonbeing, and her conduct stems from this perception.[15] *Enamorada del muro* thus lends itself to an allegorical reading as to the effects of terror on a generation that manifests its estrangement by self-destruction staged on the human body. Through her behavior of abjection, Bruma indicts society. Throughout the novel she repeats, "Me gustan las cosas repelentes" (I like repulsive things). The confined world of *La Señora*'s insane asylum and the professor's room are now Bruma's body, manipulated to isolate her from reality so she can live a make-believe existence. This behavior will inevitably lead her down the path of self-destruction.

Cama de ángeles

Isolation and abjection also characterize *Cama de ángeles* (Bed of angels), 1983, which continues Diaconú's endeavors to inscribe a marginal reality in her novels and to open up a space from which to question her society. Central to this novel are the issues of gender identity and social and political consciousness. *Cama de ángeles* narrates the story of a hermaphrodite, Angel(a), who was forced by his mother to take on a male role: "Mamá me había llamado siempre Angel . . . pues sostenía que ser hombre es mejor, que una mujer está siempre desprotegida" (Mother had always called me Angel . . . because she maintained that it was better to be a man, that a woman is always unprotected).[16] When his mother died, Angel rejected her imposition, forsaking his male identity and adopting a female identity by dressing in his mother's clothes:

Tras su muerte, fui Angela, ya que como mujer mi problema congénito se deslizaba de una manera más desapercibida.

(After her death, I was Angela, because as a woman my congenital problem would slide by in a more unnoticed manner.) (245)

Arrojé mi bufanda escocesa, deseché mis pantalones y mis sacos, mis camisas y mis corbatas, mi retrato de Angel, mi expresión y mis gestos angelicales y varoniles y dejé que el pelo me creciera en libertad, y las uñas también . . . y me escondí por el resto de la etenidad en la bata azul con ribetes violetas de mamá, su bata de invierno, flamante cuando mamá murió.

(I threw away my plaid scarf, I got rid of my slacks and my jackets, my shirts and my ties, my portrait of Angel, my expression and my angelic and masculine gestures, and I let my hair grow freely, and my nails, too . . . and I hid for the rest of eternity in mama's blue house-coat with violet trim, her winter housecoat, brand new when mama died.) (137–38)

Thus, at the beginning of the novel we find the protagonist completely isolated from the world, confined to his flat. In spite of his gesture of rebellion, he is still under his dead mother's spell. Angel never had a choice in the matter of his true gender identity: His mother made the choice for him. The mother, in this case, stands for patriarchal society, which cannot accommodate a gender identity that does not correspond to the norm. Angel's confusion is shared by the reader, who gradually discovers Angel's true nature. In the first chapter the protagonist narrator seems to be a man, projecting a male narrative voice. In the second chapter we realize that the character is dressed and looks like a female. Finally, we learn that s/he is androgynous. The predominantly male narration, fluctuating between a male and a female voice, is supplemented by other voices. The ventriloquial discourse used in previous novels is apparent in this multiplicity of voices. Previously, it was worked into the novel through the female persona of the narrator and the male protagonist. Now it takes place within the protagonist from the perspective of his duality and is reinforced by the dead mother's voice as well as by those of the other characters, whose speech is filtered through his own discourse.

When we first meet the protagonist, he has no identity. His confinement is similar to death; he spends his time in the dark flat in the company of a desiccated cat and the boxed, embalmed hands of his dead mother. These symbols of death represent the character's nonidentity, which stems from society's lack of acceptance of the Other, perceived as a threat. According to Elías Miguel Muñoz: "From its margin and its silence, Diaconú's

character poses an experience of sexuality—identity, gender—which subverts the official reality about sexuality. . . . *Cama de ángeles* suggests, in my
reading, the existence of an alternative space: the limbo space of 'non-iden-
tity.' And it presents, by giving a hermaphrodite a voice, the touching story
of an individual who is unfairly marginalized because of his genders."[17]

But during the first part of the novel, Angel(a)'s interest in the outside world is renewed when he finds out that a famous actress, Morgana,
has moved into his/her apartment building. Angel(a) carefully prepares to
meet her. First, s/he finds out everything s/he can by bribing people in her
entourage for information. Then, s/he thoroughly studies an album s/he
has assembled with all the available photos, interviews, and facts on the
actress's life. Shunning a direct approach, to create a preliminary "text"
about her, s/he approaches her by means of the ventriloquial discourse
offered by other people's narrations of Morgana's life and identity. S/he
learns that she has failed in the role of a beggar in a highly publicized play,
for an abyss separates her real-life experience from the role that she must
play. Angel(a) becomes Morgana's confidant and convinces her that they
should escape to Paris together. Morgana agrees, thinking she is going
with an eccentric spinster; but to her amazement Angela has become Angel, adopting his old male identity to become her travel escort, literally
and symbolically shedding his mother's clothes: "¡Cuál es el anonadamiento
cuando, en lugar de Angela, la vecina, el que aparece es un hombre
cuarentón, traje gris y corbata colorada" (She was stunned when, instead
of Angela, the woman next door, who should show up but a man in his
forties, gray suit and red tie) (168). Ester Gimbernat González explains
this change:

> Primero va tras la mujer que hay en él, internándose en los territorios
> domésticos, luego tras el hombre que hay en ella, se aventura por el
> terreno de afuera, los caminos de lo público, siendo siempre la pugna
> por y contra el discurso de la madre la búsqueda y el significado de la
> misma.

> (First he goes after the female within him, penetrating the domestic
> territories, then after the male within her, he ventures into the out-
> side terrain, the roads of the public sphere, the search and its signifi-
> cance always being the battle for and against the mother's discourse.)[18]

Although Angel seeks a liberation from his mother's discourse by setting off on a journey with Morgana, he also perceives a kindred spirit in
her, one who bears the stigma of a composite identity. He wants to go

beyond the facade of the great artist who appears on the covers of the popular magazines. He senses that by piercing through her masks, he will uncover both their true identities.

The second part of the novel narrates their voyage toward abjection, a mythic-oneiric journey to the underworld, as they experience misery and deprivation in the slums of Buenos Aires, a parody of their dream of a Paris escape. In her descent, the actress sheds all her disguises, losing her luxurious clothes and makeup and people's admiration. She literally becomes a beggar, finally understanding that role. As Angel(a) and Morgana journey together, they bare their souls, and Angel(a) can finally capture his/her companion's real identity:

> Su cara lavada se vuelve por lo tanto para mí, como una especie de gran entrega de Morgana. Sin artilugios, sin trucos, Morgana está dispuesta a concederme un trozo de su verdadera identidad, de su persona y no de su personaje, no la imagen inventada, no la máscara estudiada, no sus muletas, no su propia creación de sí misma.

> (Her washed face therefore becomes for me like a kind of big surrender by Morgana. Without gimmicks, without tricks, Morgana is disposed to concede me a piece of her true identity, of her person and not her character, not the invented image, not the studied mask, not her crutches, not her own creation of herself.) (198)

This understanding helps Angel to break his mother's spell by accepting her death and his own duality:

> Antes de tu muerte fui Angel. Después de tu muerte fui Angela. Y siempre, antes y después y hasta que nos reencontremos, seré los dos, —ángeles—, y seré ninguno.

> (Before your death I was Angel. After your death I was Angela. And always, before and afterwards and until we meet again, I'll be both—angels—and I won't be any.) (193)

The motif of the journey also addresses the issue of the acquisition of social consciousness and responsibility in spite of society's distortion of reality. When the characters set off on their journey, they are totally ignorant about social and political conditions in their country. The journey is the catalyst that makes them face their country's concealed plight. They enter a nightmarish space where they witness extremes of poverty, destruction, and degradation:

[C]omo si una guerra hubiera asolado esta zona de la ciudad, pues en lugar de edificios, nos topamos con paredes demolidas, construcciones destruidas por evidentes marcas de esquirlas, y un olor muy particular, que se asemeja al napalm.

([A]s if a war had razed this part of the city, because instead of buildings, we bumped against demolished walls, constructions destroyed by evident marks of splinters, and a very particular smell, which resembles napalm.) (222)

In their wanderings, they constantly come up against key events in past and recent Argentine history, which they had previously ignored. In an attempt to get closer to each other, they reminisce about their parents. Morgana remembers her father as a man who waved at her from a balcony and her mother as a young blond woman who died prematurely. Angel(a) clings to the embalmed hands of his/her beautiful mother, which s/he keeps in a made-to-order shrine s/he carries wherever s/he goes. Metaphorically, the characters who live to mourn their parents' deaths are the orphaned children of Evita Perón and Juan Domingo Perón, symbolizing modern Argentina.

Morgana and Angel's underworld voyage forces them to seek temporary shelter at a makeshift hospital in a circus tent. Here, a terrible father figure, a doctor/dictator, reigns in the midst of a bombed-out city. Under his absolute power, hunger, misery, and death prevail. In this setting, hooded men dressed in black bring to the tent the bodies of human beings screaming in agony. Near the tent Angel(a) finds a corpse with a mutilated face. In the midst of this terror, the doctor attempts to steal the embalmed hands from Angel(a), but succeeds only in getting the mother's magnificent ring. (This metaphorical reference links past and present dictators, as it reminds us of Juan Domingo Perón's stolen embalmed hands, which were cut from his corpse.) This allusion to Perón is tied to the cathartic experience of the characters, who, by finally facing the ghosts of the ruler-parents, become free. Morgana breaks her silence on the subject of her son and his disappearance. She tells about prostituting herself, to no avail, with a highly placed military man to discover her son's whereabouts. That Morgana can shed her actress's image and become a grieving mother reveals the depth of her change. Her experiences with Angel(a) allow her to pierce the official blanket of silence and give voice to her son's plight. On their journey the characters have confronted and come to terms with the parental/patriarchal discourse that molded their behavior, as well as the institutionalized discourse that had denied them a true vision of

themselves and their sociohistorical reality. Their return, narrated in the
short third section, is similar to a rebirth. They escape the whale's womb
only to find their luxurious flats flooded and their possessions ruined,
symbolizing a change in them and their lives.

Cama de ángeles presents an illustration of Diaconú's masterful efforts
to make duality and multiplicity emerge from the limitations of a single,
unequivocal vision and to deal with the tainted perceptions of Argentina's
recent past. Along with the fiction of Luisa Valenzuela and Rosario Ferré,
Cama de ángeles stands out as a text that attempts to erase the limits
imposed by gender, through a narration that strives to become genderless.

Los ojos azules

Los ojos azules (Blue eyes), 1986, elaborates upon Diaconú's theme of a
deranged character's journey and expands themes only hinted at before,
particularly lesbianism and suicide. Previously integrated themes—the mismatched couple, madness, the self and the Other, the mythic journey, and
the hallucinatory escape—are also explored. Critics predicted that this novel
would be a new direction for Diaconú. "Los ojos azules alcanza cráteres,
cimas de excelencia y ciertos espacios—entretejido de obsesiones—que se
clausuran para inaugurar otros posibles de ser desarrollados en obras
posteriores" (Los ojos azules attains craters, heights of perfection, and certain spaces—an interweaving of obsessions—which close to open up to
other possible spaces to be developed in future works).[19]

We follow the voyage of Blue Eyes, a thirtyish divorced secretary,
both attractive and mediocre, who uses all her savings to travel to an
unknown island for a night, where she hopes to meet a rich man who will
save her from her boredom and mediocrity. (Does she really set out to
commit suicide?) She is atoning for the loss of a husband who deserted
her. She perceives this loss as yet another failure, summing up an existence
plagued by failures. She is searching for the mythic lost paradise but instead descends into hell. Rather than finding Prince Charming, she becomes the prisoner of three repugnant old men, who dominate the island
and abuse her to no end. Again, the narration is a product of the
protagonist's hallucinations. Blue Eyes's nightmarish experiences on the
island of Tot (German for "dead") can be interpreted as just that—a night-
mare. In addition to the illusory island, at least two other narrative worlds
become part of the protagonist's experiences. She seems to be narrating
her life story to a psychoanalyst; at the same time she is confined to a dark
hospital room. When the reader becomes aware of this ambiguity, the text

must be reinterpreted and the sequence at Tot Island reevaluated as the nightmares or hallucinations of a deranged, hospitalized character or, possibly, the result of medication being administered as "therapy."

As in *Enamorada del muro*, another story is metaphorically inscribed in the female body. From this perspective, *Enamorada del muro* and *Los ojos azules* are interrelated and, notwithstanding critics' opinions, part of a cycle that encompasses *Cama de ángeles*.[20] The protagonist's body symbolizes territory disputed by various forces seeking to control and repress her. The regime's violence and abjection, encoded in the female body, is represented by the body's relationship with what it ingests. The struggle for control and authority centers first on the mother entrenched in the domain of her kitchen. The image appears throughout the novel in the smells associated with the mother and her cooking. This symbolizes the mother's attempts to control the protagonist through food. The use of onions—a domestic image—alludes to the mother's efforts to instill bourgeois values and passivity in her daughter. While the protagonist is in the hospital, the doctor, a patriarchal, authoritarian figure, replaces the mother. He exercises control by drugging the protagonist and feeding her intravenously when she refuses to eat. By her refusal, the daughter inscribes her protest on her body: "La sopa estaba fría y tenía gusto a trapo. La escupió no porque quisiese exasperar a la enfermera, sino por autoprotegerse, un acto de autodefensa al fin" (The soup was cold and it tasted like a rag. She spat it out not because she wanted to exasperate the nurse, but to protect herself, finally an act of self-defense).[21] Accepting or refusing to ingest food symbolizes her abuse and her attempts to recover control by the only means left to her, even though these efforts might lead to self-destruction. The allegory is further expanded in the island sequence when the three old men use drugs and liquor to victimize her. In a scene that is a nightmarish projection of national reality, Blue Eyes attends a banquet given by the old men at the hotel. The hospital sequence is transposed into this scene as she is forced to accept the delicacies that constitute the banquet but ends up being devoured by the men:

No estaba maniatada y sin embargo, todo movimiento le estaba vedado. Tal vez estaba maniatada, sí, mas con hilos invisibles. ¿Se llevaban realmente con la cucharita sus pezones?, ¿se llevaban el ombligo, le borraban para siempre la anatomía, la devoraban de verdad?

(Her hands weren't tied and, notwithstanding, any movement was impossible. Maybe her hands were tied, yes, but with invisible threads.

Were they really scooping up her tits with the little spoon? Were they scooping up her navel, were they erasing her anatomy forever, were they really devouring her?) (63)

This dream graphically represents how an authoritarian, patriarchal society devours women by denying them their identity, annihilating those who are different. The protagonist, however, deflects this attempt by using her body to enact her denial:

> ¿Vomitaría ya . . .? ¿Qué era sino su vómito ese charco pestilento en el cual se despertó . . . y su cabeza rodeada del ex caviar, del ex pescado, del ex paté, de la ex carne, de todo el festín amalgamado y en franca descomposición?

> (She wondered if she had vomited already? . . . What was that pestilent puddle in which she woke up but her vomit . . . and her head surrounded by the former caviar, the former fish, the former paté, the former meat, by the whole amalgamated feast and in full decomposition?) (65)

The protagonist's reaction has the liberating function of separating her from her victimizers: "The spasms and vomiting that protect me. The repugnance, the retching that thrusts me to the side and turns me away from the defilement, sewage and muck. . . . The fascinated start that leads me toward and separates me from them."[22] She becomes a statue of ice by emitting bodily fluids (vomit, sweat, urine) that remove her from the monsters' power as she escapes. In an alternative version, the banquet becomes the protagonist's trial, which culminates in her death sentence to be carried out by drinking liquor laced with poison. It is significant that she is condemned to ingest a fluid, as its presence in the previous scene meant removal from the abuses and evasion by means of a dreamlike journey oblivious of her body. Although her death might seem a homicide, it is the culmination of her previous efforts and can be labeled a suicide. In her confessions, the protagonist explains that she went to the island to commit suicide and free herself from a symbolic ailment:

> Creo que tengo un tumor en algún rincón de mi cuerpo. Lo siento. Hace tiempo que quiero morir. . . . Vine a esta isla, a este hotel, para suicidarme. Pero tengo suerte, porque Uds. ahora me están simplificando la labor. . . . Porque entre engullir tres frascos de pastillas y beber un delicioso licor, con el mismo resultado, la segunda opción es mucho más seductora.

(I think that I have a tumor in some corner of my body. I can feel it. I have been wanting to die for a long time. . . . I came to this island, to this hotel, to commit suicide. But I'm lucky, because you are making my task simple. . . . Because between gobbling three bottles of pills down and drinking a delicious liqueur, with the same result, the second option is much more seductive.) (238)

Her abusers have become her instrument, helping her to accomplish her goal: "En realidad la estaban salvando sin tener que ser ella la que llevara a cabo la misa negra . . . y que significaba . . . la única salida que no estuviese en contradicción con su ser esencial" (In reality they were saving her without her having to be the one to carry out the black mass . . . and which signified . . . the only way out that didn't contradict her essential self) (236). The act of ingesting the poisoned drink that will kill her represents the protagonist's rebellion, her choice to become a nonbeing, to be true to her essence. Her fate is captured by the novel's open ending, which expresses a removal of the physical being from the abusive space and a vindication of the empty spaces left by the disappeared. We can also read a vindication of the female and a restoration of her powers, which the patriarchal dictatorship had denied. By using nourishment and its effects as a metaphor for survival and power, Diaconú conjures up the scars inflicted by the patriarchy on the female body.

El penúltimo viaje

Although El penúltimo viaje (The penultimate journey), 1989, deals with some of the thematic concerns present in Diaconú's previous work—exile, journey, authoritarianism, and death—the focus of the novel is different. It is more confessional, and readers find themselves carrying on an intimate dialogue with the narrator. Treading on very personal territory, readers may feel as if they have accessed the narrator's inner sanctuary. As expressed in the title, the main focus is the journey. However, several journeys are occurring, some physical, some spiritual. Why is the journey qualified as "penultimate"? It insinuates that there is still a last journey in store, maybe the definitive one toward death.

The novel is divided into three sections, "Punto de partida" (Point of departure), "Hasta cierto punto" (Up to a certain point), and "Punto y aparte" (Full stop). In "Point of departure" two alternating stories are separated by approximately twenty years. One story, set in italics and parentheses with very short paragraphs, occurs in the present tense: An unidentified character embarks on a train journey north, from Buenos Aires to the Bolivian border. The narration focuses almost exclusively on an objective, at times lyrical, description of the landscape and its inhabitants as seen through the window of the train: "*(El viento es un viento huracanado. La lluvia cae en diagonal. El tren está detenido")* (The wind is a hurricane-force wind. The rain falls diagonally. The train has stopped).*[23]* The italicized narration alternates with the protagonist's memories of her past when she took the train through an Eastern European country. The goal of her present journey is to evoke these memories:

> *Al subir la escalerilla del tren, se prometió asumir con valor la empresa de ese viaje, cuyo único objeto era recordar en un vagón sucio y con asientos incómodos, la incómoda y poco pulcra historia de la cual hasta entonces había estado escapándose.*
>
> *(Upon climbing the stairs to the train, she promised herself to courageously face the undertaking of this journey, whose only objective was to reminisce, in a dirty car with uncomfortable seats, the uncomfortable and untidy story from which she had run away until now.)* (17)

If the outside reality is conveyed in almost totally objective language, it is because all emotion and subjectivity are reserved for the inner journey of reminiscence. Often, the two narrations feature similar themes or tonality. The story of her past is narrated in the third person and divided into alternating sections dealing with different characters, mainly members of the protagonist's family and household. The father at first occupies a high post in the Communist hierarchy, but later is disgraced and stripped of everything, becoming an exile. The father, seen almost as a divinity, is omnipotent. He has absolute control over the lives of those around him:

> Me exasperaba su mirada que nos controlaba como si fuésemos objetos, pertenencias de poco o mucho valor, no lo sé.
>
> (His gaze exasperated me. It controlled us as though we were objects, belongings of little or much value, I don't know.) (165)

> En casa, decían de él, que de noche dormía con los ojos abiertos. Y que, por eso, nada se le escapaba. Controlaba el mundillo de nuestro hogar como Dios los planetas, y no había posibilidad de engañar a ese centinela inmutable de nuestra vigilia y de nuestro sueño.
>
> (At home, they said that at night he slept with his eyes open. And that, for this reason, he didn't miss a thing. He controlled the small world of

our home like God [controls] the planets, and there was no chance of deceiving that immutable sentinel of our vigil and our sleep.) (246)

As a critic pointed out, the father is also inflexible, authoritarian, and incapable of expressing any emotion. At the same time he demands blind obedience:

El padre—llamado "Padre," sin artículo, una manera de quitarle afecto a la relación, de llenarla de un sentido de respeto y autoritarismo— representa ante los ojos infantiles una figura como la del Hermano Mayor de Orwell, sumido en un mundo de contradicciones, entre el respeto a la propaganda masificadora del régimen o el afecto al único punto que lo vincula a la realidad, sus hijos y ese micromundo en que viven.

(The father—called "Father," without the article, to strip affection from the relationship and fill it with a sense of respect and authori- tarianism—represents to the childish vision a figure like that of Orwell's Big Brother, steeped in a world of contradictions, between respect for the regime's mass propaganda and the affection toward his only link with reality, his children and that microcosm in which they live.)[24]

Amapola, the protagonist, spends a lifetime trying to understand this man and the destructive influence that he exerted over all her loved ones. Amapola is a sensitive, introspective, observing child with an artistic tem- perament manifested in her paintings. Her sister, Alelí, is totally the op- posite: egotistic, vain, self-centered, devoid of any spiritual life. She is the father's favorite child because of her beauty and conformity. The younger brother, Alisio, is outwardly weak, escaping from a reality that crushes his sensitive and creative spirit by hiding in music, books, and Christian ritual.

Their childhood and early teens are not narrated chronologically. We learn about the incidents and people that influence the formative years of the three youngsters, and the interrelations between the characters and their grandparents, aunts, governesses, and servants. The deceased mother, who haunts each family member in a different way, is an important pres- ence. There is always a setting for her at the table. The father never told the children the truth about their mother's death. He told them a story about her being ill and undertaking a journey to heal herself (the pen- ultimate journey?). This is a metaphor of the protagonist's journey through Argentina to heal her psychological wounds. The healing is also a refer- ence to her rebelliousness and nonacceptance of the regime, as the mother expresses before her death: "'Ojalá los héroes de hoy no sean los villanos de mañana'" ("Hopefully today's heroes won't be tomorrow's villains")

(273). It is significant that women characters who rebel and speak out against authoritarianism are punished by death. (Both mother and daughter succumb to similar fates.) At one point, Amapola learns that her mother, who was dying of cancer, shot herself when the children were infants. The image of the beautiful young mother haunts her and appears in her dreams dressed in veils, surrounded by mist, her eyes and nose missing from her face, ready to console her daughter in times of distress:

> The apparition of the dead mother means the world to Amapola, it's her only consolation and hope. She is her father's true daughter, the only one who holds within herself the worst of her father's sickness. . . . Her father does not know it, and, if he had known it, he would probably have been horrified, but he has triumphed: His daughter is the container of his dead wife, the medium of her frustration. He called her so much, that his wife . . . reappears . . . in his daughter.[25]

When the father falls into disgrace, the family flees to the West, traveling through many countries, first by train and finally by ship to the New World. The narration of this journey in the second section, "Up to a certain point," functions as a counterpoint to the adult Amapola's journey. It becomes obvious that we are reading Amapola's story when the narration becomes distinctly first person: "The change in strategy in the second part originates, in reality, in the desire to shift the attention toward Amapola, who becomes in this way the novel's central character."[26] It also signifies a break with her childhood and the achievement of maturity. The characters and events are the same as in the first section; the order is strictly mnemonic. The outside point of reference is the actual journey. The organization, viewpoint, and circumstances parallel the first part. Both show a protagonist undertaking a journey and reminiscing. The difference is that the first part seems more detached and objective, with a bigger time gap between events and narration. The second part has more immediacy due to the central role given to Amapola as she sorts out the puzzle of her past. Amapola's vision of her family becomes clearer as they change under the pressure of events:

> Demoré más de una década en vislumbrar con cierto desapasionamiento la personalidad de Padre, que la cercanía y una especie de extraño afecto me habían ocultado sin querer.

> (It took me more than a decade to be able to make out somewhat dispassionately Father's personality, which proximity and a sort of strange affection had unwillingly hidden from me.) (280)

Her father, once all-powerful, has become an almost penniless refugee with three children. As she sees this previously omnipotent figure crumble, it is obvious that his demise is symbolic. It represents the change taking place in their lives, the closing of a chapter, and a new beginning. The brief third part, "Full stop," deals with their failed attempts to make a new life in Western Europe and their subsequent emigration to Argentina. Nevertheless, as the protagonist expresses, things have not changed that much: "'¿Dónde estaba la libertad?', le pregunté un día cuando unos tanques salieron a la calle y un hombre viejo fue desalojado de la Casa de Gobierno" ("Where was freedom?" I asked him one day when tanks came out on the streets and an old man was evicted from the Government House) (292). In their new country, Amapola attends the university and works at several jobs; Alelí marries a lawyer; Alisio ends up committed to an insane asylum. The father becomes a civil servant working in a deteriorated building, signifying the consolidation of his downfall and mediocrity.

As the novel closes, Amapola reaches the end of her journey and confronts the legacy of her past. But this introspection has not resulted in healing, for she is still haunted by contradictory and unresolved issues. As a consequence, "Amapola's story is a journey of development in which her self-realization takes her back toward her childhood instead of progressing toward an adult personal integration."[27] This failed journey is marked by the chapter, "Balance trunco" (Balance cut short) in which the voyage ends in a forsaken station in northern Argentina. It is the poorest section of the country, a place Amapola calls "land of St. Death," dark and cold. As she sits in the empty train, shots are heard outside, and two guards drag her off the train. Her fate in their hands is not described, but it is obvious that she is trapped by the same authoritarianism embodied by her father, whom she has been trying to escape. The father, who represents patriarchy and authority both within the family and the public sphere, becomes a strong presence in her final destiny as victim to these faceless voices of destruction. Nevertheless, the story does not end in a surrender to the father. She detaches herself from reality and follows the vision of her dead mother:

La mujer envuelta en velos era su guía. No era posible perderse. En cierto momento ella suspendería su marcha y las dos se fundirían en un gran abrazo: madre-hija. Y esa fusión habría de significar que había alcanzado la meta. El destino final.

(The woman wrapped in veils was her guide. It was not possible to get lost. At a certain moment she would stop walking and both would fuse in a big embrace: mother-daughter. And that fusion would mean that she had reached the goal. The final destination.) (301)

As she rejoins her mother, we understand the title of the novel. The penultimate journey was the train ride north, which led the protagonist to another journey, the final one, where she regained her past in the company of her estranged mother. The various train rides symbolize the womb, a return to the origins, which the protagonist has achieved by finally settling accounts with a past that haunted her. The protagonist's failed voyage is a journey of integration: "The mother who is dead but present, in her ghostly figure introduces the only possible force that can be opposed to the Father. That wandering apparition of the suicidal mother impels her to seek liberation from that fate of sacrificed woman because she gradually helped her to shed the layers of guilt which tear her away from self-realization."[28]

Diaconú's ending is open and ambiguous, as unsettled and unsettling as the existence of these characters. On the one hand, Amapola is destroyed by the very destructive and repressive forces that she has sought to get away from; on the other, she transcends authoritarianism and ends her vital and existential exile by means of female spirituality and strength. In this way Diaconú empowers her female characters to recreate their existence and find their identity in a vision that rescues them from a chaotic and repressive patriarchy. Another prevailing aspect is the fictional female discourse, which transcends the authoritarian voices and acquires its own coherence and voice.

Diaconú has masterfully linked two dictatorships separated by time and space. She has shown their effects on the lives of the protagonists caught between a Communist dictatorship in Eastern Europe during the 1950s and a military regime in Argentina during the 1970s. *El penúltimo viaje* is also the story of two women, mother and daughter, trying to subvert authoritarian patriarchy in their lives at the family, social, and state level. The surface result is a family caught between the two political upheavals in a world where the nonconformist, sensitive, and artistic characters (Amapola and Alisio), whom we have come to love, are destroyed, while the conventional and accommodating characters (Alelí and the father) survive. But at a symbolic level the female characters, represented by the mother and Amapola, survive in a spiritual realm and through the reminisced and written text, as did protagonists of Diaconú's earlier novels (*La Señora, Los ojos azules*). Diaconú has crafted a masterpiece in the study of an era: a psychological portrayal of characters and linguistic richness and diversity in a "work that by means of its structure and its symbols presents effectively important reflections about a varied number of themes and circumstances, while at the same time projecting the anguished search for truth of an honest character tormented by uncertainty and dissatisfaction within the convulsed and contradictory contemporary world."[29]

Los devorados

Los devorados (The devoured), 1992, is Diaconú's seventh novel. It inaugurates Atlántida's new collection, *Voces del Plata* (River Plate voices). *Los devorados* confirms the writer's prominent position in Argentine letters of the Proceso and the postdictatorial period. The novel's skillful structure and characterization develop in an atmosphere fraught with existential anguish cushioned by irony and humor. The narration progresses from realism to the fantastic, projecting an aura subject to various levels of interpretation. The mastery with which these complex aspects are treated demonstrates that the author has reached new heights in the handling of themes and devices used in previous works.

    Los devorados is divided into five chronological parts. The titles of the first four refer to time ("Night," "Dawn," "Midday," "Evening," "A day later," "A week later," "Other days, other nights"). These are then subdivided into spatial references (Buenos Aires neighborhoods, "Retiro," "San Telmo," and "Lomas de San Isidro"). In part 4 the main narration alternates with chapters from the protagonist's notebook. In part 5 secondary characters' "testimonials" about the protagonist, Ian Gravski, are written like depositions taken in the aftermath of the main story's tragic ending. This quiltlike structure of *Los devorados*, reminiscent of a mosaic,[30] has been characterized as a "story patched together by existential remnants, by intertwining reality and fantasy, by hallucination and truths; maybe and above all, by the persecution of an utopia which ends up devouring its maker."[31]

    What at first seem to be three unrelated stories focusing on different characters gradually come to coalesce into one plot. Ian Gravski has an ambiguous story: He emigrated to Argentina with his Polish family of modest means when he was three years old. In the past he had achieved a high standard of living by means of a marriage of convenience, but when his estranged wife died, he cut his ties with his former life (as did the protagonists in *Buenas noches, profesor* and *Cama de ángeles*). As the novel opens, Gravski is unemployed and drinking too much. He lives in a furnished room in the Retiro neighborhood. His mood is one of deep despair, and his only interest, besides chasing women, is collecting and studying carnivorous plants. His story alternates with the second story, that of a beggar lying in an alcoholic stupor on a sidewalk in the San Telmo neighborhood. Formerly an architect and family man living a conventional life, the beggar lost all interest in life when his wife and daughter were killed in an automobile accident while he was driving. As a result, he now only awaits death. The third story is about Olympia Moore, a rich upper-class former marchioness, who has been married several times. Her current marriage is stale and for appearances' sake. She lives a bored, narcissistic life in her San Isidro mansion, where she is preoccupied exclusively with herself and her fleeting amorous affairs.

A skillful plot interrelates these three lives and the locations where they take place. A critic has likened the plot to "the threads in a spiderweb which slowly trap them."[32] The beggar sleeps on the sidewalk of the antique store where Gravski is supposed to be working and where the former marchioness frequently shops. Gravski develops a fascination for the beggar, whom he perceives as his double, foreshadowing his own gradual descent toward abjection. He also admires him because the beggar renounced everything and only awaits death, while Gravski still gets satisfaction from his carnivorous plants. Reviewers of the novel explain this attraction: "In him Ian sees a degraded and at the same time admirable reflection (because the choice is so absolute as to have severed all ties with 'decent' life) of his own marginal and outcast condition."[33] When the beggar dies, just before he was supposed to have lunch with Gravski, the latter renounces the ascetic existence and devotes himself to seducing Olympia. Gravski is not the only one to see a double of himself in the beggar. Olympia also perceives the beggar to be a messenger of decay and death. He represents the ravages of time, which she is trying to flee by buying youth (cosmetic surgery) and costly objects. For this reason, Olympia tries to remove the beggar from public sight by committing him to a shelter that will reintegrate him in society. He escapes and dies as an outcast on the sidewalk.

Gravski, on the other hand, chooses abjection and deceit as he seduces the aging former marchioness, pretending she is a beautiful young redhead. He ends up being devoured by the carnivorous plants in his hothouse. Reviewers have interpreted the ending as "defining the human animal as an insatiable being, lusting after objects that do not exist, devoured by the passion of his fancy."[34] They have said that "the characters of her novels (or ourselves, who definitively generate them) are being systematically and conscientiously devoured."[35] Diaconú has said that she intended to use the carnivorous plants as a symbol of life and love, that we are all insects attracted by a huge carnivorous plant that finally devours us.[36]

The story is another example of Diaconú's resistance literature. Diaconú's dissenting message, inscribed in her novel by the use of marginality, appears thematically and discursively. Ambiguity affecting narration, time, space, and structure is an allegorical reference to the destruction of patriarchal authoritarianism and the recovery of marginal and female elements.

Marginality is expressed by characters who defy the bourgeois establishment and exist on the edges of society (Gravski and the beggar). That theirs is a self-imposed condition resulting from a conscious choice shows the underlying significance of marginality. The alienation and abjection experienced by Gravski and the beggar are heightened by unusual secondary characters: a young woman with Down's syndrome, a child who cuts his veins on the sidewalk, and a blind, retarded, albino child. These characters constantly allude to despair and death (insects, skeletons, tombs). They also dwell in places frequented by derelicts, projecting an abject picture of society onto the narrative. The deep sense of marginality is heightened by the existential vision of despair that emerges from the characters' attitudes and language:

Pero Ian Gravski sabía que nadie podía consolar a nadie, que no hay consuelo. La vida era atroz para todos.

(But Ian Gravski knew that nobody was able to console anybody, that there was no consolation. Life was atrocious for everybody.)[37]

Sin embargo se le hacía que todo era un pozo sin fondo, sórdido.

(However, it seemed to him that everything was a bottomless well, sordid.) (42)

Estaba agotado de ver personajes sufrientes, oscilando entre el fantasma del hospital, del manicomio o del cementerio.

(He was worn out from seeing suffering human beings, oscillating between the ghost from the hospital, the insane asylum, or the cemetery.) (44)

The characters' marginality is reinforced by the discourse; this story is ambiguously narrated from a marginal perspective by a multiplicity of narrative voices. This particular use of discursive voices is based on Jean-François Lyotard's thesis: "[P]ostmodernism is characterized by a 'lack of dominant narrations.'"[38] When applied to the Argentine case, it dismantles the hegemonic narratives and their official language. Thus, the writer multiplies the number of spoken discourses, articulating a diversity within unpredictable surroundings.[39] The intertwining narratives lead the reader to question whose story this is. Is it that of Ian Gravski, the beggar, or the former marchioness? Or is it the story of the "fourth protagonist," the carnivorous plants (in Gravski's notebook), which take on a central role in the plot? Or is the truth contained in part 5, the "Testimonials"? Which one of these texts, posited as marginal, constitutes the true story? The critic Beatriz Sarlo interprets the use of such a multiplicity of texts—in this case, narrative, pseudoscientific, and legal—as attempts to approach, from different angles, a reality that cannot be represented in its entirety. The final product becomes a text contesting the authoritarian monologue.[40] By juxtaposing and interrelating the various narratives, Diaconú sets up a fragmentary discourse in contraposition to the hegemonic one. By making Gravski's story fragmented and ambiguous and incorporating the fantastic in the outcome, she expresses the impossibility of representing reality or individual biography. They have been distorted by the regime's and society's lies. The pseudoscientific text on carnivorous plants also fragments the narration, underlining imprecision and indecisiveness in contrast to "scientific truth."

Part 5 attempts to transgress the official version of events. The "testimonials," depositions about Gravski's past from all the characters who knew him, are supposedly detached by means of the legalistic frame in which they are placed. Their purpose is to fragment Gravski's story. Because they are partial and at times contradictory, they constitute another means of breaching the monologic discourse. This dialogic form subverts authoritarian relations and is an allegory of the attempt to include different attitudes and opinions. The critic Fernando Reati has pointed this out: "By eliminating the omniscient narrator and replacing him with the protagonists' voices, the narration denies authoritarianism."[41] By using these half-truths, Diaconú conveys the impact of the regime's silencing, which has relegated writers to work on reconstructing scattered fragments of reality. The "testimonials" provide information about Gravski that we did not have during the course of the novel. They cause readers to revise their interpretations of the material, another device that opens up the novel. Truth is seen as inconclusive and partial. The function of the novel is to render the elements that the regime has dispersed.

Ambiguity is increased by the way in which time and space are used to subvert the apparent linearity. Dominant discourse is subverted by juxtaposing ambiguous and contradictory voices. Time is similarly handled. Time is focused exclusively on the present, for the past is ambiguous and to an extent obliterated by dissenting voices. This concept of the present as a continuous "becoming" stems from existentialism and is characteristic of a female vision, which utilizes time in this way to subvert male constructs.[42] In this subversive female concept of time, continuity is ruptured: The present is not related to the past, but stems from a break with it. Linear, continuous time is replaced by a nonlinear pattern following mnemonic associations (when characters attempt to create new biographies for themselves). The writer uses this metaphor to say that in the Argentine past, inaccurate versions have emerged to deny the truth. The contrived life scripts, which obliterate the characters' biographies, underline the blocking of memory to deny a past that has been censored or has become too painful. The use of time as an eternal present depicts the anguish of the individual, who faces the passage of time and mortality. The main characters enact this drama of humankind and choose to escape by creating new biographies that deny the passage of time and death.

The three protagonists, faced with middle age, are coping with recent encounters with death, which has heightened their awareness of their own fate. While the beggar's reaction has been to give up and await death, the other characters have developed mechanisms to deter their destiny. Gravski's wife died of a terminal illness only two months earlier, and Gravski lives in fear of dying: "Acaso tenía miedo de morirse en sueños, lo mismo que Rovanna" (Perhaps he feared dying while dreaming, just like Rovanna) (25). His obsession with collecting carnivorous plants is an attempt to create a new time, different from linear time, to extract himself from his mortality and enter a new dimension. The insects (as well as the constant allusions to Franz Kafka's metamorphosed character, Gregor Samsa) constitute a leitmotif of metamorphosis. The notebooks represent Gravski's creative attempt to find eternal youth by arresting the passage of time. The same can be said of his attempts to be Olympia's young lover and his fantasies that convert her into a beautiful young redhead. By metamorphosing himself in this way, the past and the painful passage of time can be obliterated.

We find Gravski's counterpart in Olympia (an elaboration of Morgana in *Cama de ángeles*), who carries his goals to extremes. She uses all the conveniences her money and position can acquire to defeat the ravages of time on her person and surroundings. Her body is the product of the plastic surgeon's scalpel, and her home is a theatrical stage where the decor is constantly changed, as new luxurious objects must be acquired to deter permanence or deterioration. When the novel opens, she is celebrating her sixtieth birthday. The character's fear of time and death is symbolized in the funereal image conveyed by the many flower arrangements sent for the occasion: "Vio las ofrendas apiladas, coronas mustias alrededor de un féretro. ¿Quién sino ella misma estaba allí adentro?" (She saw the stacked up offerings, wilted wreaths surrounding a casket. Who was in there but herself?) (33).

She attempts to override this imagery through her amorous encounters with younger men. Before Gravski, she had a relationship with a boxer. Although he represents youth, health, and brute force, his professional defeat in the course of the story signals the illusory nature of the characters' endeavors. Furthermore, since Olympia and Gravski's attempts at seduction are described in theatrical terms, we perceive them as actors on a stage, reminding us that this is make-believe, an artificial attempt to escape from their mortal fate. Benjamin Moore, Olympia's aging husband, has adopted similar coping mechanisms. He has turned over all financial responsibilities to others and is dedicated to turning the clock back by leading a life of debauchery. Like his wife and Gravski, Ben has reverted to a younger, more seductive self: He has an affair with a younger woman and becomes addicted to cocaine. These new scripts created by the characters are futile attempts to break with the past and present reality. They signal an effort to "freeze" an eternal present and negate the flow of time. This posture questions a monologic account of history that freezes and distorts reality. The characters' denial of death and decay can be viewed as a self-censoring mechanism, responding to a society that demands this behavior in exchange for survival.

The mosaic structure characterized by alternating narrative spaces breaches the hegemonic system. It contests the unidimensional bourgeois text as well as the flow of time. Within the narrative, traditional bourgeois spaces are questioned—e.g., the house, which usually constitutes a refuge for the characters. Two of the protagonists, Gravski and the beggar, have given up their homes. Gravski lives in a sordid furnished room, and the beggar, on the sidewalk. In an attempt to shed all attributes of bourgeois existence, they have also severed ties with families, or institutions that function like surrogate families, thus giving up their traditional roles as heads of families—symptomatic of the demise of patriarchal social structures. Only Olympia remains in her house—in her palatial mansion, where she reigns supreme. She is removed from it by Gravski, to journey to an unknown place (as in *Cama de ángeles*). The mansion is replaced by the hothouse containing the carnivorous plants (representing the ravages of time). By removing Olympia from the mansion/refuge and taking her to a place where she must shed all artificial trappings (and return to her true, former identity—a sixty-year-old woman), Gravski deludes himself into thinking that he is in control: "Marquesa de Santillana, ex Marquesa, ex joven, ex invulnerable, ex omnipotente" (Marchioness of Santillana, former Marchioness, formerly young, formerly invulnerable, formerly omnipotent) (271). In the hothouse scene, time and space become inextricably related. Gravski continues his self-delusion, imagining that his partner is a young redhead instead of "esa reina que huía de la vejez" (that queen who was fleeing from old age) (261); she is also characterized as "esa tirana disfrazada de hada" (that tyrant disguised as a fairy) (261). The brutal love scene is described as a mutual victimization and has similarities with the information in the italicized metatext, the notebook with descriptions of the carnivorous plants. This notebook contains the description of a vulva that devours any insect that comes close.

> *En su interior, la hoja presenta una zona superior, erizada por pelos (apuntados hacia abajo) y un sector resbaladizo. Los insectos son atraídos por la trampa del jugo segregado por las hojas, y luego de penetrar en los pelos, llegan a una zona lisa donde resbalan cayendo así dentro del líquido.*

> (In its interior, the leaf presents an upper part, bristling with hair [pointing downward] and a slimy area. The insects are attracted by the trap of the juice secreted by the leaves, and after penetrating the hair, they get to a flat zone where they slide, thus falling into the liquid.) (221)

That Gravski's obsessions with carnivorous plants and women are related is apparent in the plant descriptions. It is significant that he becomes the victim of the plant/vulva (marchioness/redheaded young woman) while frenetically making love, representing an emergence of the female: "y el cuerpo de Yan, sin cabeza, siendo devorado por una inmensa hoja, constituía un cuadro atroz" (and Yan's body, headless, being devoured by an immense leaf, constituted an atrocious picture) (275). The act of devouring the head of the male protagonist, traditionally the seat of rational principle, ascribed to males, empowers the female element. It has its implications on the writing, as Gravski's notebook describes plants in terms of female physiology and sexuality, thus inscribing the text on the female body. Gravski at first seemed the victimizer who removed Olympia from the mansion/refuge to submerge her in his abject world, where sexual intercourse is akin to destruction and cannibalism. It has become clear that Gravski is the victim succumbing to the fate foreshadowed by his alter ego, the beggar, while Olympia escapes, returning to her mansion. The novel's ending definitely underscores the protagonists' failure in their attempts to stop time and the effects of their own mortality.

Los devorados questions and subverts traditional narrative (the characters' biographic discourse, the handling of time, spatial, and structural configurations). In this way, Diaconú metaphorically tears apart the monologic dimensions of patriarchal authoritarianism to restore the plurality of marginal, as well as female, voices. This novel reaffirms Diaconú's groundbreaking work in the areas of psychological, existential, sociopolitical, and gender literature. Her use of technical devices to break through the constraints of censorship and social taboos has carved for her a permanent niche in the rich panorama of Argentine contemporary letters and women's writing. It is not an exaggeration to count her as a figure of the magnitude of Luisa Valenzuela or to say that she has carried out Julio Cortázar's mandate to revitalize her national literature.

CONVERSATION WITH ALINA DIACONÚ

Buenos Aires, 3 April 1987

M.F.: Can you talk about your life, about the events and persons you consider to be the most important?

A.D.: I'll try to summarize. I can say that there is a notorious division in my life between my early years spent in Rumania, my native country, and the second part, which began upon my arrival in Argentina, when I was fourteen years old. This split had a profound influence in my personal life, as that change took place during puberty, a difficult time for a woman. According to the critics, it also marked my literary work, in which they detect the presence of both European and Latin American undertones. I do not have sufficient objectivity to comment about how this experience has affected my works, but I can say that it has had a profound effect on me.

M.F.: Where and how did you begin to write?

A.D.: I have gone through several stages in my literary development. I learned how to read and write at age four and started writing children's stories as a game, as I was not happy with the ones being read to me. When I was ten years old I started writing poems. Then, for many years, I was torn between two passions, painting and writing. Until finally, I felt that literature was my calling, to the point that, at age fifteen, I stopped painting altogether. Upon arriving in Argentina, I had to give up Rumanian, and I went through a very hard transition period, feeling that I didn't have a language of my own. So during the next two years, until I was sixteen years old, I wrote in French, producing several plays and poems in French. After that I started writing short stories in Spanish and then novels. I have cultivated several genres, but the novel became the main one in terms of years spent and works published. I have been publishing novels since 1975.

M.F.: You mentioned that you started writing your own children's stories out of a personal need, but was there a particular event or person that made you take up writing?

A.D.: My father was very important in this respect. He was an art critic, a man who read and wrote all the time. The memory that I have of my father is that of a person holding an open book in his hands. So I think that seeing him reading, writing, and correcting so much, as he was obsessive about correcting, must have made an impression on me as a child.

M.F.: In one of your novels there's a scene in Rumania where the protagonist's father is seen receiving the visit of his intellectual friends. Is this connected to your childhood?

A.D.: It must be one of the very few autobiographical pages that I've written, because I can state categorically that I don't write autobiographical literature. Of course, there is some autobiographical element present in all literature, but I have not written direct autobiographical literature, except those pages which you mentioned, which suddenly appeared and remained. But it's an exception. I suppose it happened at a time when I needed to narrate an event from my childhood.

M.F.: Who are your favorite authors?

A.D.: It's hard to say, because there are stages in life when you like certain writers and then your preferences change. It depends on the personal moment you are living through, which triggers a feeling of identification with a particular author.

M.F.: How about at this moment?

A.D.: Now I'm reading the works of two women writers. One of them is Anaïs Nin, the French writer who lived in the States for many years and who has written a very lengthy and interesting diary. The other writer is Lou Andrea Salomé, who was a friend of Nietzsche and Rilke. They hold a special interest for me, for both were revolutionary for their times in how they dealt with literature and psychoanalysis. The next book I plan to read is also by a pioneer woman writer, Mme. de Staël, who in Napoleon's time wrote a two-volume feminist text. I cannot say that these writers have influenced my literary production, but I read their works out of curiosity and interest.

M.F.: Can you name specific writers who have influenced you?

A.D.: I have been influenced by Russian writers like Dostoevsky, Gogol, Tolstoy and Chekov, whose works I read as a child. I would also include playwrights like Beckett, Ionesco, the philosopher Cioran, and the

American writer Carson McCullers. Among Argentine writers, Roberto Arlt and Cortázar have had a profound influence on my work.

M.F.: Do you feel an affinity with other Argentine writers?

A.D.: Especially with several writers who are not well known in Argentina, like the novelists Juan Filloy and Enrique Wernike. I am also very interested in poets like Olga Orozco, Alejandra Pizarnik, and Alberto Girri.

M.F.: Do you belong to a specific literary generation in Argentina?

A.D.: That is up to the critics to say. I don't have sufficient distance and objectivity to judge that.

M.F.: Do you need to write in a particular environment?

A.D.: Yes, I need to be at home completely alone. There can't be any noise. Even the street noise bothers me, but I have to tolerate it.

M.F.: Do you have a writing schedule or routine?

A.D.: When I start writing a novel, I keep a strict routine. Whether I'm inspired or not, I dedicate four or five hours daily to my writing, without any exceptions. For me it's the only way to write. Writing means stepping into another world and leaving the other one behind. It's like developing a parallel life.

M.F.: How do you choose a theme?

A.D.: It's an obsession. Each book starts by an obsession. I carry it with me for some time, I spend sleepless nights over it and, when I can't stand it any more, I start writing until I flesh out an outline for a novel. Before writing *Los ojos azules*, I spent months obsessed with the idea that I saw things differently. The theme of the novel became that of a young woman who is surrounded by people who have dark eyes and she's the only one that is blue-eyed, a metaphor to express that she's different from the rest.

M.F.: How do you select titles for your novels?

A.D.: Before writing *La Señora* and *Los ojos azules* I had already found the titles. But it isn't always that easy. Sometimes I have to finish a novel before I can think about the title, as was the case with *Buenas noches, profesor* and *Enamorada del muro*. There's no system. Sometimes the title jumps out at you and at other times, it's very hard to come up with one.

M.F.: What has been the critical reaction to your works?

A.D.: It has been varied and highly polemic regarding the latest works, *Cama de ángeles* and *Los ojos azules*. It's understandable because these works are irritating and strong. For me this is extraordinary, as I believe that literature has to produce an impact on the reader. I'm interested in readers who participate actively in creating the novel as they read it. Besides, several critics have made absolutely original interpretations that have enriched my own perspective on these works.

M.F.: Is it hard to publish in Argentina?

A.D.: Yes, it's very hard, especially for an unknown writer.

M.F.: How hard is it for a writer like you who has received awards and published several works?

A.D.: I have published five novels, but it's still hard for me. I know that if I write a book now, I'll find a publisher, but I don't know who it will be. My five novels have been published by four different publishers. I would have liked to work with one publishing house exclusively, but that's impossible here in Argentina.

M.F.: Are you able to live off your works?

A.D.: There are very few writers in Argentina who have been able to live off their works. Possibly Borges during his last years, or [Ernesto] Sábato, but due to sales abroad. So, I would say that no writer can live off royalties in Argentina. We all have other jobs to survive. Lately, I have organized cultural events for foundations to make a living, as I can't live off the royalties from my works.

M.F.: Have your works been translated?

A.D.: Unfortunately, not yet, but I'm optimistic.

M.F.: Is it harder for a woman writer to publish, be reviewed, and receive prizes?

A.D.: My views on the women writers' situation are very clear. There are no gender differences regarding literary activity; to write is hard regardless of gender. The differences become obvious in the recognition of a writer. For a female writer the process of publication and the successful participation in literary contests is more difficult, and the literary appraisal of her works is going to be prejudiced. Unfortunately, prejudices leading to gender discrimination exist in women as well as in males.

M.F.: Do you think that there is a female style of writing different from male writing?

A.D.: In my opinion there might be differences in stylistic traits and in the thematic content, as it is possible to distinguish between male and female themes, but that isn't very important to me. What interests me is whether a work constitutes good or bad literature. Gender determines differences in the works, but not in their quality. As I mentioned, I'm reading a lot of literature written by women because they are relative newcomers to literature. I'm interested in the sociological aspect of women struggling and writing in a man's world. But for me what's important is that a book be well written. The gender of the writer is unimportant. Women must concentrate on breaking the prejudicial barriers that make it so hard for us to function in the literary world.

M.F.: Are you a feminist?

A.D.: I don't like labels. I've written many articles defending women's rights, but I've always tried to be independent, politically and ideologically. I'm a freethinker, which is a very difficult position, because in our society you are always under pressure to take sides. Because of my writings and my expressed opinions maybe I could be considered a feminist, but I refuse to place a label on myself.

M.F.: Can you explain why one of your novels was censored by the military regime?

A.D.: One day I read in the newspaper that *Buenas noches, profesor* had been censored. I never found out why, as in those times it was advisable not to inquire. With the return to democracy, censorship was lifted for my book as well as for so many others.

M.F.: Did censorship affect your writing?

A.D.: I think it had a profound effect on my literary work. I told you how important my departure from my native country was in my personal life; in my literary work there is also a split in my production before and after the military dictatorship. Before censorship, my novels had a realistic thematic content, but in the later ones, after *Buenas noches, profesor* was censored, I found a refuge in the use of metaphor. This allowed me to express extreme critical views through symbolism and metaphor in a much more veiled way.

M.F.: Would you say that your language changed after censorship?

A.D.: It changed profoundly. And I continue using metaphor because it renders a more universal perspective to the conflicts presented in my novels.

M.F.: Were there changes in the thematic content of your novels from that time on?

A.D.: No, the themes remained the same. According to a critic my main theme is the drama of the human being facing his own destiny. I would agree; my novels always deal with antiheroes who are marginal beings undergoing solitude, failure, and death. These themes remain constant. What has changed somewhat is the mode in which they are expressed.

M.F.: You deal with Argentine reality in a different manner in each one of your novels. You might ignore it, allude to it, or give it a more important place, as in *Cama de ángeles*, but it is generally not a central concern.[43] Is it because you are interested in the psychological and existential aspects more than in external reality or because of censorship?

A.D.: In *Cama de ángeles* I allude to reality metaphorically because of censorship, but I think my novels are psychological and existential.

M.F.: An example of symbolic allusion to reality is your use of Evita and Juan Domingo Perón in *Cama de ángeles* as parental figures, and the recurrent motif of the embalmed hands. Why did you choose to include this metaphorical allusion to Argentine historical figures and events?

A.D.: It's related to a necrophilic sense that exists in Argentine society, to an idolatry for dead figures and to the perceived need of orphaned children for strong parental figures. In this respect there is plentiful material for a writer in Argentina. It has certainly inspired my use of themes like necrophilia, authoritarianism, and paternalism. Furthermore, I think the themes of dictatorship, repression, and violence are present in my works because I have lived through dictatorships both in Argentina and Rumania. I'm acquainted with two kinds of dictatorships: the rightist dictatorship of the strongman and the leftist dictatorship of the proletariat. My life has been marked by strong, authoritarian governments and that is why these traits are present in my works.

M.F.: Why do your characters select unconventional ways to escape the meaninglessness of life, such as voyeurism, prostitution, transvestism, and hermaphroditism?

A.D.: I have always been interested in the androgynous aspect of human beings. I believe artistic creation is androgynous, that when you write you become both male and female. My novels reflect that ambiguity and ambivalence, which is present in human beings but generally oversimplified.

M.F.: Why does lesbianism become more important in your later works?

A.D.: Lesbianism was alluded to as a possibility in earlier novels and in my latest one, *Los ojos azules*, I have been able to face the theme and fully develop it.

M.F.: Why do you use the "Lolita" syndrome as a recurrent trait?

A.D.: I'm interested in mismatched couples due to their marginal character. Marginality is important in my novels, and in the measure that a mismatched couple is marginal, it is part of my particular interest for what is rejected and discriminated against by society.

M.F.: Can you explain the function that the recurrence of suicide, madness, and death have in your novels?

A.D.: It responds to my pessimistic and skeptical view of life. The theme of suicide touches me deeply because I think we all fantasize about suicide during difficult times in our lives. Of course, there is a difference between thinking about it and committing suicide. I'm interested in it also because so many women writers have committed suicide, like Virginia Woolf, or in Argentina, Alejandra Pizarnik and Marta Lynch, among others. After Marta Lynch's suicide, I wrote a long article analyzing the theme of suicide in her work. I am planning to write an article on suicide and women writers, dealing with the relationship between literary creation and being a woman writer.

M.F.: Transvestism is expressed technically in the duality of character-narrator and in the interplay of different narrative planes. What is its purpose?

A.D.: I think the writer can be either male or female, or can become androgynous. That is why I was interested in writing *Buenas noches, profesor* featuring the first-person narration of a male protagonist. This is a challenge, because it would be easier for me to write about a woman of my own age and social class, which I know well, than to write about an eighteen-year-old young woman like the protagonist of *Enamorada del muro*; the life of a decadent sixty-year-old as in *Cama de ángeles,* or to put myself in the role of a fifty-year-old male character as in *Buenas noches, profesor.*

M.F.: Your first novel, *La Señora*, was very experimental. You include metatexts in the novel that derive from having the narrator become a character who comments on her text within the novel. Can you comment on this aspect of the novel?

A.D.: *La Señora* was my first novel and I consider it experimental. One of my experiments was to include the narrator in the novel as another character. I think literature has to be experimental and that each novel has to feature a new experiment, which is difficult because it is easier to be repetitive. *La Señora* was practically ignored here, but maybe because of that I feel great affection for it.

M.F.: Is this why your next novel, *Buenas noches, profesor*, also includes a metatext formed by quotations and literary allusions?

A.D.: Yes, it was another literary experiment.

M.F.: Why did you include different possible versions of the same scene in *Buenas noches, profesor* and *Cama de ángeles*?

A.D.: It reflects real life, where we are always confronted by various versions of a particular event by different people. Besides, it's related to ambivalence and ambiguity. Reality isn't clear-cut; it is always composed of facets.

M.F.: At the end of most of your novels the readers discover that what they had assumed to be an "authentic" text is the product of the protagonist's alienated mind. Why do you use this technique?

A.D.: It is a trap to make the reader reflect. I enjoy a reader who participates and questions everything.

M.F.: The use of the surprise ending is hidden by the constant, fluctuating points of view in your novels. Can you explain how you use and structure this technique?

A.D.: They are puzzles that I use in order to achieve a plurality of voices. My novels aren't linear stories, and the use of this technique is part of the puzzle that I present to the reader. It also has to do with achieving the active participation of the reader.

M.F.: According to the critics you use art "as surgery and not as therapy." What do you think of this comment?

A.D.: They're right.

M.F.: Your style captures many levels of the Spanish language, including the educated speech, Buenos Aires slang, humor, irony, lyricism, and an oneiric quality. How did you master and learn to incorporate such varied discursive modes?

A.D.: My passion for language might stem from having been born in another country, which has made me study the Spanish language closely, capture the fine tonalities, and pay attention to diverse style and dialect.

M.F.: Can you explain why your novels have a certain theatrical quality characterizing the fictional world?

A.D.: When I was a child in Rumania, I was fascinated by the theater and wanted to become an actress. I often wore costumes and disguises. When I was seventeen, I met Ionesco in Paris and was greatly influenced by his work, which was a revelation for me.

M.F.: Looking at all your works, I noticed that in earlier novels the characters say that life is more important than art, but in the later ones art becomes more important. Why the change?

A.D.: I'm not sure which is more important, so I often wonder out loud. I suppose life is more important, but at times I'm not sure.

M.F.: What are you writing now?

A.D.: I've started another novel. I'm also working on interviews of writers that I brought back from my last trip to Paris. I also write articles and interviews for several Buenos Aires newspapers. I've been working on a collection of short stories for several years now. I keep adding and deleting stories because, as a novelist, I have this sense of unity and I'm never satisfied with the volume. So maybe I'll never publish it.

M.F.: What is the title of the novel you're working on?

A.D.: I don't want to run the risk of giving it a title yet, nor to place it within my work since I haven't finished it yet.

M.F.: Can you tell me what it's about?

A.D.: The theme continues my obsession with the mythic journey (in this case, a shipwreck). The novel deals with a family from Eastern Europe at the end of the 1950s in a crucial situation. The father, an active anti-Nazi militant during World War II, has become a leader in the Communist hierarchy, but is suddenly demoted and expelled from the Party. The fall of this character, the humiliation that he and his family must suffer, the spying, and the invasion of their home by strangers drive him to seek political asylum. A succession of journeys begins: the tragic voyage of this family from country to country, from city to city, morally destroyed, without identity. They arrive to South America where dictatorship of another kind and problems of a different nature await them.

Buenos Aires, 6 November 1989

M.F.: Why did you choose the title *El penúltimo viaje*? Are you referring to the mother's and/or the protagonist's journey, which is the penultimate before death?

A.D.: How I settled on this title cannot be put into words. I have never pondered so much about a title as I did on this one. I had around two hundred titles in mind. Finally, I settled on this one because I thought it summed up the idea of the whole book, which deals with a journey, and it added an unsettling tone with the word "penultimate." Concerning your question—why is it the penultimate journey and whose journey is it—obviously I thought about the protagonist, Amapola, who somehow undertakes her penultimate journey. But there is no set interpretation. Each reader can interpret this penultimate journey in a personal way. My purpose was to refer to the protagonist's journey.

M.F.: The journey before the final one to death?

A.D.: Yes, before that final journey.

M.F.: How much of this novel is autobiographical?

A.D.: By the questions that people, including critics and journalists here in Argentina, ask me, I've felt that they wanted the novel to be autobiographical. I can't say that, because the story is in no way my own. The story of this family is not that of my family. As you know, I am an only child, and I had a father who was a wonderful person. This book features a family of three children and a tyrannical father, so it is evident that the story itself has nothing to do with my story. This does not mean that there are not many autobiographical elements that were transported in a literary fashion. I would say that I've personally experienced the setting of the story as well as some of its situations. But they are disguised, as we writers like to do when creating a fictional world. It is true that somebody who has not lived in an Eastern European country, under a regime such as the one that I depict, could not have written this book. There are some experiences that are not transferable. It is an experience that a writer who hasn't undergone it, in some fashion, cannot narrate. But it is not my personal story. In order to write that, I'll wait until I'm ninety years old and write my memoirs.

M.F.: Was the part that is in italics and describes the protagonist's journey in the present, which she sees from the train's window, influenced by the French *nouveau roman*?

A.D.: Are you thinking about Claude Simon?

M.F.: Yes, Claude Simon or Alain Robbe-Grillet.

A.D.: I read and loved that type of literature in the 1960s, as many other writers did. That period of my life is over, but it probably left its mark. It never occurred to me that my novel could be somehow related to the *nouveau roman*.

M.F.: The descriptions reminded me of *La jalousie (Jealousy)* by Robbe-Grillet.

A.D.: I would say that's probably true. There's something else that made a strong impression on me. I was very young when I read Tolstoy's *Anna Karenina*. There's a scene in the book in which she makes a journey in a carriage and reminisces during the trip. This literary creation and Tolstoy's talent in being able to enter the mind of the female character as she is thinking about something while there's something else going on impressed me a great deal. I found it very powerful. It could be that the two things are present. I don't know. But what I know is that every time I've made a trip by train, it takes me back to the past. It elicits a certain nostalgia.

M.F.: Why did you include the present in the form of a journey through Argentina, emphasizing the protagonist's uprooting, since her adult life is placed between two journeys?

A.D.: I wanted to give an impression of the Argentine landscape and, at the same time, depict an inner vision of an Eastern European country. I wanted to write about two different geographies, two different visions of these countries and continents that I knew, on the one hand Rumania in Eastern Europe and, on the other hand, Argentina. I found the best way to integrate these two was with a train journey, featuring a woman looking through the window at a changing landscape that constantly speaks to her about her present and, perhaps, the more intimate landscape of her childhood world. But the present, the train journey, is somehow the presence of Argentina in the life of this woman who has left behind another country, another story, another landscape. It's the Argentina of a certain period. The protagonist comes from an Eastern European country, with a repressive and powerful dictatorship and is now in Argentina, where repression is also a factor. There are many clues that point to the authoritarian period in Argentina.

M.F.: In the reminisced sections, what is meant by the father figure? Is he a symbol of what is left behind, of the East, of authoritarianism, of that from which one can never escape?

A.D.: Yes, it is all that. From a psychological and personal point of view it deals with the influence of a domineering man in shaping the personalities of his three children. But this can be stretched further, in the sense of defining who our parents are beyond our biological parents. Our father in politics, as an image of God, as the creator of the universe. Everything related to power, to authority. It's my personal reflection on power.

M.F.: What do the appearances of the dead mother mean? Are they a premonition of Amapola's death or of her fate?

A.D.: I like that interpretation. It can be a premonition. I created that character because I wanted to integrate death into life. It stems from the belief that the dead never leave us, that they go on living among us. And a character as mysterious as the mother—for the children know very little about her, and have very few memories of her—she somehow still lives with them. It's what happens in real life. Somehow we all coexist with certain beloved dead. In the book this is emphasized by the image that there is always a setting on the table for the dead mother. It may also have to do with that mythological and legendary quality surrounding the dead that comes from so far back.

M.F.: In the portrayal of the three siblings, whose names Alelí, Alisio, and Amapola are so similar to yours, are there different aspects of your personality?

A.D.: That I cannot answer. It was a challenge to create three characters so different from each other, for they are three different youngsters with distinct personalities. But this is what I enjoy about literature: the challenge to write about things that are not very close to my own. I suppose, though, that they ultimately have something to do with my own life.

M.F.: Is the train that leads to death and also to the mother a symbol of Amapola's return to the womb?

A.D.: Yes, I think that Amapola is a lost character. Her life has gone astray because she hasn't found an equilibrium between this extremely powerful world of her childhood, marred by authoritarianism, and this other country, Argentina, where she arrives only to find a repressive system. She is a character in search of a form of liberation. That's why she is the only one who can see her mother, the one who constantly meets her, and in these encounters there appears the desire to meet her through a liberating death, implying a return to the womb or a journey toward death.

M.F.: What is the role of fatalism in this work?

A.D.: I think that everything is predetermined. I am a fatalistic person and my fatalistic vision of the world is present in my books, perhaps much more so in this one than in others.

M.F.: The tragedy of the mother seems to accompany these characters, deciding their fates.

A.D.: Yes, it decides their fates. They cannot do anything to combat this fate, which implies uprooting, violence, the impossibility of adaptation. For at the end, the only one who manages to adjust is Alelí, the least lucid of the characters. The prevailing idea is that the lucid protagonists cannot adapt.

M.F.: That seems to be the greatest tragedy, as the two sensitive and spiritual characters, Amapola and Alisio, end up, respectively, dead or mad.

A.D.: Yes, I would say there's something to that.

M.F.: How did you find the tone to express Amapola in the different stages in her life? You depict the same character through a different voice and tone in the various sections of the novel.

A.D.: I don't know how I found the tone, but honestly, I had to search for it. Actually, that was one of the main challenges of the book: how to depict the world of adults through the critical and sensitive eyes of a girl. And then to show how this girl grows up and changes her vision of the world, according to her personal experiences. Each age has its own language and its own vision, and I was very interested in transmitting how our vision is altered by age.

M.F.: The political theme seems to be the main device that sets the action in motion. But although the characters are involved in a political turmoil, there are only hints of what is going on outside the realm of the family. Why did you choose this perspective?

A.D.: I didn't want to write a political book, nor did I want to specify where the action takes place. It is an Eastern European country, but we don't know which one. I wanted to use slight details to show how the political system can affect the life of a family. This story narrates these children's past, their childhood, the time when you experience politics through small events occurring around you. As a writer, I'm not interested in dealing with political analysis. What interests me is how politics marks a personality psychologically.

M.F.: How was this novel received in Argentina?

A.D.: These topics are new for the Argentines. In Europe they have been dealt with more frequently through the works of Eastern dissident writers like Milan Kundera. In Argentina these topics are not as closely related to local concerns. The book was received with much curiosity, as a remote story that has nothing to do with what happened here.

M.F.: Even after the experience with the military?

A.D.: I get the impression that the parts of the book dealing with life in Eastern Europe were better understood than those related to repression in Argentina. The fact that the same critical tone used in association with the regime of an Eastern country is also used to criticize authoritarianism in the seventies in Argentina went unnoticed. I'm referring here to the general reading public; this aspect was perceived by the critics. People were very interested in reading about Eastern Europe and associating the story with my personal experience. There was a great deal of curiosity and the wish that the story were my own. It became evident that there was a lack of understanding of my vision of Argentina during the dictatorship. In the book everything is metaphorical, which perhaps was the reason why it went unnoticed. It could be that some day that aspect of the book, which is of great importance to me, will be discovered.

M.F.: Are you writing another novel now?

A.D.: I'm trying to write another novel, but it has been more difficult for me than in the past to let go of my last book, *El penúltimo viaje*, and start another one. For a long time, I felt that I'd said everything I had to say, and that another story could not emerge. Nevertheless, another story is unfolding. I'm not going to tell you what it's about, only that there is another story I'm working on now.

BIBLIOGRAPHY

Primary Sources (listed chronologically)

Diaconú, Alina. *La Señora.* Buenos Aires: Rodolfo Alonso Editor, 1975.
————. *Buenas noches, profesor.* Buenos Aires: Editorial Corregidor, 1978.
————. *Enamorada del muro.* Buenos Aires: Editorial Corregidor, 1981.
————. *Cama de ángeles.* Buenos Aires: Emecé Editores, 1983.
————. *Los ojos azules.* Buenos Aires: Editorial Fraterna, 1986.
————. *El penúltimo viaje.* Buenos Aires: Javier Vergara Editor, 1989.
————. *Los devorados.* Buenos Aires: Editorial Atlántida, 1992.

Short Fiction by Alina Diaconú (listed chronologically)

Diaconú, Alina. "El cajón." *Confirmado,* 28 December 1978.
————. "¿Qué nos pasa, Nicolás?" *Claudia,* vol. 263 (1979).

———. "Otros paisajes, otras gentes." *La Nación,* 28 October 1979.

———. "La pluma." *La Nación,* 27 January 1985.

———. "El pintor." *La Gaceta de Tucumán,* 6 September 1987.

———. "Mamaya." *La Prensa,* 24 July 1988.

———. "Un cuchillo de acero inoxidable." *La Prensa,* 5 March 1989.

———. "La ceremonia." *La Prensa,* 28 May 1989.

———. "Tarde en Praga." *La Prensa,* 14 January 1990.

Critical Articles by Alina Diaconú (listed chronologically)

Diaconú, Alina. "Con Cioran, en París." *La Nación,* 17 November 1985.

———. "Mujer, creación, suicidio." *Clarín,* 9 August 1988.

———. "Victoria Ocampo: Historia de un apasionamiento." *La Nación,* 22 January 1989.

Essays by Alina Diaconú

Diaconú, Alina. "Alina Diaconú recuerda a Marta Lynch a un año de su trágica desaparición. Marta y la muerte." *Cultura* 17 (November-December 1986): 36–38.

———. "Autogeografía." In *Utopias, ojos azules, bocas suicidas: la narrativa de Alina Diaconú,* edited by Ester Gimbernat González and Cynthia Tompkins, 9–14. Buenos Aires: Editorial Fraterna, 1993.

———, comp. *Alberto Girri: homenaje.* Buenos Aires: Editorial Sudamericana, 1993.

Works Available in Translation (listed chronologically)

Diaconú, Alina. "Mamaya." Translated by Hugo Ruiz-Avila and Michael Newton. *Short Story International* 11 (June 1987): 7–9.

———. "Return Address." Translated by Magda Ibarrola. *Short Story International* 13 (August 1989): 7–14.

———. "The Storm." Translated by Richard Schaaf. In *Secret Weavers: Stories of the Fantastic by Women of Argentina and Chile,* edited by Marjorie Agosín, 194–98. New York: White Pine Press, 1992.

———. "Welcome to Albany." Translated by Richard Schaaf. In *Secret Weavers: Stories of the Fantastic by Women of Argentina and Chile,* edited by Marjorie Agosín, 199–202. New York: White Pine Press, 1992.

———. "The Widower." Translated by Richard Schaaf. In *Secret Weavers: Stories of the Fantastic by Women of Argentina and Chile,* edited by Marjorie Agosín, 203-9. New York: White Pine Press, 1992.

Secondary Sources

Antognazzi, Carlos O. "Trama sensual y compleja." Review of *Los devorados*, by Alina Diaconú. *El Litoral*, 13 March 1993.

Bailey, Kay. "Exceso y repulsión en las novelas de Alina Diaconú." In *Utopías, ojos azules, bocas suicidas: la narrativa de Alina Diaconú*, edited by Ester Gimbernat González and Cynthia Tompkins, 67–81. Buenos Aires: Editorial Fraterna, 1993.

————. "El uso de márgenes en *Cama de ángeles* de Alina Diaconú." Forthcoming.

Bilbija, Ksenija. "Hacia una búsqueda del idioma materno: *El penúltimo viaje* de Alina Diaconú." In *Utopías, ojos azules, bocas suicidas: la narrativa de Alina Diaconú*, edited by Ester Gimbernat González and Cynthia Tompkins, 23–24. Buenos Aires: Editorial Fraterna, 1993.

Borinsky, Alicia. "Ficciones de intimidad." In *Utopías, ojos azules, bocas suicidas: la narrativa de Alina Diaconú*, edited by Ester Gimbernat González and Cynthia Tompkins, 85–91. Buenos Aires: Editorial Fraterna, 1993.

Delgado, Roberto. "Viaje en tren desvelado por recuerdos." Review of *El penúltimo viaje*, by Alina Diaconú. *La Gaceta*, 15 October 1989.

Dellepiane, Angela B. "El aporte femenino a la narrativa última argentina." In *La escritora hispánica*, edited by Nora Erro-Orthmann and Juan Cruz Mendizábal, 61–71. Miami: Ediciones Universal, 1990.

De Miguel, María Esther. "Atrapante novela." Review of *Los devorados*, by Alina Diaconú. *La Nación*, 3 January 1993.

Fares, Gustavo. "This Text Which Is Not One: Escritoras argentinas contemporáneas." *Hispanic Journal* 12 (Fall 1991): 277–89.

Fares, Gustavo, and Eliana Hermann. "Alina Diaconú." In *Escritoras argentinas contemporáneas*, 57–70. New York: Peter Lang, 1993.

Flori, Mónica. "Autoritarismo, exilio y recreación feminista en *El penúltimo viaje* de Alina Diaconú." *Alba de América* 10 (July 1992): 183–94.

————. "Interview with Alina Diaconú." *Letras femeninas* 14 (Spring-Fall 1988): 97–103.

————. "La articulación de lo inexpresable: metaforización del cuerpo femenino en *Los ojos azules* de Alina Diaconú." *Alba de América* 12 (July 1994).

————. "La técnica de la inversión en las novelas de Alina Diaconú." In *Utopías, ojos azules, bocas suicidas: la narrativa de Alina Diaconú*, edited by Ester Gimbernat González and Cynthia Tompkins, 55–63. Buenos Aires: Editorial Fraterna, 1993. (First published in *Selecta* 2 [1990]: 92–96.)

———. "Madres e hijas y creatividad femenina en *La Señora* de Alina Diaconú." *Confluencia* (Spring 1993): 37–47.

Gallone, Osvaldo. "La atracción de la ambigüedad." Review of *Los ojos azules*, by Alina Diaconú. *El periodista de Buenos Aires*, 8–14 May 1987.

Gimbernat González, Ester. "*El penúltimo viaje* (A. Diaconú): la memoria de la fisura." In *Aventuras del desacuerdo: novelistas argentinas de los 80*, 11–16. Buenos Aires: Danilo Albero Vergara, 1992.

———. "*Los ojos azules* (A. Diaconú): La descompaginación de los roles." In *Aventuras del desacuerdo: novelistas argentinas de los 80*, 32–38. Buenos Aires: Danilo Albero Vergara, 1992.

———."Para eso está hecha la noche (A. Diaconú): *Cama de ángeles.* " In *Aventuras del desacuerdo: novelistas argentinas de los 80*, 163–74. Buenos Aires: Danilo Albero Vergara, 1992.

———. "Utopías, ojos azules y bocas suicidas: Un diálogo posible entre las novelas de Alina Diaconú." In *Utopías, ojos azules, bocas suicidas: la narrativa de Alina Diaconú*, edited by Ester Gimbernat González and Cynthia Tompkins, 37–52. Buenos Aires: Editorial Fraterna, 1993.

Gimbernat González, Ester, and Cynthia Tompkins, eds. *Utopías, ojos azules, bocas suicidas: la narrativa de Alina Diaconú*. Buenos Aires: Editorial Fraterna, 1993..

Gómez Vecchio, Ricardo. "Un texto violento que invita a la lectura." Review of *Los devorados*, by Alina Diaconú. *Ambito Financiero*, 9 December 1992.

Gudiño Kieffer, Eduardo. "Pesadilla para muchachas desesperadas." Review of *Los ojos azules*, by Alina Diaconú. *La Nación*, 14 December 1986.

Kliagine, Dominique. "'Breaking Free' Hard To Do." Review of *Los ojos azules*, by Alina Diaconú. *Buenos Aires Herald*, 11 January 1987.

Korenblit, Bernardo Ezequiel. Review of *El penúltimo viaje*, by Alina Diaconú. *La Prensa*, 25 June 1989.

Laiseca, Alberto. "Alina Diaconú: introducción a la guerra de todos contra todos." Review of *El penúltimo viaje*, by Alina Diaconú. *Nuevo Sur*, 4 June 1989.

Lojo, María Rosa. Review of *Los devorados*, by Alina Diaconú. *Cultura*, 15 December 1992.

M. A. "Una mirada desde el abismo." Review of *Los ojos azules*, by Alina Diaconú. *La Voz del Interior*, 1 March 1987.

Magrini, César. "Un viaje que viene desde muy lejos." Review of *El penúltimo viaje*, by Alina Diaconú. *El Cronista*, n.d.

Marbán, Jorge. "Estructura y simbolismo en *El penúltimo viaje* de Alina Diaconú." *Confluencia* 7 (Spring 1992): 131–35.

———. "Visión de lo cotidiano y perspectiva existencial en la cuentística de Alina Diaconú." In *Utopías, ojos azules, bocas suicidas: la narrativa de Alina Diaconú,* edited by Ester Gimbernat González and Cynthia Tompkins, 23–34. Buenos Aires: Editorial Fraterna, 1993.

Muñoz, Elías Miguel. "La búsqueda de un sexo 'verdadero': *Cama de ángeles* de Alina Diaconú." In *Utopías, ojos azules, bocas suicidas: la narrativa de Alina Diaconú,* edited by Ester Gimbernat González and Cynthia Tompkins, 95–104. Buenos Aires: Editorial Fraterna, 1993.

Renard, María Adela. "Juego de opuestos." Review of *Cama de ángeles,* by Alina Diaconú. *La Prensa,* 6 November 1983.

———. Review of *Los devorados,* by Alina Diaconú. *La Prensa,* 27 December 1992.

Seiguerman., Osvaldo. Review of *Cama de ángeles,* by Alina Diaconú. *La Opinión,* 15 June 1978.

Tompkins, Cynthia. "La postmodernidad de *Cama de ángeles.*" In *Utopías, ojos azules, bocas suicidas: la narrativa de Alina Diaconú,* edited by Ester Gimbernat González and Cynthia Tompkins, 107–20. Buenos Aires: Editorial Fraterna, 1993.

4

Alicia Steimberg

Alicia Steimberg was born in Buenos Aires, Argentina, in 1933. She majored in education and English at the Instituto Nacional de Profesorado en Lenguas Vivas in Buenos Aires, where she obtained teaching and English degrees in 1951 and 1954, respectively. She has taught at the high school level and at the University of Buenos Aires School of Humanities.

Steimberg has published seven books of fiction. Her first novel, *Músicos y relojeros*, was a finalist in the 1971 literary contest organized by the Spanish publishing company, Editorial Barral, and the Venezuelan publisher, Monte Avila. In 1973 *La loca 101* was a finalist in the Editorial Barral literary contest. In 1974 it won the "Satiricón de Oro," awarded by the Buenos Aires magazine, *Satiricón*. Her short story, "Ultima voluntad y testamento de Cecilia," won first prize in the 1979 Argentine Society of Writers contest. Her collection of short stories, *Como todas las mañanas*, was a finalist in the 1980 Editorial Losada literary contest, under the title *El templo de Júpiter*. Her 1989 novel, *Amatista*, was a finalist in "The Vertical Smile" contest sponsored by Tusquets, and *Cuando digo Magdalena* (1992) received the "Planeta Biblioteca del Sur" prize awarded by Planeta publishers. In 1983 Steimberg was awarded a Fulbright Fellowship to participate in the International Writing Program at the University of Iowa.

At present Steimberg combines her career as a fiction writer with teaching and translating English. For the past fifteen years she has been a translator for the Buenos Aires publishing companies, Emecé, Sudamericana, and Vergara, and for psychoanalysts through the Argentine Psychotherapy Association and the Argentine Psychoanalytic Association.

Alicia Steimberg. Photograph by Victor Sokolowicz.

ESSAY

Músicos y relojeros

Critics immediately labeled *Músicos y relojeros* (Musicians and watchmakers), 1971, as autobiographical. It describes the author's experiences of growing up in Buenos Aires in a Jewish, middle-class family during the 1940s, struggling to survive the economic crisis in Argentina. Several events from Steimberg's youth are elements of the novel's plot: the death of her father, the terrible fights among the women in her family, her failed attempts to get closer to her mother, a Jewish upbringing, which set her apart in a Catholic society, a girl's sexual awakening, and defiance of social taboos. The author, however, has contested the autobiographical label:

> Casi todas las notas publicadas sobre mi primera novela, *Músicos y relojeros*, declaran que se trata de una novela autobiográfica. Nadie me preguntó si efectivamente se trataba de una autobiografía, ni yo me preocupé demasiado por aclarar que no lo era. En realidad lo es en parte; está inspirada en hechos reales, pero en hechos reales que son recuerdos, que eran recuerdos bastante antiguos en el momento de escribir la novela.

> (Almost all the reviews published about my first novel, *Musicians and Watchmakers*, declare that it is an autobiographical novel. Nobody asked me if it really was an autobiography, nor did I bother too much to clarify that it was not. In reality it is in part; it is inspired by real events, but by real events that are memories, which were quite old memories at the time the novel was written.)[1]

Steimberg explains that she waited to write about her memories until she felt ready: "When I started to see my own childhood in a different way. My evolution in the milieu where I had been destined to live. I wrote as a way of reconstructing the story of my family origins. Of my grandmother, who arrived from Kiev in 1890 when she was eleven years old."[2] She believes what she wrote was not her autobiography in a strict sense, but the story of a large number of middle-class Buenos Aires residents who were descendants of immigrants and shared a common experience of exile in, and adaptation to, another country, culture, people, and language:

> Entonces lo que hice (sin proponérmelo, ¡yo sólo quería narrar una historia!) fue escribir no mi *auto*biografía, sino tal vez una radiografía de un vasto sector de la clase media de Buenos Aires, al que pertenezco.

(Then what I did [without planning to, I only wanted to narrate a story!] was to write not my *auto*biography, but maybe an X-ray of a vast sector of the Buenos Aires middle class, to which I belong.)[3]

Luis Gregorich, a major critic of Steimberg's work, introduces *Músicos y relojeros* as "a classic initiation story with ingredients that are clearly autobiographical, about the childhood and adolescence of a Buenos Aires middle-class Jewish girl." But he then points out that the story also contains elements belonging to a common mythic background, a statement that underlines Steimberg's objective of portraying the Argentine immigrant experience of exile and integration. Gregorich remarks that the style and content intertwine so that

> there is a familiarity, sustained by a sensible use of colloquial language and by an ironic capacity to observe the miseries and about-faces of daily life, which alleviates the frustrations of bourgeois life, the sexual and social repression which almost inevitably preside over the passage to adulthood in a big city, the conflict with the family which cannot be resolved satisfactorily.[4]

According to Gregorich, Steimberg's critical portrayal of the Buenos Aires Jewish milieu was the subject of intense criticism from the Orthodox Jewish community, which accused Steimberg of anti-Semitism, a charge that the critic disavows by pointing out Steimberg's obvious love for her origins.[5] In retrospect, it is clear that Steimberg was not interested in presenting a satire of Jewish customs, but in portraying the confusion experienced by a child who witnessed arguments and conflicts among family members divided by rejection of their Jewish identity, beliefs, and customs and a strict Orthodox commitment to them. Steimberg portrays her upbringing in the midst of this conflict, which pervaded family relations and became part of her heritage and identity. This is a prominent theme in her fiction. Her characters waver between a denial of and, at the same time, a fascination with, their Jewishness. Like the author, the characters are torn by this duality, expressed by Alicia, the protagonist:

> Soy, por lo tanto, el resultado de muchos trajines y afanes: transplantes, desarraigos, matrimonios que no se sabe si se hicieron aquí o en Rusia, peleas que no se sabe por qué empezaban, dietas alimenticias equivocadas, *lecturas de la Torah, y la religión es el opio de los pueblos.*

> (I am, therefore, the result of many comings and goings and a lot of toil: upheavals, eradications, marriages that we don't know where

they took place, here or in Russia; fights that nobody knows how they ever got started; wrong diets, *Torah readings, and religion is the opium of the people.*)[6]

Músicos y relojeros contains two mainstays of her fictional world: the emerging feminist perspective and the first Perón era. The feminist perspective depicts a protagonist growing up in a female world. Steimberg dissects several generations of the female members of Alicia's family. She presents portraits of grandmothers, aunts, the mother, and Alicia. The male characters are fleeting presences who recede into the background, allowing the female characters to stand out. Several women are alone (Alicia's widowed mother) and withstand the particular hardships of the times without male support. Male characters seem to have a gentle disposition (her brother-in-law nicknamed "Clark Gable," and the various uncles), while females, nicknamed "las fieras" (the beasts), although engaged in traditional female tasks and occupations, are stronger figures than their male counterparts—a subtle reversal of traditional roles. The central role of women in the family is implied, as the novel starts by mentioning her grandmother and her extraordinary powers: "Mi abuela conocía el secreto de la vida eterna" (My grandmother knew the secret of eternal life) (7). The grandmother dominates the novel, which unfolds under her gaze.[7] When she dies, the novel ends. Another aspect underlining the feminist vision shaping the novel is the open depiction of the protagonist's budding sexuality, as in the account of the young girl's masturbating (cushioned by her mother's epistolary reproaches):

> Pero tuve el dolor de encontrarte tirada en la cama, en mala posición, con lo cual podés causar daños irreparables a tu columna vertebral, y usando tus manos para algo que ni siquiera me atrevo a mencionar aquí, porque me moriría de desesperación y de vergüenza.

> (But I felt the pain of finding you lying on the bed, in a bad position, which can cause irreparable damage to your spine, and using your hands for something that I don't even dare mention here, because I would die of desperation and shame.) (79)

The portrayal of Alicia's development surrounded by striking mother figures takes place within the extended family, especially in the first section of the novel. But the second and third sections, when Alicia is in her teens, portray Buenos Aires in the 1940s, with its trams, popular radio programs, and idols like Clark Gable, Bing Crosby, and Frank Sinatra, as well as the political and economic reality. The rise of Peronism affects the family, which now has no choice but to participate in events shaping the country's history: "Mama tenía un revólver. El primo Quito vino a pedírselo y ella se lo dio, para que Quito saliera a luchar por la libertad y por la democracia" (Mother had a pistol. Cousin Quito came to ask her for it and she gave it to him, so that Quito would go out to fight for freedom and for democracy) (107). Peronism affects Alicia's world mainly through shortages, unemployment, and impoverishment, which become part of the protagonist's tale of development:

> "Degenerado de mierda, ¡dame manteca!" Pero el tipo había cerrado porque *no tenía más manteca.* Es una manera de decir, porque cuando ellos dicen que no hay más manteca, siempre hay un poco más de manteca: para los clientes, para el dueño del negocio y para sus familiares.

> ("Shitty degenerate, give me butter!" But the guy had closed his shop because *he did not have any more butter.* It's a manner of speech, because when they say that they ran out of butter, there is always some more butter: for the customers, for the shopkeeper, and his relatives.) (112) (Italics are Steimberg's.)

> Hubo tiempos muy malos. La desocupación. El desalojo. En un baile de beneficiencia se reunieron fondos para procurarles, como a otros pobres, un nuevo techo.

> (There were very bad times. Unemployment. Eviction. In a benefit dance funds were collected to get them, as well as other poor people, a new roof over their heads.) (17)

Although the main story centers on the protagonist's coming of age, the Buenos Aires sociopolitical environment is a fundamental element of that story, enlarging the scope of the novel. *Músicos y relojeros* transposes the delimitations of a bildungsroman to become the account of a middle-class immigrant family struggling to avoid becoming part of the working class. (This situation applied to a wide spectrum of the population in Argentine social history.) Thus, Steimberg's first novel transcends the individual and strives for the universal, something she also tries to achieve in subsequent novels. Ernesto Sábato's following characterization of fiction illustrates Steimberg's early accomplishments: "[E]ven the most extremely 'subjective' novel is social, and gives us in a direct and tortuous manner a testimonial of the universe."[8]

La loca 101

Steimberg's second novel, *La loca 101* (The madwoman 101), 1973, was also acclaimed both abroad and locally. Luis Gregorich accurately defines Steimberg's change from the traditional to the experimental:

> The writing and the world of *La loca 101* are not related to her previous work. The autobiographical intent has been pushed aside (or concealed) by a sort of narrative experimental puzzle about the world of madness, set in contrast to statements on the meaning of the narrative craft. Madness and literature mingle in a space that mixes up the roles society inflicts on its members.[9]

Steimberg too alludes to the importance of the change that took place in her writing, as she contrasts the style of her first two novels: "And while I had a tranquil and orthodox way of narrating, another [style] starts to appear, perhaps surrealist, which prevails in my whole work."[10] The surrealist style of the following excerpt portrays the world of this novel:

> un mundo de libertad, de espejismos lúdicos, de habitantes de una vida que siendo "el lapso que se extiende desde las manos de la partera hasta las de los empleados de la funeraria," es a la vez el mundo del Descuartizador, de la Pocha, de los ex delirantes, de los muertos que mueren, de Job, de Merceditas, de San Martín, del Enamorado de la Flor . . . del gato, del gratificaré y del he dicho.

> (a world of freedom, of playful mirages, of inhabitants of a life, which is the "lapse of time that extends between the hands of the midwife and those of the funeral parlor employees," and is at the same time the world of the Ripper, Pocha, the former delirious, the dead who die, Job, Merceditas, San Martín, the Lover of the Flower . . . the cat, the "I will reward," the "I have spoken.")[11]

While *Músicos y relojeros* openly depicts how social and political circumstances affect a family, *La loca 101* features very few direct references to Argentine reality in the early 1970s. As Steimberg explains in "Conversation with Alicia Steimberg," at the time there was an atmosphere of fear, and the lack of explicitness responds to these specific circumstances. It is also significant that after this novel came out, she stopped publishing for seven years. The absence of explicit discussion of political events in the novel at a time when reality was pervaded by violence is a way of drawing attention to this discrepancy and to the underlying mechanisms of self-censorship. In her study of Uruguayan literature produced under similar circumstances as the Argentine works (the dictatorship of 1973–84), critic Mabel Moraña writes that the effects of censorship produce "the need to adopt a series of discursive strategies which affect the themes and literary composition."[12] Indeed, *La loca 101* uses metaphors and an original narrative structure to circumvent censorship. According to Marta Morello-Frosch, because of censorship a realistic representation of events in fiction becomes impossible, but the themes and its elements can be related to historical events.[13] Faced with the impossibility of representing reality directly, Steimberg chose the theme of madness as a discursive strategy. The protagonist, "la loca 101," is supposedly a madwoman who narrates from within the confines of a women's insane asylum. The use of fantasy as a background suggests that the character's "madness" and her situation are to be taken figuratively rather than literally: "Lo que decidió a los médicos a internar a esta enferma fueron las fantasías vinculadas con sus jaquecas que ella, ingenuamente, relató a dichos médicos. Ese fue su gran error. Si se hubiera callado la boca, tal vez todavía andaría suelta" (What made the doctors decide to commit this sick woman were the fantasies related to her headaches, which she, innocently, told those doctors. That was her big mistake. If she had shut up, maybe she would still be free) (31). That she was committed because of her fantasies alludes to the repression against people who defy the system by expressing their views. Choosing to speak up rather than keep silent makes her a symbol of those who dare to voice their dissenting views, and end up being destroyed. Dissidence resulting in a violent reprisal is presented by the paradigm of madness and confinement. For Fernando Reati this feature is characteristic of writers of this era, as "the collective experience of this period is fictionalized by means of the overwhelming presence of enclosed spaces and asphyxiating situations in the novels, which make suffocation and enclosement a recurring paradigm to represent violence. The political experience of that which is secret, hidden, censored, leaves a mark at the fictional level consisting of the innumerable rooms, basements, bathrooms, attics, cellars, wells, and other places where the characters of many works are trapped."[14] The most prominent image of confinement in *La loca 101* is the insane asylum. Together with the recurrent images of closets, cages, tombs, and wells where human remains float in blood, Steimberg paints a picture of imprisonment and violence: "No sé bien para donde enfilo; sólo sé que me alejo de las jaulas y las tumbas" (I don't know exactly where I'm headed; I only know that I'm getting away from the cages and tombs) (85); "Los locos habían formado un círculo alrededor del pozo de sangre. . . . Los locos hundían sus brazos en el pozo, los sacaban chorreando sangre hasta el codo, levantaban los pedazos y piernas que habían logrado pescar" (The insane had formed a circle around the well of blood. . . . The insane dipped their arms into the well, they removed them dripping blood up to the elbow, they would lift the pieces and legs that they had been able to fish out) (88). The insane asylum, a contemporary re-creation of Dante's hell, is a self-contained microcosm reflecting social reality. Steimberg's hellish vision, a pervasive presence, radiates from the multiple images of confinement, which inevitably lead the reader to interpret the text as a metaphor of the prevailing political conditions. These images of enclosure show how average citizens distanced themselves from reality in physical and ideological concealment, lest they become targets for repression. The pervasive device of conveying what is horrifying by means of a metaphor of concealment is not unique to Steimberg's novel. Fernando Reati calls it an obsession of recent Argentine fiction.[15]

In contrast to the surrealist, violent atmosphere of the asylum, Steimberg inserts a few direct references to violence in the real world. Violence extending beyond a nightmarish, fantasy world to reality forces the reader to make connections: "Esos estampidos que se oyen todos los días cuando ando por la calle, cuando entro en un edificio, aunque me ría de mi miedo y me repita que no va a pasar nada, que uno termina por acostumbrarse a la presencia de la policía por todas partes" (Those detonations that are heard every day when I walk along the streets, when I enter a building, although I might laugh out of fear and repeat to myself that nothing is going to happen, that one ends up getting used to the presence of police everywhere) (83). In this way, Steimberg achieves two objectives: (1) She makes sure that there is no escape for the reader, as there is none in the real world, and that the fantastic version will not be dismissed as an imaginary construct, but will stand as a symbol; (2) she uses fantasy and humor, which distinguish her work from other works of the period, to conceal her message from the censors and enable the reader to accept an interpretation of reality that otherwise would be too terrifying.[16] The structure of the work, the narrative experimental puzzle, also contributes to that dual objective while it points out the impossibility of apprehending reality in its totality. While the hegemonic discourse expresses totality, Steimberg's fragmented and subordinate discourse strives to present the opposite in a vivid indictment of a society torn by institutionalized violence.

Su espíritu inocente

The author returns to a more traditional narrative, in both content and style, in *Su espíritu inocente* (Her innocent spirit), 1981, a sequel to *Músicos y relojeros*. Although this novel alludes to the economic crisis brought on by Peronism, its main focus lies in the narration of the author's fictionalized memories of her coming of age and first marriage. The feminist vision detected in *Músicos y relojeros* is apparent in the open and sincere account of the psychological effects of growing up female in contemporary society. The result is the emergence of a strong and healed individual who has used the experience to grow and empower herself. There is also continuity in the strong focus on female presences. Relatives are replaced by school friends and girlfriends, offering a multifaceted portrayal of female lives, which project different parts of the protagonist. By using several characters who share her own experiences as alter egos, Steimberg has attained her goal:

> "Muchos dicen que mis libros son autobiográficos," dice Alicia Steimberg, "y en cierto sentido lo son, si puede considerarse autobiografía al conjunto de recuerdos, historias contadas por otros, mentiras, omisiones y exageraciones que, junto con las alternativas del presente, amasan día a día esto que llamamos nuestra existencia. Me gusta pensar que soy todas las mujeres y todos los hombres que aparecen en mis libros."

> ("Many people say that my books are autobiographical," says Alicia Steimberg, "and in a certain sense they are, if one may consider as autobiography all the remembrances, stories told by others, lies, omissions, and exaggerations that, together with the present alternatives, knead day by day this which we call our existence. I like to think I'm all the women and all the men who appear in my books.")[17]

The narration in this two-part volume juxtaposes the traditional autobiographical first person (part 1) with other narrative voices (part 2). The first part alternates the protagonist's narration with her outpourings to an imaginary character. Although this character is not identified as a psychoanalyst but just as an imaginary conversation partner, the image of an analyst comes to mind, especially since in these conversations Alicia strives to confront and accept her childhood and adolescent self and her traumatic early experiences. These early experiences formed the core of the plot for *Músicos y relojeros*: "Yo hablaba con alguien que no estaba. Cuando hablo con alguien que no está me sonrío con la sonrisa que me enseñaron

desde chica" (I talked to someone who wasn't there. When I talk to someone who isn't there, I smile with the smile they taught me from the time
I was a little girl) (31). Fantasy in the form of recurrent imaginary scenes
helps Alicia withstand the bleak reality of her home life. The point of view
is that of the adult character, who narrates her past events in chronological order for the most part. But she breaks this order and returns time and
again to her most traumatic years. Her feeling is one of disillusionment,
conveyed by the confessional tone of anguish—cushioned by humor—a
feeling that has haunted her since adolescence. The pseudopsychoanalytic
framework focuses on the anguish she felt when she turned thirteen:

> —Me da miedo. Doy vueltas alrededor de esa época y en cuanto la
> rozo escapo a otras. Hasta mi infancia, que contiene la muerte de mi
> padre, es preferible a la época de mis trece años, que fue sin duda la
> más negra de mi vida. Creo que omití pensar en ella, durante largos
> períodos, o que sólo me permití pensarla superficialmente.

> (I'm scared. I go round and round that time and as soon as I get close
> I escape to other times. Even my childhood, containing my father's
> death, is preferable to that period when I was thirteen years old,
> which was undoubtedly the blackest in my life. I think that I avoided
> thinking about it for long periods, or I only allowed myself to think
> about it superficially.) (65)

Adolescence became especially complex, as she had to come to grips
with her sexuality as well as the deterioration of her relations with her
mentally unstable mother. In addition, her Catholic education compounded
the problem. It generated feelings of guilt in young girls who, like Alicia,
acknowledged their sexuality. She was also going through a spiritual crisis: Her Jewish-Argentine identity caused her conflicts, as she was being
raised in a predominantly Catholic, anti-Semitic milieu. These conflicts
forced Alicia to live a double life, splitting her identity in two. On the one
hand, she had to contend with the side that she wished to conceal, that of
a young Jewish girl living in a troubled home and having erotic fantasies:

> En casa dejé a la judía, la pecadora, la que subsana la falta del broche
> en el portaligas con un alfiler de gancho, la que prepara el termo con
> el café con leche para poder soportar el frío de la mañana, la que
> piensa en penes, vaginas y coitos.

> (At home I left the Jewess, the sinner, the one who makes up for the
> missing fastener in her garter with a safety pin, the one who prepares

the thermos with the coffee with milk to be able to stand the morning cold, the one who thinks about penises, vaginas, and intercourse.) (110)

On the other hand, she has her make-believe personality, the happy-go-lucky Catholic girl:

> A la escuela traigo a la chica despierta, simpática, capaz de hacer desternillar de risa a las demás, la que dice que es católica, aunque nadie la crea, la que cuenta mentiras sobre sus antepasados, pero que, en conjunto, es aceptable y hasta envidiada.

> (To school I bring the vivacious, charming young girl, capable of making the other girls split their sides with laughter, the one who says that she is Catholic, although possibly nobody believes her, the one who tells lies about her ancestors, but who, all in all, is acceptable and even envied.) (110)

The conflict is expressed in the choice of title for the novel, which comes from the lyrics of a Catholic hymn sung at school: "Su espíritu inocente de [vuestro] amor se inflama" (Her innocent spirit becomes inflamed by [your] love) (104).

The second part deals with Julia (Alicia's alter ego) and her difficult marriage to Miguel, which ends in divorce. The narrative viewpoint alternates between that of Julia and Miguel, offering the reader a more rounded view, for the protagonist's judgments are given perspective by her husband's narration. Their main problems relate to coming to terms with the end of romance, raising children in the midst of economic problems, confronting the reality of their adult selves, and finally, coping with the failure of dreams and a broken marriage.

In the second part, instead of having dialogues with an imaginary character, Julia-Alicia makes imaginary visits, using a realistic narration, to an unnamed woman who lives in a small garret in downtown Buenos Aires. The visits are short. Usually the protagonist asks the woman about her life, childhood, and failed marriage, which coincide with Alicia's own experiences. This leads us to believe the woman is the protagonist's alter ego. These scenes have the fleeting and secret undertones of a quest, the protagonist's inner voyage to uncover her hidden self. It evokes painful feelings:

> El muladar que era mi boca. El pozo negro, el sabor de las cosas putrefactas, el sabor y el olor de la basura largo tiempo escondida,

ahora en la superficie, casi en contacto con el aire. Pero mantenía la
boca cerrada, sintiendo el muladar.

(The dung heap that was my mouth. The black well, the taste of
putrid things, the taste and smell of garbage that has been hidden for
a long time was now on the surface, almost in contact with the air.
But I kept my mouth shut, feeling the dung heap.) (206)

As the novel closes, the protagonist is near the friend's garret, but we
learn that she does not visit her anymore, meaning that Alicia is cured and
can face her past reality on her own:

Desde el taxi no alcancé a ver la cúpula del antiguo edificio de Callao
y Corrientes, donde mi amiga estaría seguramente inmóvil en una
silla, sin nadie a quien ofrecer té.

(From the taxi I wasn't able to see the dome of the old building on
Callao and Corrientes [streets], where my friend was in all certainty
immobile on a chair, with nobody around to whom she could serve
tea.) (227)

As a result of Alicia's healing, the cycle of Steimberg's longer fiction with
autobiographical content has reached an end.

Como todas las mañanas

Como todas las mañanas (Like every morning), 1983, is Steimberg's only
published collection of short stories. According to the writer:

Mis cuentos, y esto debe sucederles a muchos escritores de ficción, o
tal vez a todos, nacen de una zona indecisa que no es sueño y no es
vigilia. No son relatos de sueños, si bien algunos están inspirados en
un sueño o contienen cosas realmente soñadas. Al decir *"realmente
soñadas,"* se me ocurre que lo que me propongo al escribir un cuento
es reivindicar la realidad de los sueños.

(My short stories, and this must happen to many fiction writers, or
maybe to all of them, are born in a hazy zone that is neither dream
nor waking. They are not stories of dreams, even though some are
inspired by a dream or they contain stuff that has really been dreamt.
When I say *"really* been dreamt," it occurs to me that my purpose for
writing a short story is to vindicate the reality of dreams.)[18]

The title refers to the dreamlike quality of the stories and also to a song by María Elena Walsh, "Not Asleep or Awake, / Like Every Morning," which Steimberg found herself singing one morning. In the opinion of the critic María Esther De Miguel, the stories are "enormously attractive because of their notable humor and the fascinating imagination that nourishes them. They constrain themselves to a rigorous narrative simplicity, which contrasts with the creative freedom which gives birth to them."[19]

These characteristics are evident in the volume's last short story, "Ultima voluntad y testamento de Cecilia" (Cecilia's last will and testament). This story illustrates the writer's tendency to use humor in situations society deems especially serious—in this case, death and all the legal and ceremonial rituals that accompany it. In a dreamlike setting, a friend discovers a will in Cecilia's empty house after her unexplained departure. As the protagonist settles down to read the will, a storm comes up, which, coupled with the preposterous contents of the will, points to the possibility that the whole experience is a dream. The fact that Cecilia is still alive and that she is giving away very unusual gifts, like the last ten years of her life, moments of freedom, and a recurring fantasy, are aspects that underline the humor as well as the oneiric quality of the tale. (Also, the friend has no idea who these people are who are named to receive her gifts). As is characteristic in Steimberg's prose, the language becomes another source of humor. The will reads like an informal conversation instead of a legal document. The critic De Miguel comments:

> Sin duda, en el panorama de la literatura actual, más bien solemne cuando no aburrida (o aburridísima), los relatos de Alicia Steimberg (como su literatura en general), traen un fresco aire tonificante, la oportuna cuota de algo "distinto," y la seguridad de una escritura que tras su aparente fantaseo intrascendente, está poniendo banderillas a muchos prejuicios, imposturas, astucias y/o estereotipos canonizados por una sociedad castradora.

> (Undoubtedly, in the present literary panorama, which is quite solemn when it is not boring [or very boring], Alicia Steimberg's stories [like her literature in general], bring an invigorating breath of fresh air, the opportune quota of something "different," and the confidence of a writing that beneath its apparent unimportant fantasizing is pointing a finger at the many prejudices, poses, tricks, and/or stereotypes sanctioned by a castrating society.)[20]

The stories could be characterized as fantastic and surrealistic because they present a gallery of characters (the majority are women) who, among other qualities, can transport themselves to other times and societies ("Vals vienés" [Viennese waltz]) or be present at their own funeral ("Juan, el hombre que asistió a su propio entierro" [John, the man who attended his own funeral]). Some can walk on air ("Belleza árabe" [Arab beauty]), and almost none can distinguish dream from reality. The recurring themes of death and madness link these stories with Steimberg's previous works. Concrete details about death appear in almost every story, like this description from the child's viewpoint in "Vals vienés":

> Nilda apoyó los labios sobre esa mejilla dura y fría, se apartó y observó que todos los que rodeaban la cama de la abuela estaban llorando.

> (Nilda placed her lips on that hard and cold cheek. She stepped aside and observed that everybody who surrounded the grandmother's bed was crying.) (30)

Or the death of the female protagonist in "Arab Beauty":

> Alma murió. Yo le crucé las manos, sus manos grandes y claras, sobre la blusa pintada, le bajé los párpados, modifiqué el gesto despectivo de su boca hasta convertirlo en la sonrisa de la muñeca de los ojos vaciados.

> (Alma died. I crossed her hands, her big and light hands, over her painted blouse, closed her eyelids, and changed the contemptuous gesture of her mouth until it became the smile of the doll with the emptied-out eyes.) (24)

These existential themes are presented in a perfectly designed format often ending with a surprise. In "Cómo es Ana" (The way Ana is), which received a special mention in a contest sponsored by the journal *Hispamérica* in 1977, Ana, the middle-aged protagonist, is presented like any other character in the collection: a woman stifled by routine, domestic life and work. At least that is what she believes, but the third-person narration reveals that she is a vain woman who dreams of becoming an artist but has no talent or desire to work. She is just a complainer. Ana escapes her reality through dreams of affairs with handsome men; these are humorously and ironically narrated to show how out of proportion her dreams are to reality. In the last paragraph, the point of view changes to first person. The narrator presents herself as the young Ana of the dreams, who is fed up with the real Ana and decides to leave her and enact her fantasies.

Throughout the stories, characters like Ana, who lead monotonous and routine lives and try to create a new fantasy life for themselves, emerge. Steimberg uses universal themes and situations. But by erasing the borders between the real and the fantastic, she creates an unstable world where the surreal can take place. As readers, we are left with a desire for these stories to be more developed. Nevertheless, the feeling that the stories are too schematic can be overcome if we look at the volume as a whole, presenting a self-contained universe.

El árbol del placer

El árbol del placer (The tree of pleasure), 1986, shares certain themes and characters with *Su espíritu inocente*. It deals satirically with a phenomenon in vogue since the sixties in Buenos Aires: psychoanalysis. Specifically, it portrays long and expensive psychoanalytic therapy as a fad undertaken to avoid taking responsibility for one's life. That responsibility is relinquished to the analyst, who acquires divine might and proportions in the eyes of the patient:

> Sabía mucho más de nosotros que nosotros mismos, y eso no cambiaba con el correr del tiempo: después de diez, quince o veinte años de tratamiento, seguíamos esperando que él nos revelara si estábamos alegres o tristes, con quién queríamos tener amores o a quién deseábamos matar. A veces sospechábamos algo sobre nuestros propios sentimientos, pero nunca lo confesábamos a los demás hasta haber oído la confirmación de Alcázar.

> (He knew more about us than we did ourselves, and that didn't change with the passing of time: after ten, fifteen, or twenty years of treatment, we kept on expecting him to reveal to us whether we were happy or sad, with whom we wanted to have an affair, or whom we wished to kill. At times we suspected something about our own feelings, but we never confessed it to the others until we had heard Alcázar's confirmation.)[21]

The novel's title refers to the analyst as the symbolic tree of life, virility, and procreation. The analyst and his wife, who is also his assistant, become parental figures for the patients, who cluster around them for guidance and protection, as the clinic becomes a substitute home. The two central characters exemplify the relationship of dependence established between Alcázar, the analyst, and his patients. A married couple, Ana and Enrique, think that part of their problem is that they have lost the ability to feel pleasure. By undertaking a twenty-year treatment with Alcázar, they hope to regain the power to experience pleasure. Ana's first-person narration satirizes the treatment they receive in individual and group sessions, the analyst's total control over their lives, and the way he imposes fads on his patients:

> En la época florida de los años sesenta los pacientes acudían por docenas, y no preguntaban cuanto duraría el tratamiento. Que un tratamiento dure veinte años, o más, le llama la atención a cualquiera. Por otra parte un tratamiento que dura veinte años ya es una forma de vida.

> (During the good times of the sixties patients would come by the dozens, never asking how long a treatment would take. That a treatment would last twenty years or more draws anyone's attention. On the other hand, a twenty-year treatment has already become a way of life.) (29)

The humorous and satirical criticism of the psychoanalytic situation constitutes only the surface of the work, which presents an underlying "rhetoric of sickness."[22] The narration is anchored in disease, concentrating on the characters' illnesses, their symptoms, and treatment. The tradition of the literary portrayal of disease is an important one. Leo Tolstoy, Thomas Mann, Albert Camus, and Alexander Solzhenitsyn dealt with this theme in their fiction. Disease might stand for a flaw in a character, or it can be an experience that makes the character perceive himself and the world around him from a new perspective (Tolstoy's *Death of Ivan Illych* is a case in point.) In Steimberg's novels disease is a means by which characters attain knowledge to heal themselves. The use of sickness in fiction also indicates evil in society (Camus's *The Plague*). Disease in Steimberg's later novel represents a socially and politically repressive system. The main elements that incorporate this metaphor in *El árbol del placer*, besides the constant references and descriptions of the characters' symptoms, are the clinical setting and the allegorical relationship between the analyst and his patients. The clinic, according to Gimbernat González, is "the microcosm, where a repressive system is made evident, hidden by a good montage of controlled transgressions, a scaled-down model of a system of government imposed by force."[23] The analogy becomes obvious: The clinic, where Alcázar reigns, is a place from which it is almost impossible to escape:

> [L]a seducción de Alcázar era tal que se consideraban dichosos de haber podido acercarse, y no pensaban en irse. A los pocos que se

atrevieron a preguntar, jamás se les dijo que su tratamiento no tenía
término y que nunca se les daría de alta.

([A]lcázar's seduction was such that they considered themselves lucky
to have been able to approach him, and they were not considering
leaving. The few who dared to ask were never told that their treatment had no end and that they would never be allowed to leave.)
(29)

Thus, the clinic becomes a place of reclusion, fear, and intimidation. It is
reminiscent of the spaces described in *La loca 101*, and provides continuity to the writer's allegorical inscription of her vision of the country. The
clinic, like the insane asylum, is described as an enclosed and confining
space (like a uterus), a place where the characters are behind bars, where
they cannot breathe, where they suffocate. Even the analyst's name, Alcázar,
denotes a fortress, which, in this case, instead of protecting those seeking
shelter, becomes the space where, under his direction, all sorts of transgressions against the patients' physical and spiritual well-being occur in a
parodic reversal of what is expected from medical treatment. The patients
are constantly tormented by a chain of so-called cures that Alcázar imposes on them, such as experimentation with LSD, violent sessions ending in beatings, sexual therapy bordering on abjection, and any fad that
will keep them under his control. The result is fear:

[N]os comunicábamos nuestros miedos: miedo a la ironía y a la
crueldad de Alcázar, miedo a los sufrimientos físicos que podíamos
experimentar con las diversas técnicas, miedo a la violencia que solía
desatarse con el psicodrama.

([W]e communicated our fears to one another: fear of Alcázar's irony
and cruelty, fear of the physical sufferings that we were able to feel
with the diverse techniques, fear of the violence that usually became
unleashed with the psychodrama.) (72)

In this setting and relationship, which exacerbate sickness and dependency,
we accompany Ana through the vicissitudes of her analysis, including a
romantic fixation with her analyst, sexual involvement with his patients as
a form of therapy, and divorce from Enrique. An important aspect of her
journey is that her experience with Alcázar's outrageous methods serves as
a catalyst that makes her seek freedom, transcending the patriarchal, repressive manipulation that she has suffered in the clinical setting. Her
journey helps her to get out of analysis after a twenty-year stint and to try

other therapeutic treatments, like homeopathy, which she finds equally unsuccessful. She finally frees herself from dependency and is healed in the process of writing her story:

> El motivo inicial que me llevó a contar esta historia me parece ahora muy fútil: aquellas tenues insinuaciones amorosas de Alcázar debido a las cuales, o más bien gracias a las cuales terminé con mi estúpida y peligrosa dependencia.

> (The initial motive that made me narrate this story seems very futile to me now: because of those tenuous amorous insinuations from Alcázar, or thanks to them, I finished my stupid and dangerous dependence.) (166–67)

The novel closes with two dreams that symbolically convey Ana's recovery. The first features Alcázar, his clinic, and an independent Ana who devises ways of letting him know she is free. It is followed by a dream of her father's burial, signifying that she has come to terms with his death. She symbolically buries her father and thus breaks away from Alcázar, the father figure. In the "Conversation with Alicia Steimberg," the writer expresses the profound influence her father's death had on her life. Therefore it is fitting that her novel of a psychoanalytic catharsis signaling freedom should end with symbolism related to that tragic experience. She has strived to transform the traumatic experience of his loss into a constant source of inspiration and creativity, while using a playful and ironic style. The ending depicts the female's emancipation from patriarchal father figures. Ana is alone, but she has transformed her former diseased and dependent self by coming in contact with an inner, spiritual force, and using writing to restore her femaleness.

Cuando digo Magdalena

Cuando digo Magdalena (When I say Magdalena), 1992, has a deceptively simple plot that utilizes elements reminiscent of *El árbol del placer*. The characters, who are taking a course in mental control, spend a weekend with their families at the estate of one of the group members. While they are there, a traumatic event takes place, unexplained in the novel, because the protagonist narrator has erased it from her memory. As a result, the present time of the story features conversations between Iñaki, her old family doctor, and the protagonist, who has also forgotten her name and so is called Magdalena, Sabina, Gertrudis, Lili Marlene, Maggie, or Magui.

Although the conversations are from the perspective of that weekend, they expand during the novel to cover events that took place throughout the protagonist's life. The doctor is not a psychoanalyst. He is a sympathetic listener who guides Magdalena in her introspection.

The novel uses strategies that evolved during the repressive years. The techniques developed by writers to circumvent censorship in the previous decades must still be applied in the nineties in response to the silence generated by society's collective denial of recent Argentine history. As the newly democratized society emerges from a political pact based on memory loss and denial of its recent violent past, artistic and intellectual creativity renews its commitment to awaken our moral social conscience, a responsibility undertaken by Steimberg in *Cuando digo Magdalena.* For this purpose it uses an allegorical narrative to underline the regime's discourse of reconciliation in efforts to erase the past from public conscience. The novel is also about the process of creating an avant-garde, postmodernist text from a female perspective. In this respect, it is a self-conscious narrative, which tells a story while referring to the strategies employed to create the text. Susan Rubin Suleiman has defined this type of text as one that

> defies, aggressively and provocatively, the traditional criteria of narrative intelligibility, and correlatively the reader's sense-making ability: where the reader expects logical and temporal development, avant-garde fiction offers repetition or else the juxtaposition of apparently random events; where the reader expects consistency, it offers contradiction; where the reader expects characters, it offers disembodied voices; where the reader expects the sense of an ending, it offers merely a stop.[24]

These goals are attained in the novel by presenting two distinct yet interrelated stories within the framework of a conversation between a female patient and her doctor. At one level the plot parodies the detective novel with its traditional elements: a murder, a disappearance, characters posing as detectives seeking to solve a crime, as well as apparent motives and an adulterous love triangle that may have unleashed the violence. The choice to use this genre is not fortuitous; it is a favorite of dissident writers. According to Andrés Avellaneda, it is the perfect genre to metaphorically express reality without alluding to it directly: "[I]n it crime is inherent to the genre, assassination forms part of its internal legality. It is the ideal genre to talk about crime and violence."[25] Steimberg uses this genre as metaphor as her story narrates the protagonist's failed efforts to unveil the hidden mystery regarding the event that took place at the estate. The lack of resolution and the metaphor of the amnesiac are an oblique reference to the present social climate, where it has become impossible to uncover the real story and assign responsibility for past violence.

The failed detective plot, the apparent topic of the dialogue, reveals another story: the protagonist's search for her lost identity. The "rhetoric of sickness" employed in the previous novel is present as the narration of an amnesiac's discourse, an elaboration of the theme of disease as a means of attaining self-knowledge. The story is a somewhat failed version of the female journey of self-discovery, as memory is only partially recovered. Although Magdalena is unable to confront what went on at the estate during the tragic weekend, she successfully retrieves diverse biographical data including "houses all of them enclosed but open to exploration; Jewish origins and condition, family, social group, languages, an ambiguous or at least conflictive sense of belonging to the country."[26] The exploration of her past and the detective plot come together as the protagonist suspects that she had a role in the events but chooses silence, a parallel to the silencing of conflicting voices in society: "[Y]o había hecho algo para que todo eso sucediera, y decidí que era mejor, por mi propia seguridad y la de él, que me callara" ([I] had done something for all that to happen, and I decided that it was better, for my own safety and for his, to shut up).[27]

The narration resists a homogeneous and inflexible mimetic discourse, as the author proposes a discourse that departs from that of institutionalized texts. Her feminist avant-garde literary structures are placed in contrast to a conventional plot and repetitive descriptions of the estate grounds, the house, and the objects it contains, focusing exclusively on the characters' outward appearance and actions without analysis. Magdalena's reading material provides a clue to the treatment of the embedded plot:

Elijo para leer relatos tranquilos del siglo pasado, donde la gente procede con parsimonia; nadie piensa en voz alta ni se desnuda en público. Todo sucede ordenadamente hasta que llega alguna catástrofe.

(To read I choose tranquil stories of the last century, where people proceed unhurriedly; nobody thinks out loud or bares himself in public. Everything happens in an orderly fashion until some catastrophe takes place.) (111)

In contrast, the narrative style she has chosen to tell her story subverts the canon, as evidenced in the treatment of spatial, temporal, structural, and discursive strategies. Space becomes a central element, as it is the locus that contains and shapes the protagonist's discourse. Magdalena and her doctor have returned to Las Lilas, the estate where they are almost totally alone (Flora, the doctor's wife, occasionally intervenes), and it is mainly from this space that the novel is narrated. Las Lilas, where they meet, is also the space where the detective novel unfolds, affecting the flow of time in the novel, as past and present intermingle in the dialogue. Denying the past by making it coincide with the present points to a female concept of time, one that restores the capability of a continuous re-creation of experience not conditioned by the past.[28] Besides, temporal progression becomes fragmented as it follows the protagonist's memories and mental associations, which are not linear and which reappear time and again, defying traditional views supporting the existence of an order predetermined by experience:

> Los relatos detallados me agotan. Creo que debería decir "ordenados."

> (Detailed stories wear me out. I think that I should say "orderly.") (159)

> —¿Contar esta historia? Es como ir haciendo un ovillo de una madeja muy enredada. Pero la madeja existe de antemano. Hay en ella cosas conocidas; aparecen y vuelven a aparecer las mismas cosas. Parece que estoy condenada, por ejemplo a hablar una y otra vez de la laguna.

> (To tell this story? It is like making a ball of wool out of a very entangled skein. But the skein exists beforehand. In it are known things; the same things appear and reappear. It seems that I'm condemned, for instance to speak once and once again about the lagoon.) (109)

The temporal progression is also fractured by interrupted dialogue when the protagonist digresses, tires, or feels too much pain to continue. These are marked in the text by nonverbal cues, such as the activity of swimming or sunbathing. This silencing, characteristic of female writing, attempts to subvert traditional linearity and the logic of cause and effect, giving the female narrator a device to temporarily distance herself from the narration and turn inward. The sense of fragmentation evidenced in the treatment of space and time also affects the novel's form and discourse. The title and the concluding phrases of the novel are indicative of a format and discourse based on elliptical, inconclusive statements defiant of male logocentrism based on rational interpretations of reality. "Cuando

digo Magdalena" (an allusion to Marcel Proust's *madeleine* and its function in the recuperation of memory) indicates the beginning of a statement or anecdote that we expect to continue. But it is truncated, and
reading the novel does not complete it. It is significant that the title (the
first thought) is incomplete and projected into the future by the concluding questions posed by the characters: "—¿Estoy mejor? —¿Mejor?" (Am
I getting any better? Any better?) (216). These questions cast a veil of
doubt over the whole story and indicate that the dialogue is attempting a
healing process that might continue endlessly. They also project the unresolved issues outside the realm of fiction to involve the readers and society
at large. This intention is expressed in the references to the novel's technical creation and its attempt to dismantle literary conventions to adopt a
tempo that fits a female style of writing with its repetitions, hesitations,
and open-ended patterns. These denote an interest in an experiential approach to reality rather than interpreting it according to preestablished
concepts: "¿Por qué hay que contar la historia? Todos los días hay millones
de historias que quedan sin contar. Pero si se empieza a contar una hay
que terminar de contarla. ¿Y si no se termina de contarla? Eso sería un
fracaso" (Why is it necessary to narrate a story? Every day there are mil-
lions of stories that remain untold. But if one starts to narrate one, it is
necessary to finish narrating it. And if one doesn't finish narrating it? That
would mean failure) (135). The truncated spatial, temporal, and structural
dimensions are related to the duality and fragmentation within the narrator and her discourse. As the story is told by the protagonist to another
person, she is divided into the voice that narrates and the subject of the
action narrated. Her amnesia has also divided her into the conscious part
of herself and the one buried in her memory. Her duality is obvious in the
crisis regarding her self-knowledge, the novel's central theme. This crisis
is symbolized by the absence of a single, permanent name for the protagonist, who hides under different identities. The fragmentation is also apparent in that there is no attempt to include the voices/versions of other
characters. What we read can be construed as a mutilated text, as these
other voices might have been erased. This technique, which reviewers
have consistently labeled as conversation or dialogue, becomes, after a
closer reading, a monologue. For example, the doctor does not actively
participate; he just prompts the protagonist to keep going. When the
reader is faced with a single perspective, it is assumed that it is an uncon-
tested view of events. However, *Cuando digo Magdalena* intentionally
does just the opposite: the protagonist ignores or cannot face the truth, so
there is no resolution that reestablishes normality, and the monologue form
is characterized by ambivalence. The adoption of this form of narration,

which discards the possibility of a single harmonious voice bringing forth the multiple versions of the characters, points to the impossibility of any dialogue. In this respect, the narration is articulated to subvert dominance and to defy dominant discourses. The subversion of dominance and the emergence of a female voice in a central position are also evident in the treatment of the traditionally powerful medical figures, represented by Iñaki and Alcides (the leader of the mental control study group), who relinquish their positions of authority in the novel. In Iñaki's case, there has been a transformation of the medical situation, as his discourse has been almost relegated to silence and he is stripped of his healing powers; Alcides, a reincarnation of *El árbol del placer*'s Alcázar, is first excluded from the group and then symbolically disappears.

Alicia Steimberg's novel, narrated from the chaotic perspective created by the protagonist's loss of memory, weakens the centers of power and control and dismantles the authoritarianism of an inherited political and literary text. The novel stands as a milestone indicative of the maturation achieved in both the content and style of her writing. Her progression is also indicative of a strengthening of her feminist intent and style, which, especially in later novels, indicates an empowerment of the female spirit through self-knowledge and the creative process. Her narration emerges in opposition to patriarchal, repressive voices in an effort to inscribe a female and a dissident reading of history inspired by the knowledge and healing resulting from the characters' exploration of their inner depths.

CONVERSATION WITH ALICIA STEIMBERG

Buenos Aires, 8 April 1987

M.F.: Could you talk about your life, about the events and people you consider to be the most important?

A.S.: There were several important events, but a tragic event that stands out and that marked my childhood and my life was my father's death at age forty-one. I was eight years old at the time and I was terribly affected by his premature death. I think it determined several things in my life, among them, possibly, the fact that I became a writer. My father was a writer. He was a poet and essayist, a person who loved literature and was dedicated to his studies. He left us (my brother is also a writer) this vocation of writing. Among many other events that marked my life are my two marriages and my three children.

M.F.: Would you say that your father and, specifically, his death, was one of the events that made you begin to write?

A.S.: Without a doubt. I worked it into *La loca 101* in the shape of an old fantasy I had after my father's death. I was always a rather solitary child who fantasized a lot. But after my father passed away, I imagined how I could bring him back through fantasy. Although both sides of the family were Jewish, religion wasn't stressed in my upbringing. I think I substituted what could have been a religious belief for that fantasy, which was the idea that father was present somewhere in the world, that I hadn't lost him altogether. I imagined what had really happened was that someone else had come here and died, that it hadn't been my father.

M.F.: What role did these fantasies have in your literary development?

A.S.: They were short stories, my first short stories.

M.F.: What other events were important in your becoming interested in literature?

A.S.: Our book collection was important. I can still remember it by heart. The collection was kept inside one of those old-style libraries with three doors. My mother locked the door where the forbidden books were kept, but since there were no partitions inside, I could reach through the unlocked door next to it, get it open and read. I had a real passion for our book collection, a passion I had evidently inherited from my father.

M.F.: Do you belong to a generation of Jewish-Argentine writers with Mario Szichman and Cecilia Absatz, among others?

A.S.: Yes, of course, although it's not a constant preoccupation for me or them, nor do I have an all-encompassing feeling of belonging to a generation. But we share common activities. For instance, this year we participated in a congress on the search for identity for Jewish-Argentine writers.

M.F.: What is the role of the Jewish identity in your works?

A.S.: The Jewish identity appears in *Músicos y relojeros*, a novel about my childhood. It's childhood memories seen through the critical vision of an adult, which is the only way to write childhood memories. It's because of this novel that I'm classified as a Jewish-Argentine writer, not for any other. I never went back to this theme, although it's present in other works in some ways.

M.F.: Yes, there are allusions, but they are more veiled.

A.S.: There are allusions, but in *Músicos y relojeros* the whole story is the Jewish theme. I plan to take it up again, in fact, in what I'm working on now. It's a script for either a television miniseries or a movie (the format still hasn't been decided) on the history of the tango. The idea is to sell the script in the United States. I'm working on it with another Argentine writer,

Elsa Osorio. The whole Argentine social spectrum in the [almost] fifty years from 1890 to 1935 is contained in the history of the tango. One of the characters, a singer, is Jewish. We wanted to show how difficult it was for Jews to integrate in Argentina.

M.F.: Besides the script, what else are you writing now?

A.S.: I'm always writing short stories. My last novel, *El árbol del placer*, was published last year. I'm not writing a novel right now, so that means that I'm working on short stories.

M.F.: Do you feel an affinity with other Argentine writers?

A.S.: I feel closest to the writer Hebe Uhart; it's as though we had a common origin. She also comes from an immigrant family. Her grandparents came from southern Italy. She's an excellent short story writer. I also identify with Cortázar, as many writers do, and with Pedro Orgambide and Cecilia Absatz. It's easier for me to name contemporary writers with whom I feel affinities. When I received the Argentine Society of Writers' prize, my work was compared to that of a compatriot of yours, Felisberto Hernández, regarding the role of fantasy.

M.F.: What other writers have influenced you?

A.S.: It's hard for me to tell, but obviously what I read during my adolescence—Russian writers like Dostoevsky and Tolstoy, because their works were part of our home book collection. I think the Jewish writer Shalom Aleichem also influenced me.

M.F.: What are you reading now?

A.S.: I'm reading a book by Borges that's a compilation of notes which appeared in the magazine *El Hogar* in the thirties.

M.F.: How do you select a theme?

A.S.: I always say that in reality the theme selects me, it takes hold of me. When I'm working on something like the script for the history of the tango, I select the theme; but when I'm about to write a short story it's a different process. The story begins before I start to write it down. For instance, there's a story of mine that hasn't been published yet in book form, that started as an encounter I had with a vegetable vendor. I went into his store and he asked about my mother. My mother had died years before. But I thought, "I come in here for a few minutes. Am I going to explain that he's wrong, that mother died years ago, that he's thinking of someone else?" And so I answered, "Fine, thanks." From then on, something strange happened. The vendor looked puzzled while he answered, "I'm so glad." I started wondering what had become of the real lady he was inquiring about. Maybe she was dying or near death, and I had confused him by telling him that she was fine. And then I started imagining things that got the short story going. I had painful memories of my mother's death a few years ago. Those two elements, the imaginary mother the vendor asked about and memories of my mother's last moments, came together. A painful experience was transformed by another experience and became a story.

M.F.: Do you have a writing schedule or routine?

A.S.: Unfortunately, no. I'd like to. It happens sometimes. For a while, years ago, I'd write late at night till daybreak and then I'd sleep during the morning, because I was able to then. Lately I can't, because my circumstances have changed, so now I don't have a writing schedule. However, sometimes I do nothing but write for three or four months; and then I stop writing for another three or four months because I have to earn a living.

M.F.: You can't live off your works?

A.S.: Here in Argentina, writers are not only unable to make a living off their works, but they usually go broke writing.

M.F.: Is it harder for a woman to publish, to be reviewed, and receive prizes?

A.S.: In my case, I'm sure it hasn't been harder because I'm a woman. But I couldn't say whether in general it's harder or not. What allowed me to make rapid headway was that my work received recognition abroad, and that's very important in Argentina. If a work is favorably recognized in a country considered more prestigious, then it is accepted here.

M.F.: Do you think there is a female style of writing different from male writing?

A.S.: I've discussed this issue many times. I think there may be certain experiences that affect the themes in "female writing." But I don't know if there's a female writing style that's demonstrably different from male writing.

M.F.: Are you a feminist?

A.S.: I consider myself a feminist when I make feminist demands at home on my family, or when I participate in panel discussions on women and women writers. I'm always ready to support feminist demands. However, I'm not a militant feminist in that I don't belong to a feminist movement.

M.F.: Do you include your feminist views in your works?

A.S.: I think so, but not because I specifically deal with feminism or classify them as feminist. But there's feminism in them because they reflect my liberation, my independence from a patriarchal value system.

M.F.: Where were you during the years of the "dirty war" in Argentina?

A.S.: I was in Buenos Aires.

M.F.: Did you feel the effects of censorship or self-censorship?

A.S.: Very strongly. To the point that after my second novel, *La loca 101,* was published in 1973, I didn't publish anything for seven years. In 1981, *Su espíritu inocente* was released. In some ways it was the sequel to my childhood memories. Half the novel is the protagonist's memories of adolescence, early youth, and her first experiences of marriage. It's free of any reference to what was going on in Argentina at the time.

M.F.: Did you feel personally threatened?

A.S.: Yes, I feared for my safety and the safety of my children.

M.F.: Is that why you stopped publishing during those years?

A.S.: Yes, except that *Su espíritu inocente* was published in 1981 when we were still under the dictatorship, but it was totally marginal to what was taking place in the country. My next volume, a collection of short stories, *Como todas las mañanas,* was released in 1983. I didn't write about the dictatorship in those works, but in *El árbol del placer,* published in 1986, there is an allusion to the dictatorship, because the novel deals with a group of people in Buenos Aires under an oppressive leader.

M.F.: According to the critics your work is autobiographical. Do you agree with that?

A.S.: No, it's only partially autobiographical. My autobiographical novel is *Músicos y relojeros* and to some extent, *Su espíritu inocente.* There are always autobiographical elements present because writers usually draw on their own experiences.

M.F.: Why did you title your first novel *Músicos y relojeros?*

A.S.: My maternal grandmother always proudly stated that all her direct ancestors had been either musicians or watchmakers, because among Jews, and maybe also Gentiles, in Russia, occupations were passed on, and to be a musician or a watchmaker was a distinguished profession.[29]

M.F.: What is the meaning of the almost exclusive focus on the family in *Músicos y relojeros* and the exclusion of outside reality? Is that a portrayal of Jewish life in Argentina at the time?

A.S.: That wasn't my intention. I took the point of view of a child isolated from reality, because in early childhood she is confined to the home and school environment. At that time, the 1940s, a child wasn't as knowledgeable about what was going on in the world as today, for there was no television. In the second part of the novel, the protagonist has more contact with the outside world than in the first part, because she lives through hard times and shortages. That's when the external reality comes into play.

M.F.: Why are female characters so traditional in this novel? Is that how you see the Jewish-Argentine woman?

A.S.: Yes, the characters portray reality. They are traditional women of the 1940s who didn't work outside the home, and if they had to it was seen as a sort of punishment. They were forced to work, but didn't see it as form of personal growth or development. My mother, whose fictionalized characterization is only sketched, except for certain aspects related directly to me, was a precursor; she was a dentist.

M.F.: In this novel as in others there is constant mention of physiological functions. Why?

A.S.: I cover the whole life of my characters and that includes bodily functions.

M.F.: Are you trying to transgress social taboos?

A.S.: That's possible, although it wasn't my intent. My works, and especially *El árbol·del placer*, deal with the medical aspects of life and also with the natural processes of daily life.

M.F.: Why does your second novel, *La loca 101*, incorporate madness so prominently? What is the meaning of the recurring imagery linking madness with cages and tombs?

A.S.: I think that madness, like the cages and tombs, is related to my personal experience. My mother was mentally disturbed. She never went mad, she wasn't committed to an institution, but my brother and I suffered greatly because of her sickness, especially when my father died and left her widowed at age thirty-four. So it represents my experience with the mental problems of my family.

M.F.: In this novel reality is only alluded to in a veiled manner. Was this the result of censorship or self-censorship?

A.S.: Yes, because I wrote this novel in 1973 and, at that time, there was already fear and intimidation in Argentina.

M.F.: Critics characterized this work as an "experimental narrative puzzle." Can you explain your purpose in writing this type of novel?

A.S.: It wasn't intentional. I thought if I could rave while thinking, I could also rave while writing and see what came out of it. I got tired of narrating long stories. While writing *La loca 101*, I started by narrating enthusiastically and, suddenly, I didn't feel like continuing that story; another story appeared through free association. And so I ended up narrating this other story. The novel is the result of interweaving several stories in this manner. I would say that *La loca 101* happened once and will never happen again.

M.F.: What was the critical reaction to this novel?

A.S.: *La loca 101* had several critics who weren't convinced, and it also had enthusiastic supporters. I don't know how seriously the critics took that novel. There is a critic here, Luis Gregorich, who has taken my work seriously.

M.F.: Are there different stages in your work?

A.S.: I would say rather that there's zigzagging between two styles: the orthodox narrative style and the more fantastic, like in *La loca 101*.

M.F.: After the complex experimental style of *La loca 101*, what made you change to a more linear and accessible style in *El árbol del placer*?

A.S.: It was totally deliberate. *El árbol del placer* was written in the most orthodox possible language without any literary innovation. It was what I wanted for that type of story.

M.F.: Do you plan to continue writing in this orthodox style or will you return to the "puzzle"?

A.S.: I'm sure I'll return to the "puzzle"; I always have. Some of the short stories I'm writing now resemble *La loca 101* and others are closer to *El árbol del placer*. It's a luxury to write in the experimental style of the "puzzle" because it's hard to sell such works. However, there's an audience for works like *La loca 101*. A lot of readers loved that novel. I'll write in that style again, but it's a risk and therefore, somewhat frightening.

M.F.: What is the meaning of the title, *El árbol del placer*?

A.S.: The protagonist, the psychoanalyst, is an individual who promises and gives pleasure. That's the goal of his treatment. And he's the tree. Without him, there's no pleasure and that's the tragic aspect.

M.F.: He's the tree in the Freudian sense, as a phallic symbol?

A.S.: Yes, the tree as he who renders pleasure, besides being a phallic symbol.

M.F.: Why did you use erotic-psychological language in this novel?

A.S.: I wanted to describe a common phenomenon in Argentina, especially in Buenos Aires—that is, the introduction of psychoanalytic language into everyday life. I consider it an absurdity and I present it as absurd.

M.F.: Were you psychoanalyzed?

A.S.: Yes, for many years.

M.F.: Did your own experience with psychoanalysis help you write the novel?

A.S.: Yes, it was a firsthand experience.

M.F.: Does the social satire in this novel correspond to your vision of Buenos Aires society?

A.S.: It's my view of a sector of Buenos Aires society. I call it "middle-middle class." It's neither upper-middle class nor lower-middle class, it's a middle-middle pseudo-intellectual class. Many members of this class underwent psychoanalysis, but this has diminished somewhat because of the economic crisis.

M.F.: The novel is set in Buenos Aires during the 1970s but the characters seem oblivious to reality. Is this because of censorship or was it your intention to show that they were cut off from reality?

A.S.: In this case it wasn't due to censorship, but because I was dealing with the issue of prolonged treatments that helped people ignore or escape reality in the midst of the terrible events happening in this country.

M.F.: At first the female narrator appears as the central character, but later on she becomes an observer and the psychologist and the group become the protagonists. Why does this change occur?

A.S.: My interest in the other characters grew. It wasn't a literary choice.

M.F.: Why does the novel end with an image of death?

A.S.: The death of the father is the separation from the psychoanalyst in this case.

M.F.: Is that autobiographical as it was in *La loca 101*?

A.S.: It's partly autobiographical.

Buenos Aires, 1 November 1989

M.F.: Tell me about what you have published since our last conversation.

A.S.: I sent my novel *Amatista* (Amethyst) to a literary contest in Spain in 1988 and it was one of two finalists. The novel that won the prize didn't win unanimously, but by a majority. A portion of the jury voted for me.

M.F.: Which contest was it?

A.S.: The contest was "The Vertical Smile" sponsored by Tusquets Publishers (in Barcelona.) Are you familiar with it?

M.F.: No, tell me about it.

A.S.: It's a contest for erotic fiction that has been held for eleven or twelve years. It features a jury including writers like Juan Marsé, as well as movie directors like [Luis] Berlanga. It's a specialized jury, specializing in erotic literature.

M.F.: Why did you choose to write erotic literature?

A.S.: How did I end up writing erotic literature? I had written a story years ago, but kept it in a drawer, I think due to lack of encouragement. I kept that unfinished material for years and didn't even think of submitting it to a contest because, here, if a work can be construed as sinful or if there's a hint of sexuality, it's repressed. You're probably wondering what is censored. Pornographic magazines on the stands aren't censored; neither are films or television, for the most part. Censorship of books is quite uncommon. However, there's opposition to freedom of sexual or erotic expression in Argentina. That's not true in Spain. It used to be so backward, but now Spain is a much more progressive country than Argentina concerning these matters. The erotic novel contest was encouraging to me, so I sent my novel and the results were very positive. The book was published and it's just now being distributed to Spanish booksellers. It will be available here in a few days.

M.F.: What is the novel about?

A.S.: It's a didactic novel featuring a woman who gives a man a series of theoretical and practical lessons on eroticism. Both characters are anonymous. She's "the woman" and he's "the doctor." It's humorous, especially the language. It also contains erotic humor. The problem I had was not whether I was going to describe one of my erotic fantasies, but how to describe it so it made sense and would have the same effect on Spanish speakers in a different part of the world. You know how ridiculous it is when you see a movie and a word is used to describe something sexual or erotic that isn't the word used in your language. It sounds awfully funny and, of course, it doesn't make the slightest impression on the viewer, because the vocabulary is devoid of connotations. So instead of being erotic it becomes ridiculous. In trying to make the language make sense to both Argentines and Spaniards, I confronted an unsolvable problem, because you must either use the Argentine or the Peninsular Spanish terminology. I solved it by using jokes. Humor is the salient aspect of the book, much more than eroticism.

M.F.: What kind of jokes did you incorporate?

A.S.: There are jokes and parodies of various things. Nowadays self-help books on lovemaking are fashionable everywhere, especially in the States. Translations of the North American books are available here. There's a parody of these ridiculous texts. Another problem I confronted was that I was sending this book off to Spain and I know that they don't care about the *voseo*,[30] and besides, there is a clash that generates humor, because while they are having sex, they use delicate and refined speech, addressing one another formally with "Sir," "Madam," and "Doctor." The plot deals mainly with stories the woman tells the doctor, somewhat like Scheherazade, but these are erotic tales with very curious and somewhat surrealist erotic characters. The woman and the doctor aren't surrealistic; they could be real people if you use your imagination. The characters also resemble characters in children's stories, except that they have a perversion, and what happens between them doesn't have anything to do with the world of children. The entire book is written this way, thus allowing me to write an erotic novel in a humorous vein. No book can be erotic from start to finish. It can contain erotic parts, but it's improbable that it can sustain eroticism from the first to the last page. The only way to do it is as I did, as a joke.

M.F.: And why did you title it *Amatista*?

A.S.: I thought of *Amatista* by chance and used it as the name of one of the characters. In the tales the woman tells the doctor, Amatista is the main character. She's a young woman from the fifties by the way she dresses (her clothes are always described), the places she goes, and the music she listens to. Although she's placed in the fifties, there are flashes to other time periods and other characters. I didn't think of the amethyst, the stone; maybe I liked the name because it has to do with love and Amatista seems to be the one who loves or dedicates herself to love.[31] I read up on the amethyst, a stone that has healing properties and is used by the Orientals to meditate. So it was a good choice. There are no other reasons for the title. The novel was mainly a literary exercise to see whether I would be able to carry it off; my first drafts didn't have much in common with the final product.

M.F.: What were your first drafts like?

A.S.: They were surrealistic erotic fantasies I spontaneously wrote without any outline in mind. Later I cleaned up the draft and deleted lots of material that had nothing to do with the erotic content. Let's say my draft became a more "normal" narrative that contained other stuff, too. And I used it pragmatically as a stylistic exercise. I made up the story that I already told you and was very satisfied with the outcome. I also had a lot of fun writing it.

M.F.: Was the book well-received in Spain?

A.S.: The reception was excellent. I have just received two reviews from Spain. And although nobody has read it here yet, it has made a great impact because it's about the forbidden subject. I have had write-ups, interviews, and I have been on television programs.

M.F.: What are your future plans?

A.S.: For the first time, I'm working on a book in essay form titled, *La claridad lechosa del amanecer* (The milky brightness of dawn). It's unusual for me to title a book before I start writing it, but the book has already been written in my mind. It's an essay on the writing of fiction. I reflect on how fiction is produced. I stress that it's about the writing of fiction and not the art of fiction. I don't think it's an art that's learned, but something that happens to a writer over a long period of time, not just when the writer settles down to write. That story has already been written—you don't make anything up while you're putting it down on paper. A very complex process takes place before that. I deal with many subjects in my essay. I trace the process of how a trivial dialogue with a fruit vendor at a grocery store stirred up many issues for me and resulted in a short story. I'm showing how fiction originates and develops. I envision the writing of fiction as the last stage of a process that maybe unfolds throughout an entire life. Let's take any fictional character, for example, a character of mine that is a recurring obsession: a blond English aviator. What I remember is that when I was twelve or thirteen years old, the Second World War had just finished, and I was in love with the British and the Americans. They seemed like movie heroes. I could visualize them cruising the skies, blond and handsome like movie stars. That is a fantasy. When I was about twenty, I met some British youngsters in Buenos Aires and they introduced me to an English aviator. We went to a café and chatted and I never saw him again. That was all that ever happened between us, but it was like a dream come true, as if the person of my dreams had suddenly taken shape. Later on he became a fictional character—an episode, a memory, a strong shock in life; for instance, an early death can be perceived in many different ways later on. I wouldn't be able to express what I felt when I was eight and my father died; what I can express are my feelings and reactions to it at different stages of my life.

M.F.: Do you have any plans for writing fiction?

A.S.: Not right now. I have unfinished short stories, so I suppose I'll eventually compile another collection of short stories. I've only published one. But I don't have any immediate plans to write a novel.

BIBLIOGRAPHY

Primary Sources (listed chronologically)

Steimberg, Alicia. *Músicos y relojeros.* Buenos Aires: Centro Editor de América Latina, 1971.
——. *La loca 101.* Buenos Aires: Ediciones de la Flor, 1973.
——. *Su espíritu inocente.* Buenos Aires: Editorial Pomaire, 1981.
——. *Como todas las mañanas.* Buenos Aires: Editorial Celtia, 1983.
——. *El árbol del placer.* Buenos Aires: Emecé Editores, 1986.
——. *Amatista.* Barcelona: Editorial Tusquets, 1989.
——. *Cuando digo Magdalena.* Buenos Aires: Planeta, 1992.

Critical Articles by Alicia Steimberg (listed chronologically)

Steimberg, Alicia. "La autobiografía, ese género inexistente." Paper delivered at symposium on Latin American Women Writers. San Miguel de Allende, Mexico, 23 June 1978.

————. "Prologue." Foreword to *Como todas las mañanas*, by Alicia Steimberg, 11–12. Buenos Aires: Editorial Celtia, 1983.

Short Fiction by Alicia Steimberg (listed chronologically)

Steimberg, Alicia. "Gratificaré." *Hispamérica* 2 (July 1972): 99–104.

————. "La flor de lis." *Hispamérica* 5 (April 1975): 90–92.

————. "Belleza árabe." *La Opinión*, 10 August 1975.

————. "Juan, el hombre que asistió a su propio entierro." *La Opinión*, 10 August 1975.

————. "Cómo es Ana." *La Opinión*, 30 October 1977.

————. "La salita de música." *La Opinión*, 17 May 1978.

————. "Vida social en Pisaflores." *La Opinión*, 17 May 1978.

————. "El templo de Júpiter." *Escandalar* (April-June 1979): 63–66.

————. "Modas." *Siete días*, 3–9 July 1980.

————. "Tránsito." *Clarín*, 14 October 1982.

————. "El grano." *Acción*, 15–30 January 1986.

————."Con trípode y bastón." *La Razón*, 29 June 1986.

————. "Blues del gatito." *Acción*, 1–14 September 1986.

Works Available in Translation (listed chronologically)

Steimberg, Alicia. "From *Musicians and Watchmakers*." Translated by Miriam Varon. In *Echad: An Anthology of Latin American Jewish Writers*, edited by Roberta Kalechofsky, 45–54. Marblehead, Mass.: Micah Publications, 1980.

————. *Erotische Lektionen*. Translated by Veronika Schmidt. Frankfurt am Main: Eichborn Verlag, 1989.

————. "Cecilia's Last Will and Testament." Translated by Christopher Leland. In *Landscapes of a New Land: Short Fiction by Latin America Women*, edited by Marjorie Agosín, 102–11. New York: White Pine Press, 1989.

————. "From *Musicians and Watchmakers*." Translated by Lea Fletcher. In "Argentine Writing in the 80s." *Literary Review: An International Journal of Contemporary Writing* 4 (Summer 1989): 578–81.

————. "García's Thousandth Day." Translated by Lorraine Elena Roses. In *Secret Weavers: Stories of the Fantastic by Women of Argentina and Chile*, edited by Marjorie Agosín, 227–29. New York: White Pine Press, 1992.

————. "Segismundo's Best World." Translated by Lorraine Elena Roses.

In *Secret Weavers: Stories of the Fantastic by Women of Argentina and Chile*, edited by Marjorie Agosín, 230–40. New York: White Pine Press, 1992.

―――. "Viennese Waltz." Translated by Lorraine Elena Roses. In *Secret Weavers: Stories of the Fantastic by Women of Argentina and Chile*, edited by Marjorie Agosín, 221–26. New York, White Pine Press, 1992.

Secondary Sources

Antognazzi, Carlos. "Sobre nosotros mismos." Review of *Amatista*, by Alicia Steimberg. *El Litoral*, 14 March 1992.

Ayats, Dolors. "Lliçons eròtiques." Review of *Amatista*, by Alicia Steimberg. *Set dies*, 27 October 1989.

Barone, Roxana. "La memoria antojadiza." Review of *Cuando digo Magdalena*, by Alicia Steimberg. *El Cronista Comercial*, 9 September 1992.

Battista, Vicente. "Buscando a Magdalena." Review of *Cuando digo Magdalena*, by Alicia Steimberg. *Clarín*, 3 September 1992.

Cicco, Juan. "Sobre un orden extraño." Review of *Como todas las mañanas*, by Alicia Steimberg. *La Nación*, 29 May 1983.

Comas, José. "Alicia Steimberg gana el primer Premio Planeta de Argentina." *El País*, 20 June 1992.

C. R. "Ajena a la bohemia y la taquilla." *La Epoca*, 24 October 1992.

"Datos para una ficha." Review of *La loca 101*, by Alicia Steimberg. *Crisis*, 10 December 1973.

De Miguel, María Esther. "Ni dormida ni despierta." Review of *Como todas las mañanas*, by Alicia Steimberg. *El Cronista Comercial*, 27 April 1983.

"El desarraigo." Review of *Músicos y relojeros*, by Alicia Steimberg. *Análisis*, 28 January–3 February 1972, 47.

Flori, Mónica. "Cecilia Absatz y Alicia Steimberg: dos narradoras argentinas contemporáneas." *Chasqui: revista de literatura latinoamericana* 17 (November 1988): 83–92.

Gimbernat González, Ester. "*El árbol del placer* (A. Steimberg): retóricas de enfermedad." In *Aventuras del desacuerdo: novelistas argentinas de los 80*, 289–94. Buenos Aires: Danilo Albero Vergara, 1992.

Gómez, Carlos Alberto. "Los personajes son co-autores." Review of *Cuando digo Magdalena*, by Alicia Steimberg. *La Gaceta*, 18 October 1992.

Gregorich, Luis. "La autora." *La Opinión*, 17 May 1978.

―――. "¿Un nuevo 'boom' de la narrativa argentina?" *Salimos*, 1–30 April 1982, 51.

Herrera, Francisco. "La literatura erótica femenina tras los pasos de su propia mitología." *La Prensa*, 6 March, 1990.

Itkin, Silvia. "Encuesta: ¿Existe la literatura femenina? Ellas tienen la palabra." *Puro cuento* 17 (July-August 1989): 6.

"Las mil y una variantes de los cuentos eróticos." Review of *Amatista*, by Alicia Steimberg. *Página 12*, 2 March 1989.

Magrini, César. "Rosario de asombros." Review of *Como todas las mañanas*, by Alicia Steimberg. *El Cronista Comercial*, 21 September 1983.

Mercado, Tununa. "Romper la amnesia." Review of *Cuando digo Magdalena*, by Alicia Steimberg. *Carnets* 3 (24 October 1992).

Monge, Carlos. "Alicia en el país del erotismo." *Siete días*, 11 May 1989, 43.

N. L. Z. Review of *La loca 101*, by Alicia Steimberg. *La Prensa*, 31 March 1974.

Peltzer, Federico. "Con buena prosa y humor." Review of *Como todas las mañanas*, by Alicia Steimberg. *La Gaceta de Tucumán*, 12 June 1983.

Pinto, Antonio. "Alicia Steimberg." *Cultura* 17 (November-December 1986): 22.

Poblet, Natu. "Natu Poblet sale a comer con Alicia Steimberg." *First* (May 1989): 36–38.

Pomeraniec, Hinde. "Alicia Steimberg ganó el Premio Planeta argentino." *Clarín*, 20 June 1992.

———. "Alicia Steimberg: la fuerza de lo cotidiano." *Clarín*, 25 June 1992.

Renard, María Adela. "Entre sueño y vigilia." Review of *Como todas las mañanas*, by Alicia Steimberg. *La Prensa*, 22 May 1983.

Review of *Amatista*, by Alicia Steimberg. *Tiempo*, 16 October 1989.

Roffo, Analía. "Alicia Steimberg: vivir una experiencia única." *Tiempo Argentino*, 21 March 1984, 9.

Russo, Miguel. "Alicia Steimberg obtuvo el Premio Planeta." *La Maga*, 24 June 1992.

———. "Alicia Steimberg recuerda su larga trayectoria literaria y prepara un libro acerca de la ficción." *La Maga*, 8 July 1992.

Seijas, Gustavo. Review of *Músicos y relojeros*, by Alicia Steimberg. *Gaceta de Tucumán*, 23 April 1972.

Senkmann, Leonardo. *La identidad judía en la literatura argentina*. Buenos Aires: Editorial Pardes, 1983.

Soares, Norberto. "La sintaxis de los sueños de cada mañana." Review of *Como todas las mañanas*, by Alicia Steimberg. *Tiempo Argentino*, 24 April 1983.

"Sonrisas verticales." Review of *Amatista*, by Alicia Steimberg. *El Periódico*, 7 October 1989.

Sosnowski, Saúl. "Alicia Steimberg: enhebrando pequeñas historias." *Essays on Foreign Languages and Literatures* 17 (1987): 104–10.

Vassallo, Marta. "Las voces secretas del erotismo." Review of *Amatista*, by Alicia Steimberg. *Sur*, 17 January 1990, 15.

Verlichak, Victoria. "Ideas premiadas." Review of *Cuando digo Magdalena*, by Alicia Steimberg. *Noticias*, 6 September 1992, 28.

Vilas, Irene. Review of *Músicos y relojeros*, by Alicia Steimberg. *La Prensa*, 26 March 1972.

"Voz libre en la cultura." Review of *La loca 101*, by Alicia Steimberg. *Voz libre*, 11 November 1973.

Zeiger, Claudio. "Alicia Steimberg: un Planeta a sus pies." *Cultura*, 1 September 1992.

5
Cecilia Absatz

Cecilia Absatz was born in Buenos Aires, Argentina, in 1943. She studied philosophy and psychology at the University of Buenos Aires School of Humanities, and then pursued a career in public relations and journalism. She was publicity editor at the Agens, Martín Propaganda, and Cícero Publicidad agencies from 1965 to 1970, when she was named creative director at the Nueva Agencia de Publicidad. In 1973 Absatz became the communications manager of Asesores de Empresa y Consultores de Dirección. She worked as a columnist and then assistant editor for *Status* magazine in 1977, and from 1978 to 1980 as its director. She then became editor of *Claudia* magazine and a columnist for *Vosotras* magazine during 1983 and 1984, in addition to other journalistic positions. She has been a columnist for *Claudia* since 1984. In 1985 she coordinated literary workshops for the Buenos Aires "Neighborhood Cultural Projects." During 1991 and 1992 she wrote a weekly column titled "Mixed Media" for *Somos* magazine. At present, she contributes notes and columns to the daily newspaper, *La Nación*, and to *Playboy*, *Competencia*, and *First*. She also writes television scripts for a miniseries, *Where Are You, Love of My Life, Whom I Cannot Find?*, based on the film by the same name directed by Juan José Jusid. Her short story, "Un poco de paz" (A bit of peace), from *Feiguele y otras mujeres* (Feiguele and other women) was the basis for a sequence in the movie.

Essay

Cecilia Absatz admires writers of short works. Her three short volumes of fiction attest to her own literary maturity in that genre. As I sat in Absatz's

Cecilia Absatz. Photograph by Graciela Ocampo.

flat discussing her life and work, I was reminded of apartments where her female protagonists lived: spacious and well-lit, with a big terrace where geraniums bloomed. The writer reminisced about her first book, *Feiguele y otras mujeres* (Feiguele and other women), 1976, and the vicissitudes it encountered before and after publication. Especially difficult were the eight years the work was censored by the military as immoral.

Feiguele y otras mujeres

The unity of the volume (a novella, *Feiguele*, and six short stories) hinges on the narrations, which portray both adolescent and young women, Absatz's alter egos struggling to attain an authentic female identity in a patriarchal society. When asked her motive for writing the novella, Absatz said, "Desperation, I suppose. At the time it didn't seem to be a question of motives, but an unspecified order. Today I think that the motive always ends up being the desire to deeply understand the story one is writing."[1] The result is the story of Feiguele, a fourteen-year-old girl growing up in a middle-class Buenos Aires neighborhood in a Jewish-Polish family. The novella, narrated in first person, covers approximately one year of Feiguele's family and school experiences, as well as a vacation in Mar del Plata. We feel for Feiguele, an adolescent who suffers ostracism and rejection for being fat. Her overweight body acquires symbolic proportions. It makes her different, an outcast, as can be perceived in the way she introduces herself in the opening sentences of the work:

> Me llamo Feiguele y soy muy gorda. Tengo catorce años, y aunque ustedes se rían, conozco bastante del dolor del mundo. Como la mayoría de la gente cuando tiene catorce años.
>
> (My name is Feiguele and I am very fat. I am fourteen years old, and even though you may laugh, I know quite a bit about the pain of the world. Like most people when they are fourteen years old.)[2]

But what makes Feiguele special for the reader, compared to her mindless adolescent acquaintances, are the critical powers of perception and the sarcastic linguistic abilities that Absatz has given her. Her ironic vision, underscored by humor, makes us identify with this precocious antiheroine who struggles against the traditional socialization imposed on her. Her plight becomes that of every woman. In retrospect, the story, and especially Feiguele, become the foundation for Absatz's fictional world: Feiguele is a precursor for her later protagonists. Absatz has said, "In reality, the protagonists of the three novels [*Feiguele*, *Té con canela*, and *Los años pares*] are the same character, at different ages and in different situations."[3] Absatz values power above other traits. Her heroines seem content when they have attained a certain degree of power, which frees them to develop their own identities: "Each one, according to her age and her place, hopes to escape the stereotype and be free to inquire into who she is, without being obligated to do what others expect her to do."[4] In Feiguele's case, the reader realizes (and Feiguele learns as she matures) that what sets her apart is her intelligence, imagination, and ability to manipulate language. When her peers mock and trick her, she learns that the only possible relationships are based on her dominating by means of her wits. Feiguele refines these weapons (reminiscent of Steimberg's protagonist Alicia) to protect the very qualities that make her different and defy the narrow constraints that gender imposes on women in her society. Absatz also cultivates in her work strong images of women who empower themselves by choosing to be alone instead of becoming dependent on a man, a lesson that Feiguele learns early, for she is disappointed by men. These lessons, which shape the characters early in life, are woven into the complex tapestry of human relations portrayed in the volume's short stories.

The six short stories, though not as fully developed as the novella *Feiguele*, are vignettes about women. They can be read as one story, because we feel Absatz's unifying presence behind each protagonist. "La siesta" (The siesta) can stand alone or as the novella's epilogue, for it is still Feiguele's story. Dealing with Feiguele's first amorous experience, it is also a transition between the novella and the remaining five short stories. The focus on her awakening sexuality establishes a transition between the novella's childlike character and the young women whose sexuality and eroticism are central to the stories. One such woman is the protagonist of "La teta" (The breast), who has managed to break into the male professional world by becoming a successful executive, only to be destroyed by her lack of self-esteem. Her crisis, symbolized by the worms that she imagines are taking over her life, including her sexual life, cause her to seek refuge in the comforting presence of her mother. "El aborto" (The abortion), "Un poco de paz" (A bit of peace), and "Un ballet de bailarinas" (A ballet for ballerinas) deal with the issue of women and sexual relations in an attempt to rebel against stereotypes in a Latin male-dominated society. "El aborto" shows the high price women pay for independence and equality in sexual practices. As the story opens, the protagonist has just had an abortion. Although it is explicit in the title, it is not directly mentioned in the text, as if emphasizing the character's attempt to push it out of her mind.

The description of the lonely park she crosses creates an appropriate atmosphere to transmit her stifled feelings of disgust. In her mind, scenes from her present predicament blend with the past as she enters a bookstore, maybe the same one where she met the man who got her pregnant. The rest of the story narrates in a matter-of-fact tone the casual encounter and the lovemaking in a hotel room. The protagonist's present feelings are constrained, as are her reminiscences. That is, they are not explicit. The hotel room (like the park) conveys her feelings of indifference and boredom: while making love, she concentrates on the room's dampness and cobwebs. Used to subvert Latin machismo, this device takes away from the male the ability to seduce and sexually dominate women. By trivializing the stereotypical seduction scene depicted from the protagonist's perspective, Absatz strips it of romantic connotations. H. Ernest Lewald has aptly defined these unconventional aspects of Absatz's characters and situations:

> Las protagonistas femeninas de Cecilia Absatz encaran las relaciones humanas con un completo abandono del tradicional código moral latino, y tratan el sexo con una casual indiferencia que bien podría pertenecer al ambiente de los bares de solteros de Nueva York o Londres. En su prosa encontramos una irónica despreocupación que permite a sus personajes femeninos examinar, condenar o ridiculizar la condición masculina. Cecilia Absatz ha logrado sobre todo describir una nueva moralidad basada en la necesidad de sobreponerse a la alienación y la hostilidad en el mundo de la porteña moderna.

> (Cecilia Absatz's female protagonists face human relations with a complete abandonment of the traditional Latino moral code, and deal with sex with a casual indifference that could belong to the atmosphere of singles bars in New York or London. In her prose we find an ironic lack of preoccupation, which allows her female characters to examine, condemn, or ridicule the male condition. Cecilia Absatz has especially achieved the description of a new morality based on the need to overcome the alienation and hostility in the world of the modern female Buenos Aires dweller.)[5]

"El aborto" ends as the lovers reach what for the woman is a mechanical and nauseating climax. Nausea gives the story a circular structure, as it links this scene from the past with its present consequences. Even though Absatz uses a matter-of-fact tone in her narrative, her stories touch contemporary readers. The contrast between the narration and the subject matter allows the reader to feel the loneliness experienced by her contemporary female characters living by Lewald's "new morality." The indifference of the tone expresses alienation in the hostile urban sites—street, car, and hotel—as backdrop for the stories of people who have severed ties with family and home, and have only fleeting relationships. "Un poco de paz" also opens and closes on a street. The main part of the story takes place in a car, where total strangers are thrown together in an unsettling experience. The story begins as the central character battles the Buenos Aires traffic after walking out on an abusive husband. She accepts a ride from a passerby who turns out to be a psychopath. He insists that she looks just like his dead wife and abducts her so that they can get married and recreate his former life. The story closes as the protagonist barely manages to jump out of the car at a traffic light. The point of the story, illustrated by her relationship with her husband and the episode in the car, is the victimization of women by males and the institution of marriage. That the protagonist reminds the psychopath of his dead wife emphasizes the way women lose identity in marriage and become the stereotypical wife. The story also presents women's physical victimization, for the protagonist's husband beats her. It is probable that the stranger killed his wife, and he intends to abuse and kill the protagonist as well. In this context, marriage becomes self-destructive for women. "A bit of peace" is what the protagonist seeks in struggling to flee victimizing relationships.

The last story, "Lisa," underscores the volume's central theme: the subversion of taboos that subjugate women, freeing them to become whatever they want. An economically independent married woman who works at a news agency suspects that her husband is cheating on her when he goes away, supposedly on an assignment. So, she becomes a highly paid prostitute for that weekend. The experience is related objectively by the narrator without any trace of moral judgment. On Monday morning when she tells a coworker about the weekend, she radiates a sense of innocence and joy, certain that she has returned to her old role of traditional wife. For once, we see a woman protagonist having sexual encounters without becoming emotionally involved. She not only profits from them, but is in absolute control. We can share the protagonist's sense of fulfillment in gaining sexual freedom and equality.

"Las flores rojas de los semáforos"

"Las flores rojas de los semáforos" (The red flowers of the traffic lights) and "El descubrimiento de Barracas" (The discovery of Barracas) were published separately, but provide continuity to the situations and characters portrayed in the collected stories. Cecilia Absatz considers "Las flores rojas de los semáforos" her best short story:

> Este cuento fue escrito en 1977 y abandonado hasta 1983, cuando lo encontré herrumbrado en una carpeta. Sé que es uno de mis favoritos porque no me siento avergonzada cuando lo vuelvo a leer. Cosa que me sucede a menudo con otros textos.

> (This story was written in 1977 and abandoned until 1983, when I found it yellowing in a folder. I know it's one of my favorite short stories because I don't feel ashamed when I read it again, which is something that often happens to me with other texts.)[6]

The brief story depicts an evening in the life of a typical Absatz protagonist. An independent and liberated young urban woman has had an exhausting day in Buenos Aires traffic trying unsuccessfully to track down a cabalist who prophesied an important encounter that never materialized. The woman cruises Buenos Aires, oblivious to everything but her false hope of attaining inner peace through her guru and his prediction. Her state of mind is described:

> Hay días en que me siento así, como un testigo estrábico de la vida. Días en que todo el tiempo parece estar pasando algo, algo que me concierne, pero cinco minutos antes o diez metros más allá. Días en que la cólera de no estar en el lugar correcto me enceguece, y me impide ver cuál es el lugar correcto.

> (There are days I feel like this, as a squinting witness of life. Days when something seems to be going on all the time, something that concerns me, but five minutes before or ten meters away. Days when rage blinds me for not being at the right place, and prevents me from seeing the right place.)[7]

At the end of the day, the "right place" seems to be in bed with another cabalist she meets by chance, a handsome French poet whom she finds irresistible. She spends the night with him, and thus the original prophecy unexpectedly comes true.

"El descubrimiento de Barracas"

A similar frantic mood, atmosphere, and protagonist appear in the story, "El descubrimiento de Barracas." According to Absatz the story was conceived "para investigar cuál puede ser la mitología erótica femenina, si es que hay alguna: 'no sé si lo logré' —dice—, 'pero al menos me eroticé escribiéndolo'" (to investigate what the female erotic mythology might be, if there is one: "I don't know if I achieved it"—she says—"but at least writing it was an erotic experience").[8] The story is divided into two parts. The first narrates the female protagonist's attempts to pick up several men, and gives a description of her lovemaking with one of them, followed by an erotic fantasy. It is complemented by a section titled "Balance del ejercicio" (Balance of the exercise), featuring the writer's confession that she had to drink and take amphetamines to write the previous section. The second part of the story is a monologue delivered to an unavailable man the protagonist desires. According to critic Francisco Herrera, this short story is an example of the new writing by Argentine women (Griselda Gambaro, Alicia Steimberg, and Tununa Mercado) who, like Absatz in this story, "express a more ample phenomenon: women advancing, whether they are writers or not, in the task of reformulating their sexuality and constituting their own eroticism."[9]

Té con canela

Té con canela (Cinnamon tea), 1982, Absatz's favorite among her novels, is developed from situations in "El descubrimiento de Barracas." Mirta Reyes points out that it is not by chance that the novel came out in 1982, when democracy and freedom started gaining ground in Argentina. The novel is an example on how to assert "the freedom to be female." Reyes says that "the novel is a vital testimonial of a woman's inner world."[10] The emphasis on a female perspective and introspection, asserting a woman's right to freedom, was praised by female critics like Reyes. Nevertheless, it was not appreciated by some male critics, who remarked that readers might find the novel too personal and react negatively to a work based on reflections originating from a state of indifference and an "apparent absence of narrative."[11] The experimental format used to convey the personal exploration (pointed out by the critics) was conceived as a tribute to television, with its characteristic blanks, cuts, and rhythm:

> A mí me gusta pensar que es moderna. Pero ese modernismo fue muy criticado. Por un lado, respetaba el flujo de pensamiento femenino, y muchos lo consideraron una falla de estructura, dijeron que no era una novela. Por otro lado, lo hice como un homenaje a la televisión. Me gusta mucho mirar televisión y aprecio enormemente la forma cómo las series norteamericanas cuentan historias. Yo observé

los tiempos, cómo llevan la narración de modo que lo único que cuentan es lo esencial. Y la novela, con sus cortes, responde a ese ritmo narrativo.

(I like to think of it as modern. But that modernism was highly criticized. On the one hand, it respected the flux of the female thought process, but many considered that a structural flaw. They said it was not a novel. On the other hand, I did it as a tribute to television. I like to watch television very much and I enormously appreciate the format used by American series to narrate stories. I observed their use of timing, how it leads the narrative so that only the essential is told. And the novel, with its cuts, reflects this narrative rhythm.) [12]

Absatz made explicit her intention to tell the story of a woman's quest for identity by using the flux of the female thought process: "ver cómo una puede reconciliarse con su condición de mujer, empezando por su manera de ver el mundo desde su condición de mujer" (to examine how we come to terms with our female condition, starting with how we perceive the world from our female perspective.)[13] Sandra Gilbert and Susan Gubar have pointed out that the fiction of women typically contains under a surface plot "a woman's search for her self-definition."[14] Elaine Showalter writes that the main theme in women's literature since the 1920s has been "self-discovery" and a "search for identity."[15] For Sharon Keefe Ugalde, this type of fiction poses particular issues:

> [T]he question that arises is what are some of the emerging character-istics of female essence or experience? A tentative list might include the following aspects: plurality, multiplicity and ambiguity; bonds with the mysterious depths of the irrational and the subconscious; knowledge of female eroticism; the presence of active, energetic fe-male figures; and synthesis of opposition.[16]

Absatz's novel incorporates these aspects in a feminist framework. She adapts the traditional bildungsroman as the structure for the story of the protagonist's quest to make sense of her life and present identity. Revising the bildungsroman genre is in itself an act of defiance, for women were traditionally excluded from a genre conceived to express the male experience of development. Women writers have reclaimed this obsolete genre and use it in unorthodox ways to signify their marginality in relation to traditional patriarchal structures. As these feminist fictional works revise the traditional bildungsroman, we are presented heroines who shun integration with a social order in favor of integration with a female inner self.[17] Because their search means rebelling against society's rules and expectations for women, female characters experience an inner split in this journey fraught with anguish and solitude:

> Repeatedly, the female protagonist . . . must chart a treacherous course between the penalties of expressing sexuality and suppressing it, between the costs of inner concentration and of direct confrontation with society, between the price of succumbing to madness and grasping a repressive "normality."[18]

The traditional male hero searches for his identity in the public domain, but, in women's fiction, the female protagonist disassociates from society, choosing confinement in "a room of her own." *Té con canela* is an example of this type of fiction. As the novel opens, the protagonist is confined to her flat on a three-day holiday weekend, nursing a hangover and reconsidering her life. She lies in bed and the following runs through her head:

> [M]irando esta estúpida lluvia de domingo que ni siquiera sabe caer para abajo, preguntándome qué va a ser de mi vida. Considerando una vez más la tremenda posibilidad de que todo haya sido en vano.
>
> ([W]atching this stupid Sunday rain, which does not even know how to come down straight, wondering what might become of my life. Pondering one more time the terrible possibility that everything might have been in vain.)[19]

The image of confinement and alienation is also signified by the format of the novel: the personal diary. Writing a diary implies a private activity kept secret from a prying and censoring external gaze. It is confinement within oneself, a fitting image for the Argentine writer in the eighties. The personal diary written by the protagonist on her bed, within the confinement of her bedroom, signifies women's inner exile during the Proceso. The structure of this diary deviates from the traditional diary chronologically organized; only the first and last sections have dates as headings—respectively, 24 May and 25 May. Significantly, it is the Argentine Independence holiday. This has contradictory connotations: Independence evokes the liberating function of the diary, but signifies male achievements and official commemorations, symbolizing the protagonist's constraints in that particular historical moment. That she confines herself indoors, refusing to take part in the celebrations, signifies her rebellion, which, in these times, can only take place behind closed doors and within the pages of her diary. Instead of chronological entries, headings refer to events, names, and nicknames of importance in the protagonist's recent life. These are flashbacks, placed in a purely subjective and mnemonic order, reflecting women's experiential mode rather than the traditional male-centered chronology. They contrast with the chronological frame enclosing them, symbolizing the rigid social structures that have always constrained women and devalued their experiences.

By piecing together the dispersed elements of the story, we learn that the protagonist is a thirty-three-year-old divorcée who left her family home when she was eighteen to assert her independence. She is also a professional woman, a public relations executive facing a midlife crisis after a divorce and several unfulfilling affairs. Her present despair is not explicitly explained until the novel and her self-analysis reach a close, coinciding with the moment when she becomes conscious of how much she has been affected by a recent occurrence. She has been slighted by the man she loves, who, ironically, has had sexual relations with every woman who crossed his path, except her. And that, she thinks, is what gives her power over him. When she goes to his place intending to seduce him, he tells her to leave, as he is busy playing poker with his buddies. She learns that she had deluded herself into thinking that she had the power to control relationships. As a result, the unexpected humiliation triggers her seclusion and introspection tinted by self-pity and shame. The use of a male character with whom the protagonist is romantically involved as the catalyst for her introspection shows that Absatz wants to transform women's romantic delusions, sanctioned by our society, into empowering experiences transmuted by lucidity:

> Domingo eterno de ayuno y silencio y Ella es presa de la dolorosa lucidez que da el sufrimiento. Pero por ahora su única lucidez es la de estar consciente del hecho de tenerse lástima. ¡Vamos! ¿Dónde está la Condesa? La Condesa se hace esperar.

> (Eternal Sunday of fast and silence and She is seized by the aching lucidity that suffering renders. But for the time being her only lucidity is to be conscious of the fact that she feels self-pity. Come on now! Where is the Countess? The Countess makes us wait for her.) (108)

The Countess is one of the disguises adopted by the protagonist as she examines her past. Because she does not have the guts to face it directly, she distances herself by assuming various roles that represent different parts of her. But that the Countess keeps us waiting reveals a self-assured and poised aspect of the protagonist's personality:

¿Quién es Ella? ¿Lili Marlene? ¿Petra von Kant? ¿Victoria Ocampo? ¿Zully Moreno? El secreto está en su diario, abierto bajo su mano. El apagado murmullo de la lluvia termina por reemplazar todo otro sonido en el interior de su mente. Ella se duerme, suavemente. La mano que todavía retiene la lapicera entre sus dedos, cae a un costado. Las hojas del diario, libres ahora de la presión, comienzan a volverse con ritmo impar. No se percibe ninguna brisa: sólo puede impulsarlas la inercia previsible de la memoria.

(Who is She? Lili Marlene? Petra von Kant? Victoria Ocampo? Zully Moreno? The secret is in her diary, open under her hand. The stifled murmur of the rain ends up replacing any other sound inside her mind. She falls asleep, gently. The hand that still retains the pen between its fingers, falls to one side. The diary's pages, free now from the pressure, start turning following an uneven rhythm. No breeze can be perceived: they can only be propelled by memory's foreseeable inertia.) (22–23)

By using disguises the protagonist can confront repressed issues not fully understood when they took place. She focuses mainly on a series of sexual and highly erotically charged episodes, which established the protagonist as a sexually liberated woman. These include fleeting affairs with strangers, reminiscent of those featured in Absatz's short stories, and potential lesbian relations that were never fully pursued. Absatz's depiction of a protagonist attracted by other women suggests androgyny, the merging of sexual traits to transcend gender limitations.

Yo era el hombre que la amaba, sí, pero también fui una mujer, y cuando una mujer quiere que le hagan el amor no espera que le pidan permiso, no quiere preámbulos ni explicaciones.

(I was the man who loved her, yes, but I have also been a woman and when a woman wants somebody to make love to her she does not expect to be asked for permission, she does not want preambles or explanations.) (71)

These possibilities suggest new roles for women, who have attained the freedom that until recently had been a male prerogative. They also present a new morality and an independence from social rules that used to regulate women's behavior concerning their sexuality.

Té con canela closes with her being rejected by the man she loves, giving the work a circularity symbolizing an unending quest. The circular pattern alludes to the female psyche and is an image of her soul-searching, which can only take place in confined material and mental enclosures, within the pages of her diary. The weekend has been a learning process for the character, who has gained invaluable self-analytical tools and a deeper understanding of a female-centered experience of the world: "De pronto el mundo era un lugar diferente, y ahora yo tenía mucho interés en averiguar quién era la dama del vestido plateado, qué hacía cuando hacía lo que le daba la real gana" (Suddenly the world was a different place, and now I was very interested in finding out who the lady in the silver dress was, what she did when she did whatever she felt like) (98). What she learns about the lady in the silver dress (another facet of herself) is that sexual freedom is not equivalent to personal freedom. She also discovers that her so-called independence was based on deception, because self-legitimization does not come from an outside source, but from within herself:

> Quince años de mi vida creyéndome tan viva para rebelarme contra todo lo que me obligaban hacer, y luego otros quince años creyéndome tan viva por hacer todo aquello que me prohibían. Pero siempre cumpliendo órdenes, del revés o del derecho, siempre bajo control, y para peor, creyéndome tan viva.

> (Fifteen years of my life thinking I was so clever rebelling against everything that they made me do, and then another fifteen years thinking I was so clever doing everything that they forbade me. But always carrying out orders, one way or the other, always under control, and to top it off, thinking I was so clever.) (97)

Her growth teaches her humility, as she becomes conscious and accepting of her limitations: "Me creo que todas las cosas del mundo me están permitidas y compruebo, presa del pánico, que en efecto me están permitidas, si las puedo tolerar" (I believe everything in the world is permissible for me and I confirm, panic-stricken, that, in effect, everything is permissible for me, if I can tolerate it) (72).

The novel is an original achievement in terms of its technical format, which conveys the specificity of the female experience. By using a feminist version of a traditional genre, the bildungsroman, and a structure and temporal flux suited to the female psyche, Absatz expresses the multiplicity and plurality characteristic of women's experience. In addition, she successfully portrays the process experienced by women as they develop their identity, as opposed to the traditional male depiction of women as recipients of an identity shaped a priori. Female confinement is used to underscore women's inner exile in an ideologically constraining society and to represent an inner journey to recover their fragmented selves. As we finish reading the novel, we realize that to change patriarchy women need to understand and love the woman within.

Los años pares

After *Té con canela* was misunderstood by the critics, Absatz decided to write an orthodox novel. The result was *Los años pares* (The even years), 1985, which was well-received by both the critics and the reading public. This novel is divided into four sections: "1980," "1976," "1978," and "1980" again. The novel opens in 1980 when the protagonist, Clara Auslender, is at a police station in Buenos Aires unsuccessfully trying to renew her identity card. Her difficulty in renewing a document establishing her official identity suggests that her true identity is at issue. She runs into a problem because of a report from Jujuy, dated 1976, made while she was in the custody of the local police. The report says that she lied by saying she was single, when in reality she was divorced. There is a simple explanation: She obtained her papers before her marriage and never bothered to change the information about her status. But once she started lying, she had to keep it up during successive interrogations. She did this at great personal risk. To lie about her marital status meant that she could be lying about the reason she and her companion, a Dutch painter, were traveling. The police, suspicious that the couple were guerrillas, would think they were right. Thus, the couple ran the risk of becoming "dirty war" casualties.

In 1980 Clara is an executive of a magazine financed by American capital. But in 1976, her situation was similar to that of *Té con canela*'s protagonist. Her husband, Teo, had left her for another woman, who earned her livelihood by replacing Clara in their puppet-making venture. The protagonist was barely making a living when she met Eric, a striking Dutch artist who was passing through. He invited her on a trip to the northern Argentine provinces, Bolivia, and Peru. Upon reaching Jujuy, they were interrogated by police, who were looking for guerrillas. Clara never understood why they were suddenly set free, in spite of her obvious lie, and in 1980 the idea still haunts her.

On the surface, Absatz sets up an intrigue, blending many elements of a detective novel. At a deeper level, however, there is a much more fascinating psychological and introspective intrigue. The motif of the outsider who proposes a journey (an escape from the "enclosed room") to a female protagonist is a recurrent one in contemporary Argentine novels by women writers. The outsider and the journey function as catalysts for the protagonist to question her past life at a time of upheaval and turmoil, and to open new perspectives.[20] Throughout the novel, we encounter several levels of conflict and resolution reflecting Clara's efforts to come to terms with herself. Just before the characters meet, a fortune teller suggests that Clara study English, as she will be traveling. This turns out to be useful advice, for Clara needs English to communicate with Eric. The next scene, a nurturing female world, contrasts with the intimidating police station. The fortune teller connotes female spirituality and a visionary and unconscious knowledge. When Clara meets Eric, she allows herself to be swept off her feet by romance. After her abandonment by Teo, she is afraid of losing Eric, as can be seen in the subservient position she assumes in their relationship:

> [E]l es un ángel, se decía, viene y va. Es mejor toparse con un ángel un ratito, se decía, que no haberlo encontrado nunca.

> ([H]e's an angel, she would tell herself, he comes and goes. It is better to run into an angel for a little while, she would tell herself, than not having met him ever.) (49)

> Eric era tan bello . . . siempre caminaba un poco detrás de él y veía el efecto radiante que su paso producía.

> (Eric was so beautiful . . . she always walked a short distance behind him and saw the radiant effect that he would make in passing.) (62)

The motif of the outsider serves a dual purpose. At first, he serves to present Clara's alienation from her real self, but then he evolves to trigger her understanding of her real self and the surrounding world. Gradually Eric becomes an agent of change for the protagonist by virtue of boons he offers her. He gives her two portraits of herself, which make her realize that she has lost her identity in their relationship: "El alma de Clara emigró de ella y ahora tambaleaba en la punta de un lápiz. Ella ahora es de él y no puede hacer más que mirar desde afuera" (Clara's soul migrated from her and was wobbling now on the tip of a pencil. She belongs to him now and may only look from the outside) (52); "el rebote permanente de la mirada del otro, los otros, lo otro, contra el límite de la piel, volviéndola una cosa" (the permanent bouncing of the other's gaze, the others, the other, against the boundary of the skin, turning her into a thing) (56). His gaze has turned her into an object, and the portraits have captured Clara's estrangement from herself and made Clara aware of it. Although at this point she does not have the knowledge to mend the broken link with her real self, or to face the relationship in a more positive way, she is about to undertake a journey that will lead her to freedom. The journey, another offering from Eric, establishes his role as agent of change in Clara's maturation. Absatz portrays this process by means of an ongoing dialogue between the couple during the journey. As Clara and Eric discuss their cultural differences (Eric is Dutch; Clara is Argentine) and the way their cultures make them perceive reality, Clara's narrow assumptions about the world change. Absatz uses a female approach to reality, a dialogue, and an interpersonal and cross-cultural relationship as a framework for the protagonist's questioning. Clara also confronts her own European and Spanish-American identity when she faces the indigenous elements of South America on her journey and feels as alien to her surroundings as her European companion:

> Ella podía estar diciendo algo tan simple como Buen día, o Cómo se llama este pueblo. Entonces la miraban con una desconfianza amasada durante quinientos años y en el mejor de los casos le contestaban con señas.

> (She could be saying something as simple as Good Morning or What's the name of this town. Then they would look at her with a distrust kneaded during five hundred years and, in the best of cases, would answer with gestures.) (126)

This conflict also reflects the struggle within Clara Auslender ("foreigner" in German), a Jewess of Polish descent born and raised in Argentina, who has always felt caught between two cultures. Clara is constantly required to exert herself to the limit during a journey in which she is deprived of comfort, and must eat frugally, sleep in cold, cheap lodgings, and trek through inhospitable territory. The physical constraints force her to see herself in a different light, and she realizes that she is not as independent or as totally in control as she thought.

There is still another boon: Eric takes Clara to a boxing match at the Luna Park, and Clara feels that she is crossing into an unknown territory; "al atravesar las puertas del Luna Park, Clara creyó entrar en otro país" (when they crossed the Luna Park's doors, Clara thought she was entering another country) (57). She experienced the same feelings of crossing over a threshold when she first met Eric at a party and offered him a piece of cake:

> Ella había creído que el viaje por el extranjero comenzó con ese pedacito de torta, pero ahora había cruzado otra clase de frontera. Se encontraba en el seno del espacio extraterrestre. Sin previo aviso y de una reverenda patada.

> (She had believed that the trip abroad started with that small piece of cake, but now she had crossed another kind of border. She found herself in the bosom of extraterrestrial space. Without any previous notice and by means of a tremendous kick.) (72)

The experience at the boxing match triggers her awareness of the country's political situation and wakes her up to violence:

> Podía sentir los juegos del miedo y del poder, la presencia del dinero, el agotamiento y la súplica, la devoción y el ensañamiento, la fuerza de la verdad en una sola gota de sangre brotando de una ceja herida. La sangre estaba allí, a unos metros de ella.

> (She could feel the games of fear and power, the presence of money, the exhaustion and the pleading, the devotion and the cruelty, the force of truth in just one drop of blood spurting out of a wounded eyebrow. The blood was there, a few meters away from her.) (59)

The boxing match imagery foreshadows the violence they encounter during the journey in a country fraught with repression: "Las brigadas militares los detenían con frecuencia: estaban en el centro neurálgico de la guerrilla" (The military brigades stopped them frequently: They were in the nerve center of the guerrilla) (60).

The last two sections of the novel take place in 1978 and 1980, when Clara attains independence. When Eric returns in 1978 to exhibit his paintings in Buenos Aires, he finds Clara established in her career. Conscious that the entrapment of romantic love confines women and their feminist ideals, she feels completely out of love with Eric. She does not want him around and arranges for him to stay somewhere else. She avoids him and refuses to attend parties in his honor. Only when she hears that he is exhibiting paintings of her does she consent to attend. Although the two paintings from before the trip showed Clara as alienated from herself, the portraits of their travels depict her as a strong woman, occupying the center of the canvas and illuminated by a strong natural light, signifying her self-confidence and independence from Eric's luminosity: "una mujer magnífica de pecho amplio y piernas gruesas, sentada sobre sí misma, tomando mate" (a magnificent woman with an ample chest and thick legs, squatting, drinking mate) (128). Clara's independence is made explicit by the exhibit and by the realization that her previous romantic dependence on Eric has turned into utter hatred and contempt for him (a reversal of the Sleeping Beauty myth). At the time she does not quite understand why she feels this way. In 1980, as the novel closes, she learns why.

It is Christmas Eve 1980. A drunk Clara attends a party with Eric, who is back for another exhibit. Clara gets terribly sick and returns home by herself to throw up the food she ate at the party, which is described as the same as what she had eaten four years ago on the trip. The scene symbolizes her repugnance over what transpired between her and Eric over the past four years, vividly expressed in the ritual of assimilation and expulsion inscribed in her body:

> Vomitó un fricassé de cerdo condimentado con rencor y locotos cuatro años atrás. Defecó una explosión, roca y almíbar negro. Menstruó un único coágulo, del tamaño de una granada. Transpiró y lloró su propio villancico de nochebuena.

> (She threw up a pig stew spiced with animosity and hot peppers four years ago. She defecated an explosion, rock and black syrup. She menstruated only a coagulum, the size of a grenade. She perspired and wept her own Christmas Eve carol.) (160)

The elimination of body fluids symbolizes her feelings of abjection unleashed as a culmination of a process put in motion by her relationship with Eric. It also signifies the expulsion of her old, subjugated self and the birth of a new, conscious self. The idea of rebirth is underscored, as the scene takes place on Christmas Eve. The exaggerated description evokes a birth followed by a contented aftermath: "Clara estaba viva. El sudor se hizo rocío y la refrescaba. Se durmió en el mundo, pronto amanecería" (Clara was alive. The perspiration became dew and refreshed her. She fell asleep in the world, it would soon be dawn) (160). Her transformation and rebirth are expressed linguistically as negative images, implying effort and darkness are transmuted into a dew-covered dawn ushering in Christmas Day.

The next day, Christmas, she thoroughly cleans the flat, throwing out everything that reminds her of her former husband and Eric. While she works, she starts piecing together the incident at the Jujuy police station. As she cleans the kitchen windows, she sees her reflection and suddenly understands the reason for their fast release. She realizes that Eric betrayed her to the police in exchange for their release, an action that explains her disgust for Eric for what she considers inexcusable deceit and cowardice. The actions of cleaning up and perceiving are symbolically linked in this scene to reflect the character's new understanding. Thus, the mystery that opened the novel is solved by Clara's attainment of knowledge, and she has shed the trappings of romantic fantasies, which characterized her past amorous entanglements. Symbolizing her inner transformation by means of a female activity, cleaning house, is an explicit choice by Absatz, who treats elements of women's daily life as literary devices.[21] Cleaning house, which usually means subjugation and domesticity, is given a new meaning; she transforms it into a liberating one for her protagonist. The literary treatment of female physiology and domestic chores (symbolizing women's coming of age) relate these scenes to the prophetic scene with the fortune teller in 1976 at the chronological beginning of the story. Clara has come full circle and a symbolic transfer of the fortune teller's vision and knowledge to her is achieved. Clara has become whole as a result of her journey.

At the end of the novel, Clara is alone on Christmas Day. She does not have a family or a man. The magazine she worked for is folding, so she has lost her job. Although her relationship with Teo had left her with just an empty workshop where they used to make puppets, Eric and the journey have left her with new ways of perceiving the world and herself. Their travels have opened the way for her to undertake an inner journey that has set her free from dependence. We have witnessed her development into a self-sufficient and independent being, fully knowledgeable and accepting of her heritage and identity:

> Se siente fuerte y liviana. Baja por la escalerita de metal y vuelve a su terraza. Cuando termina de ducharse, el living de su casa la recibe con un abrazo tibio. Las cortinas la protegen de la luz de Navidad que pretende avasallar su ventanal, ahora que está tan limpio.

> (She feels strong and light. She climbs down the small metal ladder and returns to her terrace. When she finishes taking a shower, her flat's front room greets her with a cool embrace. The curtains protect her from the Christmas [sun]light, which tries to take over her large windows, now that they are so clean.) (175–76)

Throughout the novel the dirty windows impaired her vision. Now they are clean, indicating that Clara has recovered her powers of perception. The character's state of mind, her inner peace, and strength show her development. Clara does not have to resort to crutches. Even though to an outsider her situation has not changed much, Clara has proven that she has the courage to assume her own identity and place in life.

Absatz's three books trace a female tale of development from adolescence to maturity, obviously reflecting her own search for identity. This gives the characters' quests an air of authenticity. At the same time they are couched in ironic language and vision. Absatz has learned to laugh at herself, to adopt a playful attitude even with extremely sensitive and profound issues. Each of her works aids us in our own experience of self-discovery and the uncovering of a female world in a voyage marked by patterns of submission, rebellion, and search. The protagonists strive to transcend the limits of their confinement by journeying through territories marked by male codes, which they question and subvert. Absatz uses the male character who entraps her protagonists in submissive, romantic relationships as a device leading to their rebirth; they open up to external reality and their true selves. Her stories chart journeys of self-recognition for her female protagonists, which enable them to transcend the territory where patriarchy has confined them.

CONVERSATION WITH CECILIA ABSATZ

Buenos Aires, 25 May and 2 June 1987

M.F.: When and how did you begin to write?

C.A.: Writing is my natural mode of expression. I've always written. As a child I kept a diary. My former husband was instrumental in making that private writing become one with literary ambitions. When I was twenty-two years old and married, I started writing a story as a personal quest. Instead of undergoing psychoanalysis, I worked on that story, which became *Feiguele*. I wrote it over and over again, exactly fourteen times. As soon as I would finish writing it, I'd read it, but I was never satisfied from a literary point of view. After rewriting it thirteen times, I realized, as if by magic, what was not working. Then I wrote it in a flash, and because I felt good about it, considered that my final version. My husband suggested I take it to [Daniel] Divinsky, the publisher at De La Flor, a possibility that had never occurred to me. I took it down and Divinsky said that it was very good, that he was interested in publishing it. However, he added, because it was so good it was worth revising. I thought that was an elegant way of turning down my work. I continued working on it, but never took it back. A year later several work acquaintances said that Divinsky had mentioned he was expecting my stories. At that point, I quickly finished it up and submitted the manuscript, and it was accepted. That was how I started getting my work published.

M.F.: What problems did you run up against during the publication of *Feiguele y otras mujeres*?

C.A.: My first book had a difficult story. After it was accepted in 1974, publication was delayed for two years because of a financial crisis. At that time, Divinsky had a list of 180 books accepted for publication, out of which he was able to publish eighty. Mine didn't make it because I was an unknown writer. I was working in public relations, which is an anonymous type of work. Besides, my last name, as well as the book's title, were difficult to pronounce. So all the odds were against me and I had to wait for two years.

M.F.: How did you come up with the name Feiguele?

C.A.: Feiguele is a common name in Yiddish. It means "little bird."

M.F.: What happened to the book then?

C.A.: It came out on December 31, 1975, and was censored in March 1976. It circulated for two months and in that time sold over five hundred copies. It remained banned for eight years until 1983, when the new government lifted censorship. It was one of the first books to be released.

M.F.: How did censorship affect your literary production?

C.A.: The only thing that happened to me was that my book was censored for immorality (it contained some four-letter words), not for political reasons. It was clear to me that the censorship had to do with the persecution of a publishing company that had leftist leanings. They had prohibited five books, four for political reasons and mine for immorality. I considered it an adversity, not a persecution, and that enabled me to continue writing.

M.F.: Did the censorship of your first book affect your later works written during the years of the Proceso?

C.A.: No. I had heated discussions with a lot of people who took adversity for persecution. Many writers, including some whose works were prohibited at the same time as mine, left the country because they knew that they weren't going to get reviews and publicity in the media for a while. You leave your country if you're afraid of getting killed, but not because you don't get any publicity. Lack of publicity doesn't prevent you from writing at home.

M.F.: Censorship didn't affect your second book, *Té con canela*?

C.A.: I was watching out for possible prohibition for immorality. Besides, I had read Proust, who dealt with very risqué scenes without using any four-letter words. *Té con canela* is a much harsher work than *Feiguele*

from a moral standpoint, but it doesn't contain a single four-letter word.
Everything is achieved through literature.

M.F.: Can you name specific writers who have influenced you?

C.A.: In *Feiguele* there's the very obvious influence of Salinger. After
that, I wrote a novel I never published because I didn't consider it good
enough, called *La trompada del diablo* (The devil's punch), influenced by
Thomas Mann. Proust's influence split my life in two in the sense that
throughout my life I had been accused of being an intellectual and my
work was dismissed because my discourse was pure literature. Then I read
Proust's *Remembrance of Things Past*. In its last volume, *The Past Recap-
tured*, it says on the writing of a novel that true life, life that is finally
elucidated, is literature, and that vindicated me. It was an amnesty with
myself, a reconciliation. Now I'm proud of the fact that my life is pure
literature.

M.F.: Are there any Latin American writers who have influenced you?

C.A.: For me there's one great novel among all those novels of the
boom, and it's *Cambio de piel (Change of Skin)* by Carlos Fuentes. Other
than that, I see novels based mostly on research data that present only a
smattering of literature, like in [Fuentes's] *Terra Nostra* or [Vargas Llosa's]
La guerra del fin del mundo (The War of the End of the World), but that
doesn't interest me. What interests me is literature. The worst thing that
can happen to a writer or a literary generation is to be successful. When I
see that all published books are systematically around six hundred pages
long, I feel distrust because I can see business looming behind it.

M.F.: Do you feel affinity with Argentine writers?

C.A.: Among Argentine writers my favorites have published no more
than two [or three] books each. I admire Rodolfo Fogwill and his novels
Mis muertos punk (My punk dead), *Pájaros en la cabeza* (Birds in the
head), and *Música japonesa* (Japanese music). Eduardo Belgrano Rawson,
a favorite of mine, wrote two short books, *No se turbe vuestro corazón* (Do
not perturb thy heart) and *El náufrago de las estrellas* (The shipwrecked of
the stars), and leaves his life in each one of them. Everybody said Ricardo
Piglia's *Respiración artificial* (Artificial breathing) wasn't a novel but a philosophical essay. I maintained that it was indeed a novel and that if the basis
was a philosophical essay, it didn't matter. I recognize a good novel when
I read one.

M.F.: Do you belong to a specific literary generation in Argentina?

C.A.: I feel affinity, though unrelated to literary or temporal issues,
with marginal writers like Reina Roffé, Rodolfo Fogwill, and Eduardo
Belgrano Rawson. We are not connected to the official literary establishment. I don't attend congresses or seminars, nor do I seek prizes or grants

M.F.: Do you consider yourself belonging to a generation of Jewish-Argentine writers like Alicia Steimberg?

C.A.: I feel affinity with Alicia Steimberg, but not because of the Jewish-Argentine theme. The use of humor links us. Both of us inject humor into our writing. One of my favorite novels is Alicia Steimberg's *Músicos y relojeros* (Musicians and watchmakers).

M.F.: Are there definite stages in your work?

C.A.: Some people consider *Feiguele* my best work, but others disagree because it was my first book. Personally, I discovered in my critical reading of *Feiguele* that, in this first stage, I couldn't look beyond myself, that the only character with literary consistency was the protagonist and the rest functioned as her background. That was my deficiency, a rather blown-up pride that hindered me from becoming a good writer. A friend who's a brilliant writer, Rodolfo Fogwill, told me to write literature using that pride to make fun of myself. The result was *Té con canela*, which is my favorite work. In it there's myself and "She," a totally unassailable and ridiculous character. My intention with this novel was to create a modern dramatic structure for literature. That's why I structured it very carefully. It's a tribute to television. None of the critics understood that, though. Although the reviews were very favorable, the reviewers questioned whether the book was a novel. I thought maybe I had been too hasty in writing a modern work before showing that I could write a traditional novel. Therefore, I began writing a linear novel, the kind of work that wouldn't leave a trace of doubt in anybody's mind that it was a novel. And the result was *Los años pares*. That's why its success didn't surprise me. It was an exercise and the critics adored it. Now I can write whatever I want to.

M.F.: Can you comment on this new stage where you can write what you feel like writing?

C.A.: I'm working on the theme of women's anger, which is present at the end of *Los años pares*. In general, women are depicted in love or in pain, but nobody writes about their anger. And, in what concerns me, I am angry. I think that the only way to approach this current work is to channel my anger.

M.F.: Is it going to be a novel?

C.A.: I don't have the slightest idea, because what I've written up to now, approximately forty pages, contains a degree of violence that frightens me and, because of that, I've set it aside for the time being.

M.F.: Why does it have such an effect on you?

C.A.: What frightens me, and the reason I stopped writing, is that the text shows a certain outlook on life and the world that could hurt several people close to me.

M.F.: Is it very autobiographical?

C.A.: It's not that, it's the worldview that might make it a literary work of great interest. But I have to continue living and to publish this text would mean social suicide for me.

M.F.: How did you go about writing it?

C.A.: I started writing viscerally, without worrying about literary form, but what came out was so strong it made me feverish. So, I stopped for a while and now I'm writing again.

M.F.: What does writing mean for you?

C.A.: Writing is my salvation. I'm a marginal being and I don't belong to any type of structure, so when I feel the world collapsing around me, the only thing that can save me is to sit down and write. When I stopped writing for four years (between *Feiguele* and *Té con canela*), I realized that the secret was not to think about publishing. If I set out to publish, either I'm unable to write or I lie. I have such a sense of responsibility toward myself and literature that I'm not going to lie. Therefore, the solution I found, which satisfies me very much, is that I'm going to write and not think about publishing.

M.F.: What is the main theme of *Té con canela*?

C.A.: I believe it's our inability to love or difficulty with love. The protagonist suffers because the guy she loves doesn't pay any attention to her, and she starts to understand what love is all about in her relationship with the young girl.

M.F.: According to the reviewers this is a lesbian relationship. Was that your intention?

C.A.: No, it wasn't. Charo, the young girl, wants it to become a lesbian relationship, not for love but to obtain power. The protagonist doesn't want any part of it. She loves her because she recognizes herself in Charo, who reminds her of herself when she was Charo's age. The relationship is not lesbian; it's described ambiguously because it is ambiguous. Somebody said that this novel is an inquiry about all the possible forms in which women can relate to one another, only one of which is lesbianism. When the novel came out everybody assumed that the relationship was lesbian and that I was also lesbian. For a long time that hurt me because of my loved ones. Now, I don't mind anymore. It's almost attractive because it makes it even more impossible to classify me with any certainty.

M.F.: Who is *Té con canela*'s protagonist, whom we encounter as the narrator, "She," Marlene Dietrich, and the Countess?

C.A.: I like this protagonist. She's an adult Feiguele and, in her anger, she's me. I don't worry anymore about the fact that I can't transcend my own self. If I were able to dig deeply within myself, I wouldn't imitate my own inner world because it's limited, not because I'm unable to explore beyond myself, but due to the fact that I don't dare probe the depths.

M.F.: And that's what the protagonist is up against?

C.A.: Exactly.

M.F.: Your protagonist, who spends a weekend confined in her apartment with a hangover, reminisces about fairly recent events. Why doesn't she have a past?

C.A.: The truth is that I didn't have the guts. When I wrote this novel, I had taken up writing after a four-year pause and a lengthy divorce. Besides, I was afraid that my universe was very limited, due to the fact that I had been unable to create a Tolstoyan character. That's why there's no family, and I don't address pain, love, or the past, which are the requirements for a good novel.

M.F.: However, there's a section in the middle of the novel where the protagonist evokes her Polish father and his death. Is there a reason for that?

C.A.: There's a secret story related to a rather magical game that has to do with dates, numbers, attitudes, and the father. But it's secret, in the sense that it was an almost cabalistic discovery I made when I finished the novel. It started as a diary I was keeping and suddenly, I discovered that I had hit upon a tone, so I set the diary aside and started writing the novel, endowing it with a dramatic structure that I called my "proposal for a modern novel." It begins on May 24 and closes on the following day and is set during a long weekend, characterized by the acute boredom of a working person whose only passion is her work. When I finished the novel, I had to close all the anecdotal clues that I had given directly. So I made a chronogram.

The year is 1981, and there's a clue when a guy named Jorge Salcedo invites the protagonist to celebrate Independence Day because it's a *capicúa*[22] holiday commemorating 171 years of independence. It all started the eve of the 24th, when she got drunk. That's why she's at home nursing a hangover. And the reason she got drunk is that the man she loves kicked her out of his flat when she visited during a poker game. He has seduced every woman he ever met, and her power over him is that she's never slept with him. She knows he loves her and saw him get jealous when she wore an expensive present from Salcedo. That happened a week before when she met Salcedo, on a Friday, and he fell for her because she refused to talk. She played this marvelous and rather erotic game of remaining silent and refusing to talk. I calculated all this after I wrote the novel and realized that May 15, the day when the protagonist played her silent game, was my father's birthday. The relationship with the father was basically one of language and silence. When I discovered that, I shuddered. So when you ask me why the theme of the father appears in the center of the novel, I confess that I don't know why but there is all this secret and protective configuration that encloses it all in an unbelievable fashion.

M.F.: Did the protagonist's game of language and silence reflect your relationship with your father?

C.A.: My relationship with my father was exactly what I described in the novel. My father didn't speak Spanish and I refused to speak Yiddish. My father knew how to speak Spanish. It was all a power game. The tragedy that I narrated in that chapter is that I foolishly participated in that power struggle and lost out on getting to know my father in the process. I spoke Yiddish, I could have talked to him in Yiddish, or I could have been like my sister, who didn't speak Yiddish but played gin rummy with him. I was fifteen years old and I refused to give in. At that age we don't consider the possibility that someone might die. So the scene appeared as my way of understanding too late that I had been foolish enough to miss having a personal relationship with my father.

M.F.: The critics have wondered about the hybrid structure of this novel. Can you comment on that?

C.A.: The structure responds to me, to my thought pattern. It's a system of flashes based on memories under the influence of liquor. The structure is sustained by a system where one chapter is "real," and the next one is a mnemonic association triggered by the "real" scene.

M.F.: Why did you choose the title *Té con canela*?

C.A.: I chose the title because I wanted to give it an attractive, feminine name with a good ring to it. It didn't have any other private meaning, but later on I found out from Marta Lynch that, when she was young, cinnamon tea was given to young girls when they menstruated because it was supposed to be good for them.

M.F.: In *Los años pares* there's a change in your treatment of female characters and male characters became more important. Can you explain this change?

C.A.: Clara, the protagonist of *Los años pares,* is an independent woman, a woman who's by herself. That independence makes her different from the others; she's not defined by her relationship to a man. She's defined by her relationship to herself and to her world. My relations with women are stronger than those with men, and that has allowed me to know them and work with them better in my novels. My male characters are secondary, but in this novel they become more important, a trend that started in my unpublished novel, *La trompada del diablo.*

M.F.: While traveling with this man, the Dutch painter, through South America, the protagonist's quest for a South American identity is expressed by confronting her European lover and the indigenous elements of the journey. Can you explain this?

C.A.: There's a dialogue between America and Europe behind the dialogue between the Argentine protagonist and the Dutchman. It's an ideological discussion between two ways of seeing the world, the South American and the European way.

M.F.: Why do you include the female element through traditional female activities, like when Clara furiously washes her kitchen windows?

C.A.: Cleaning the windows is a metaphor for woman's anger, which in real life can't be expressed directly, but only through actions. It is also related to vision and it's a catharsis after breaking up with her lover.

M.F.: Why do you include it as a final scene after the protagonist has kicked her lover out of her apartment?

C.A.: It's a metaphor for putting your house in order, in this case the inner abode. It's also a means to return to herself and getting rid of the man who provoked her anger.

M.F.: Can you explain the structure of *Los años pares*?

C.A.: In *Té con canela*, a tribute to television, I imitated the structure and rhythm of television. *Los años pares* is a tribute to the detective story. The novel begins in a police station with a procedure for renewing a document. I started with intrigue and used a detective-story style to recall events that took place four years before, to discover the explanation of the intrigue.

BIBLIOGRAPHY

Primary Sources (listed chronologically)

Absatz, Cecilia. *Feiguele y otras mujeres*. Buenos Aires: Ediciones De La Flor, 1976.
———. *Té con canela*. Buenos Aires: Editorial Sudamericana, 1982.
———. *Los años pares*. Buenos Aires: Editorial Legasa, 1985.

Works Available in Translation

Absatz, Cecilia. "A Ballet for Girls." Translated by H. Ernest Lewald. In *The Web: Stories by Argentine Women*, edited by H. Ernest Lewald, 153–61. Washington, D.C.: Three Continents Press, 1983.

Short Fiction by Cecilia Absatz (listed chronologically)

Absatz, Cecilia. "Las flores rojas de los semáforos." *Puro cuento* 17 (July-August, 1989): 42–43.

———. "Rosenberg." In *Rencontres: Encuentros: Ecrivains et artistes de l'Argentine et du Québec,* edited by Gilles Pellerin and Oscar Hermes Villordo, 25–36. Québec: Les Editions Sans Nom, 1989.

———. "El descubrimiento de Barracas." In *Antología del erotismo en la literatura argentina,* edited by Francisco Herrera, 17–24. Buenos Aires: Editorial Fraterna, 1990.

———. "Rosenberg." In *Buenos Aires: una antología de la nueva ficción argentina,* edited by Juan Forn, 145–54. Barcelona: Editorial Anagrama, 1992.

———. "Balance del ejercicio." In *La Venus de Papel,* edited by Mempo Giardinelli and Graciela Gliemmo, 67–73. Buenos Aires: Beas Ediciones, 1993.

Secondary Sources

Castello, Cristina. "Cecilia Absatz: reflexiones literarias con té y canela." *Tiempo Argentino,* 1 December 1982, 3.

"Cecilia Absatz." *Babel* 1 (January 1989): 34–35.

"Cecilia Absatz: una escritora en busca del libro que cuente sólo lo esencial." *La Nación,* 6 April 1986.

"Cecilia Absatz: expresar los deseos resulta peligroso." Review of *Los años pares,* by Cecilia Absatz. *Tiempo Argentino,* 17 April 1986, 5–6.

Checa, Elizabeth. "Cecilia Absatz: entre la necesidad y el narcisismo." *La Opinión,* 4 September 1979.

Dellepiane, Angela B. "El aporte femenino a la narrativa última argentina." In *La escritora hispánica,* edited by Nora Erro-Orthmann and Juan Cruz Mendizábal, 61–71. Miami: Ediciones Universal, 1990.

Fernández Sampecho, Carmen. "Escritoras: Cecilia Absatz y el enojo de las mujeres." *Tiempo Argentino,* 14 November 1985, 8.

Flori, Mónica. "Cecilia Absatz y Alicia Steimberg: dos narradoras argentinas contemporáneas." *Chasqui: revista de literatura latinoamericana* 27 (November 1988): 83–92.

———. "Identidad y discurso de la femineidad en *Los años pares* de Cecilia Absatz." *Explicación de textos literarios* 22 (1993–94): 87–97.

Gimbernat González, Ester. "En los nones de *Los años pares* (C. Absatz)." In *Aventuras del desacuerdo: novelistas argentinas de los 80,* 94–99. Buenos Aires: Danilo Albero Vergara, 1992.

Herrera, Francisco. "La literatura erótica femenina tras los pasos de su propia mitología." *La Prensa,* 6 March 1990.

Kreimer, Juan Carlos. "Mate con Ginseng." Review of *Té con canela,* by Cecilia Absatz. *Humor,* 2 December 1982, 117–18.

"Natu Poblet sale a comer con Cecilia Absatz." *First* 69 (June 1992): 52–54.

Reyes, Mirta. "La literatura de la democracia." N.p., n.d.: 18.

Zimmerman, Héctor. Review of *Los años pares,* by Cecilia Absatz. *Claudia,* 10 February 1986, 22–23.

Reina Roffé. Photograph by Silvia Sanz.

6

Reina Roffé

BIOGRAPHY

Reina Roffé was born in Buenos Aires, Argentina, in 1951. She obtained a bachelor's degree from Domingo F. Sarmiento College in 1970. From 1970 to 1973 she studied journalism and public relations at the Instituto Superior Mariano Moreno in Buenos Aires, obtaining a master's degree in those subjects. From 1973 to 1977 she studied literature at the University of Buenos Aires School of Philosophy and Literature.

Roffé has made a career in journalism and public relations. In Buenos Aires, she collaborated with *Latinoamericana*, *Siete días*, and *Crisis* magazines, and the newspapers *La Opinión*, *Clarín*, *La Razón*, *Página 12*, and *Tiempo Argentino*. She has been a book reviewer for *Convicción* and an editor of *La Razón*. She has been a publications editor for several public relations agencies (J. Walter Thompson, Diálogo, and Gowland-McCann Erickson) and a freelance writer for Gente de Comunicación and Carlos Gallardo. Roffé has worked at various publishing houses and formerly headed the press and public relations department at Editorial Planeta Argentina. She has also served as literary advisor at Editorial Per Abbat.

In 1975 Roffé received the Sixto Pondal Ríos Prize (best book by a young author) for *Llamado al puf*. In 1981 she was awarded a Fulbright Fellowship to the University of Iowa International Writing Program. While in the United States, she wrote for the New York–based newspaper *Noticiero Argentino*. She went back to Buenos Aires in 1982 but returned to the United States in 1983 to be the literary advisor for Ediciones del Norte in Hanover, New Hampshire, where she produced videotaped interviews with contemporary Latin American writers (also published in book form). In 1984 she produced a weekly radio program, *No sólo para nosotras*, and a cultural program on the lives and works of contemporary Latin American writers. In 1986 she received for *La rompiente*, the only prize awarded

215

at the first Biennial International Short Novel Contest in Córdoba, Argentina.

Roffé returned to Buenos Aires in 1985, where until 1988 she wrote for *Crisis* magazine and coordinated reading and writing workshops for the Alfonsina Storni Library. In 1988 she moved to Madrid, Spain, where she currently resides and writes for *Cambio 16*, *Marie Claire*, and *Guía del niño* magazines. From 1988 to 1990 she coordinated literary workshops for the Madrid Telephone Company Cultural Association and Biblos bookstore; from 1990 to 1992 she was director of foreign relations for the State Society for the Quincentennial Library in Madrid. While in Madrid, she completed the novel, *A la intemperie*.

ESSAY

Although Reina Roffé's publications span several genres, including short fiction and essays, she is best known for her novels. Roffé does not identify with a particular literary generation, but acknowledges that there are similarities between her work and that of a group of young Argentine writers who started publishing in the 1970s (Cecilia Absatz, Alicia Steimberg, and Mempo Giardinelli). Critics labeled these writers "marginal" to the literary establishment in terms of lifestyle, values, and writing. Roffé's background, worldview, and approach to content and form justify the "marginal" label. Her novels are somewhat autobiographical, and the feeling of estrangement that characterizes her work comes from her own background. She was raised by a Sephardic family in her grandmother Reina's house. Her parents did not figure significantly in her childhood or upbringing, as indicated in her book *Llamado al puf* (Calling Puf), a fictional account of her early years. She grew up with an immigrant family and was raised by surrogate parents but became detached from the values of the immigrant and local culture. Roffé's spiritual break with her family contributes to her ironic treatment of the bourgeois values and ethics of her culture.

Her themes and characters often reflect a worldview alien to bourgeois morality, and one weighted by issues and behaviors taboo in both the Jewish and Argentine traditions.

In Roffé's novels the supreme drama of the outcast is acted out by female characters who experience separation, degradation, and isolation. They usually sever ties with their families and loved ones, set out on a destructive course, and engage in relationships set in transitory and degrading environments. Her young female characters rebel to escape from stifling families, only to form surrogate families of friends and straight, gay, or bisexual lovers (*Monte de Venus*). Roffé deals with sexuality and eroticism in a way that transgresses the cultural mores and literary tradition prevalent in Argentine society. Her female characters' sexual and erotic practices are vividly portrayed. They go through life seeking independence from men and finding sexual fulfillment outside marriage, or by pursuing their education and writing. The thematic content is reminiscent of work by Roberto Arlt and Julio Cortázar. Both portray voyages of degradation through the underworld. Roffé's language has traces of Cortázar's playful style, injecting a strong dose of humor to lighten the despair. A closer look at Roffé's novels illustrates how she uses content and style to create her fictional world.

Llamado al puf

In *Llamado al puf*, 1973, Roffé's award-winning first novel (written when she was only seventeen years old), we witness the author's transmutation of her personal myths into a work of art. Partly autobiographical, this work features the writer's fictional alter ego, Celia, a seventeen-year-old protagonist who evokes the story of her childhood and adolescence to understand her embittered present self. The novel critiques the era in Argentina during the early fifties, the end of Perón's first regime. The depiction of the deteriorating middle-class society represented by Celia's family is reminiscent of that in Steimberg's *Músicos y relojeros* in that the domestic setting depicts a larger social reality:

> *Llamado al puf* is Reina Roffé's first novel, but this circumstance is not important for a work such as hers, which breaks away from trendiness [and] captures a complete generation while attempting to reveal a socio-historical reality. The novel represents a search for the elements that sustain the present and it does not use literature to mythicize or deform life. For Reina Roffé, for the protagonist of *Llamado al puf*, to look at the past means to recover the journey she was destined to trace. With that certainty, she sets forth to that big, old house on United States Street, sheltering a family ruled by a strict matriarchy, until she finds, among the shadows, among interested protections and cruel dependencies, the hand that might lead her to the surface once more, shedding light on her own existence. But in the adventure of that descent to hell, she cannot avoid attacking, with refined ferocity, the surrounding world, the class where she originated, the stifling mores of a society in disgrace. A precise style, assured, and unpretentious, renders the sounds of her desperation, of

her loneliness, presenting a novel that, in all its violence, stands as a true cry for freedom.[1]

The prologue points out that the intent of the novel transcends the portrayal of a family and social class. It is an indictment of Argentina's place within the imperialist international system:

> And it is then when the ferocious x-ray tearing apart the social strata points directly to the system, to the relations established in a peripheral country, sunk in the most faraway corner of a capitalist spider web. There is almost no pity in that outrageous attempt to ridicule the tics and craftiness of a small bourgeoisie in disgrace. They fight just to escape the working class, while unknowingly sustaining the values and ideas of an oligarchy—an underdeveloped bourgeoisie, mediator of colonization and support for the current imperialism— which has taken strong roots in these poor and wretched immigrants, corrupted by their condition as foreigners, as well as by misery and misfortunes. They are forgotten in a huge house, lonely, savage travelers, and accomplices of a treason that also belongs to them, for which they suffer or pay with devouring loyalty.[2]

The corruption and decay of Argentina's social fabric at the hands of the Peronists is obviously a metaphor for the Argentina of the 1970s. That the novel seems to take place in a void, in contrast to what was happening when it was written, has been noted by Francine Masiello, who considers that Roffé's novel "withdraws her characters from history by isolating them in the safety of an illusory past." She says that Roffé "turns to the comfort of nostalgia as a meager compensation for the present," and that "her characters live outside history."[3] Because of this, Masiello notes, *Llamado al puf* fits within the context of the particular fiction that emerged in Argentina in the 1970s. It is a fiction that offers minor dissent (such as the feminist novel, the detective story, and the neonaturalist saga) and a liberal text as official evidence of freedom. These novels became the "accepted discourse that had passed the check-point of the censors."[4] To escape censorship, and to survive, the "novel of the seventies" encodes ideology, tying Roffé's text to the fiction of Diaconú, Steimberg, and Absatz, who resorted to similar strategies of withdrawal from current events.

Roffé expresses her dissent through subversive use of domestic space and the concept of family, a technique used by other contemporary Argentine women writers, such as Marta Traba (*Conversación al sur* [*Mothers and Shadows*], 1981) and Silvia Molloy (*En breve cárcel* [*Certificate of Absence*], 1981). These writers use domestic space to flee (but also to question)

exterior repression. The home serves a dual purpose: it momentarily protects but it also confines women. The protagonists reclaim that home
space to analyze their individual stories and liberate themselves. The protagonists also analyze family ties (reflecting a repressive ideology and hierarchy) to gain an understanding of themselves. Questioning the patriarchal
home and family is a way of attacking repressive institutions of the state,
for the two institutions are founded on similar principles, principles that
the writers would not be able to critique openly.[5] As the protagonist makes
the transition from adolescent to adult, she realizes that to become an
independent woman she must first settle accounts with her past, whose
secrets lie within the confines of the family home:

> Celia estaba otra vez en el patio con todo el frío de ese momento y de
> antes porque dónde, pero dónde, iba a hallar la puerta que escondía
> una realidad horrible—no sabía qué—, sólo que era necesario
> encontrarla de una vez por todas.

> (Celia was once again on the patio with all the cold of that moment
> and of the past, because where, but where, was she going to find the
> door that hid a terrible reality—she did not know what—only that it
> was necessary to find it once and for all.)[6]

The structure of the house—its doors, the tiles on the floors and the walls,
and the glass windows—become Celia's Proustian *madeleine*. They assist
her in evoking the past. The elements that help her to recapture her past
are in disrepair, alluding to the difficulty of the process of confronting
painful memories:

> Miró la puerta del caserón y advirtió que conservaba aún, en la parte
> alta, el vidrio roto como una media luna. Sí, el horror tenía que estar
> detrás de esa madera barnizada que guardaba muchas cosas, porque
> el horror de hoy siempre está en el pasado de ayer que complica los
> días venideros.

> (She looked at the big house's door and noticed that its upper part
> still kept the glass broken like a half moon. Yes, the horror had to be
> behind that varnished wood that preserved many things, because
> today's horror is always in yesterday's past, which complicates the
> future.) (24)

Celia discovers the "terrible reality" and "the horror" behind the house's
symbolic doors and other rundown structures: the idols of her early years
that stunted her development and nurtured dependence have fallen. As

Celia reminisces, she audaciously and ferociously dissects the family members, resulting in an ironic and humorous portrayal of them: "The Old
Bag" (a grandmother who controls the lives of her thirty-year-old offspring), "The Idol" (an uncle whom Celita admires only to become disappointed), "Mrs. Doesn't-Have-a-Say" (her self-effacing mother), and "The
Piano Owner" (the grandmother's sister, a hypochondriacal spinster who
runs a piano academy in the family dining room). As the characters of this
Jewish lower-middle-class family cling to their bourgeois aspirations and
ideals, they sink economically into the lower working class, transmitting a
vivid and accurate portrayal of the socioeconomic decadence of the 1950s.
Roffé's satirical commentary exposes the hypocritical beliefs and attitudes
of the family members and their stifling interaction while they are confined to the decrepit house, an appropriate background for their useless
and destructive life rituals. As Celia recalls this vanished world, she finally
fully understands the impact her relatives had on her when she was growing up:

> y los años que te abren los ojos y te parten el alma, porque es terrible
> . . . sospechar que hay otro mundo mejor y a la vez dolerse por los
> desperdicios humanos que uno ha descubierto tan recientemente y
> qué golpe cuando se vienen abajo, cuando dejan de ser unos monstruos
> divinos, para ser unos psicópatas sin psiquiatra que no te dejan crecer
> las alas.

> (and the years that open your eyes and tear your soul apart, because
> it is terrible . . . to suspect that there is another world that is better
> and at the same time feel hurt because of the human discards one has
> discovered so recently and what a blow when they crumble, when
> they are no longer divine monsters, and become psychopaths with-
> out a psychiatrist who do not allow you to grow wings.) (133)

What hurts her now is the awareness that she grew up in the midst of
these "human discards," who gave up their ideals and the will to attain
their dreams. Instead, they sought the protective matriarchal home and
family structure to avoid facing reality and taking responsibility for their
lives. To Celia "The Idol" (her uncle) is the most vivid example of the
transformation of these characters, because he was the most promising. A
student of economics during Celia's childhood, a young, bright intellectual, both resourceful and dependable, her uncle was the one whom the
family always turned to when they had problems. Celita admired him
because he was her mentor. The Idol taught her about books, revolutionary heroes, and social justice. She recalls how proud she felt when The

Idol distributed clandestine newspapers. But in the end, The Idol betrayed them by turning into a bureaucrat and a conformist: "Celia pensó que ese hombre pequeño e insignificante, vestido de traje azul, corbata y camisa blanca, como los muñequitos de las tortas de casamiento, había sido su Idolo" (Celia thought that the small and insignificant man, dressed in a blue suit, a white tie and shirt, like the tiny dolls on wedding cakes, had been her Idol) (128). Celia's disappointment is acutely conveyed in the new name she has coined for him: The Dead Idol. He crumbles under her scrutiny: "¿[C]ómo voy a mantener aunque sea uno de esos ideales que un día tuviste, *pase lo que pase* si para vos pasaron de largo?" (How am I going to maintain at least one of those ideals that you once had, *come what may*, if they passed you by?) (129; italics are Roffé's). The process suffered by The Idol alludes to the death of illusions of the Argentine youth and the middle class caught in the political and socioeconomic turmoil of the Peronist years. Realizing that her life will waste away like his and the other members of her dysfunctional family gives Celia the strength and courage to leave:

> Sí, Celia, querías libertad. No pedías mucho sólo necesitabas abrir un poco tus alas para no olvidarte para siempre de tu individualidad, algo tan difícil de acordarse como de las individualidades. Habías tomado conciencia de la nada perniciosa de la gente que te rodeaba en un círculo cerrado que se estrechaba cada vez más hasta oprimirte. Te aterró la rutina de esas vidas que respiraban por arte de magia.

> (Yes, Celia, you wanted freedom. You did not ask for much, you only needed to spread your wings a little not to forget about your individuality forever, something so hard to recall as individualities. You had become aware of the pernicious nothingness of the people surrounding you in a closed circle, which was closing in on you more and more until it was crushing you. You became terrified by the routine of those lives that breathed as if by magic.) (139)

Two years later, as Celia evokes this process, she is able to pierce through the pain and confront her past. She is now able to leave the decrepit house and its ghosts for good, returning to the external world as an independent adult:

> Los pasillos intentaron atrapar a Celia en su falso laberinto sin conseguirlo. Los vidrios de la mampara se negaron a iluminar su fuga; tropezó con una baldosa floja que parecía detenerla en ese recuerdo pisoteado, amarillo y negro. Cuando bajó por las escaleras sintió que

las piernas le temblaban. Dejó atrás el caserón por la calle Estados Unidos llevada cuadra tras cuadra hasta donde el aliento le permitiera llegar.

(The hallways tried unsuccessfully to trap Celia in their false labyrinth. The screen's glass windows refused to shine on her as she was running away; she stumbled over a loose tile, which seemed to retain her in that trampled reminiscence, black and yellow. When she went down the stairs, she felt her legs shaking. She left the huge house behind, by way of United States Street and kept going, block after block, as far as her breath would allow her to go.) (141)

This tale of an adolescent's flight from a stifling and repressive authoritarian environment to freedom stands as a metaphor for her country. The decaying house and family represent conditions in Argentina during her generation. Disillusioned with the system, Roffé offers a blueprint for subverting it. Although the home is questioned, it is also a haven where the protagonist can escape conventional expectations and the outside authoritarian world. Roffé has converted the concept of the ideal traditional family into one where women's liberation can be forged.

Monte de Venus

While writing her second novel, *Monte de Venus* (Mount Venus), 1976, Roffé heeded the advice she received after *Llamado al puf* came out:

> I sat down to listen attentively to everything that was being said by those who said they were—and at times, let's admit it, they truly were—experts in the rules of the game, I mean the craft.[7]

> The novel that I undertook afterwards had—as I had listened attentively—less "personal content" and more "social content." *Monte de Venus* was my first "planned" novel, where—I betrayed the individual, subjective, "female" message—I sought to render a realistic portrayal of the transformations of a social fringe immersed in, and conditioned by, the tyrannical conventions that ruled society in general.[8]

Roffé fulfilled her objective so well that *Monte de Venus*, published during a turbulent time, was censored on charges of immorality. The novel was censured for its open depiction of lifestyles and sexual practices considered taboo in mainstream Argentine society and its explicit political content. The text, like other contemporary Argentine novels, results from "the intensity of the novelists' meditation about Argentine history and society," and is "part of a long tradition that could be called the literature of silence."[9] According to Pierre Macherey, the discourse in such works has its origins in

> a certain silence, an issue that is given shape, a terrain where a figure is traced. Thus the book is not self-sufficient, it is necessarily accompanied by *a certain absence,* and it would not exist without it. Knowledge about the book must include consideration of that absence.[10]

Macheray suggests two kinds of silence in a text: (1) what is erased (the absence of meaning) and (2) what is illegible (present but hidden).[11] Roffé's *Monte de Venus* includes both the "erased" and the "illegible" text. Roffé has erased allusions to present events in her novel by inscribing them metaphorically in the past. Therefore, there is a marked absence, as present reality is not explicitly recorded. This absence generates a hidden text, concealing political events (especially during Juan Domingo Perón's return to Argentina and his presidency) reflected in "two years of Argentine history: The last year when Lanusse was in power, the 1973 elections, the student movements, the Peronist government's move to the right, and the disappointment of those who believed in a change."[12] The reader has to find the connection and read the plot as a *mise en abyme* of another story, which, although silenced, is expressed in the text's violence and the political framework.

According to Roffé, *Llamado al puf* and *Monte de Venus* are totally unrelated: "The former is the family novel, autobiographical, a novel of atmosphere, where I perform a sort of homemade analysis of my childhood. . . . But *Monte de Venus* transcends that limited context of the individual, to contain another world, other beings."[13] Nevertheless, the two novels use similar devices to depict political chaos: the dissolution of the family, the generational struggle, and the corruption of institutions (including the family and the educational system). Both focus on young female protagonists and their loss of innocence and attainment of independence. Roffé uses the female world as a point of departure, then extends it to present female characters trapped in the larger social context:

> When I started writing *Monte de Venus*, my purpose was to describe the closed universe of a young woman's intimate life: her relationship with her body, with men, her daily life, and, especially, her questions about herself. The political scene gave women the illusion of power and, above all, tried to persuade them that their own enigma had been solved by history. The novel is influenced by all these contradictory

currents. The characters are women who not only question their lives, but also history, which brings them alive only to dehumanize them. And they are surrounded by men, castrated rodents who complete the scene. [The novel portrays] an era, a night high school, a beehive where the problem of women's condition unfolds as the pretext that shapes the plot. Besides the successive themes that intertwine and unfold, *Monte de Venus* shows the generational problem of young people my age, not only those of women. What the text transmits, in its totality, is great hopelessness; the protagonists are torn apart without quite understanding why. Somewhat like *Gatopardo*. Everything must change so that nothing at all changes.[14]

The novel is divided into two alternating stories with contrasting structures that are linked at the end by a central character, Julia Grande. Julia's first-person narration of her life story alternates with a third-person narration of events taking place at a night school. The prevailing mood—betrayal, solitude, and defeat—permeates both stories, unifying the novel.

Julia's story is being recorded by her female literature teacher as material for a novel she intends to write. We read Julia's "Transcribed Recordings." The elaborate framework (Julia's original narration, the recordings, the transcriptions) suggests that the real story (concealed present reality) cannot be told directly. It must be hidden within a fictional story that is closely related to national events.

In Roffé's novels, the family is a context where dominant values and ideologies are questioned and subverted: *Llamado al puf* presented a family dominated by a matriarch, and *Monte de Venus* portrays a reversal of traditional roles within the family. In Julia Grande's family, the mother dominates the family and mistreats Julia, never showing her any love, while the father cultivates a maternal side, which Julia mistakes for weakness. She yearns for her mother's love, and mocks her father by abusing his kindness. Symbolically rejecting an oedipal love, she unsuccessfully seeks to return to a pre-oedipal stage by fusing with her mother. Julia defies her father and society's patriarchal structures with her (frankly depicted) lesbian behavior and aggressive male roles in her relationships. She is unconsciously attempting to usurp her father's role and win her mother's affection. When Julia's father finds her making love to a female friend in the family home, he kicks her out. The transcribed recordings detail her further misfortunes as Julia degrades herself in the Buenos Aires underworld. She embezzles, commits homicide, becomes a prostitute, and has an unwanted pregnancy, encumbering her with a baby boy. As she lives through these experiences, Julia behaves as she did while with her family. She tries to destroy protective male acquaintances, as though seeking revenge on her father and reestablishing, in ill-fated lesbian affairs, the broken bond with her mother. Several characters who become father figures in her life are destroyed by Julia, who unconsciously seeks to appropriate their roles: She embezzles from an elderly man who protects her, causing him a nervous breakdown, and she kills her male lover in a drunken brawl. The symbolic patricide that undermines the father's position represents the text's undermining of the patriarchal political and social system. David William Foster emphasizes the link between the character's behavior and the text's critical intent: "[A] novel that gives voice to an aggressive lesbian, one whose inverted behavior threatens sacred institutions by parodying them with notable fidelity, clearly represents a new threshold in the corruption of the national moral fiber."[15]

Julia's story is further developed in the night school sequence. She unsuccessfully tries to reform, forsaking her previous life and continuing her studies so she can find a job and provide a home for her baby. But she still seeks to bond with her mother and she thinks she has found a stand-in in her female literature teacher, Victoria Sáenz Ballesteros, the only person who seems sympathetic to her plight. Victoria sets up weekly meetings with Julia to record the story of Julia's past adventures. On the one hand, Julia feels attracted to her as the ideal friend and lover who will provide a stable life and home for her and her son. But, she also sees a mother figure in Victoria, due to the teacher's concern for Julia's baby, which Julia thinks extends to include her. Julia and the other students project onto Victoria all the qualities that their own mothers lack: "[S]e destacaba por ser una mujer inteligente, sobria, ajena al ambiente que las rodeaba y para algunas, el ideal de madre, de la madre que les hubiera gustado tener" ([S]he stood out because she was an intelligent, serious woman, impervious to the atmosphere that surrounded them and, for some of them, the ideal of a mother, of the mother they would have liked to have had).[16] But events prove the students to be deluded in their quest for a role model. At one point, the teacher threatens to discontinue Julia's recording sessions, pretending there is not enough material for the novel. In her desperation to continue her relationship with Victoria, Julia is tricked into revealing her worst past transgressions (including how she murdered her lover). With Julia's recorded confessions, Victoria is able to claim Julia's illegitimate son. The death of Julia's real mother underlines the symbolic death of the surrogate mother who has betrayed her. As a result, Julia plunges into deep despair, her quest for maternal affection recurring in the novel's final image:

Sé que hoy estoy sola y me da miedo, mucho miedo. "Todos fuimos estafados," me dijo Baru; pero eso a nadie consuela. Mi dolor sólo es mi dolor. Qué no daría por una pequeña caricia, como ese viento suave que anda, allá entre las ramas de los árboles, agitando sus manos, contra la noche cercana.

(I know that today I'm alone and it frightens me very much. "We were all taken for a ride," Baru told me, but that does not console anybody. My pain is only mine. I yearn for a single caress, like that gentle wind that blows, there, between the tree branches, moving its hands back and forth against the approaching night.) (270)

The disintegration of the family, inscribed realistically in Julia Grande's account and in the night school segment, is a hidden representation of Argentina's national reality at the time the text was written. It also alludes to the corruption of institutions, a theme developed in the night school, where two generations confront each other. The night school stories are vignettes of everyday happenings. They focus on the dissolute and disillusioned existences of young, lower-class women who attend night school to complete their secondary education, and the apathetic staff, also characterized by low moral standards. Although the students create havoc in school and in the staff's personal lives, the staff members "appear to have been trained as insane-asylum wardens rather than torchbearers of 'Liberating Knowledge'. The administrators are tin-badge tyrants—iron maidens whose sadism would be exquisite if they were not presented so ridiculously as poor copies of Argentine military figures."[17] They represent an authoritarian world, one that Roffé aptly captures in her ironic descriptions:

La Pechugona, firme como un sargento, se colocaba en la puerta del colegio a inspeccionar a las alumnas que entraban. Con la cabeza erguida, un tanto imperativa, el traste saliente y las piernas flacas, parecida a una gallina bataraza, la vice, con sus dobles pechugas listas a estallar en cualquier momento, humillaba a las chicas que tenían la cara demasiado pintada o las polleras muy cortas o algún escote por debajo de la clavícula.

(Busty, standing at attention like a sergeant, would place herself at the door of the school to inspect the students who came in. With her head held high, somewhat imperative, her protruding fanny and her skinny legs, looking like a speckled chicken, the Vice, with her boobs ready to burst at any moment, humiliated those young girls whose faces were painted too much, or whose dresses were too short, or whose necklines were below their collarbones.) (123)

Incited by members of the Peronist Youth who infiltrate the school, the students revolt against the staff's authoritarianism. At the same time, they participate in political events such as demonstrations and organize a welcoming committee to greet Perón upon his arrival at the airport. At first these events and the students' participation bring new hope for change and renewal, both in the microcosm of the school and in the country. The diary entries of Baru, one of the students, "chronicles point by point the economic, cultural and political chaos of the early 1970s, the time in which the novel is set."[18] As a result of the students' revolt, the authorities are forced to resign. Then they are reinstated, pointing out that Perón's return and presidency will not change anything in society at large or in the students' lives. As Baru remarks, "Esto es lo del *Gatopardo*, todo tiene que cambiar para que nada cambie" (This is like the *Gatopardo*, everything must change so that nothing at all changes) (269). By intertwining the complete collapse of authority at the school and in national events, the novel indicts institutions. Institutions betray the average citizen, especially young people who, like those in the novel, are corrupted and depleted of their ideals. As noted by Eduardo Gudiño Kieffer:

> [I]t is necessary to say that the main characters are **young women,** high school students, and that most of them are domestic servants or blue-collar workers; and that the story was the one experienced by Argentine youth, leading them from frustration to frustration, or **from illusion to frustration,** in a period so similar to the present one that it still feels wretchedly painful and, in more than one sense, shameful. . . . It deals with young people without a goal, lost after so many unfulfilled promises; youngsters who believed they would participate in the process of creating a country and were surrounded by lies, fraud, corruption, and the ineptitude of those who broke their promises.
>
> *Monte de Venus* **is susceptible to many readings and many interpretations.** But at this moment in Argentine history—which is also literary history— **it is worthwhile to consider it as an open testimonial and a document** that conjugates a difficult but indispensable verb: **to reconstruct.** Because it is not possible to reconstruct without having as a basis a sincere confession, without recognizing the situations that preceded the present.[19]

Julia's and Baru's stories, recorded in the transcriptions and the diary, embody the degradation that every citizen has suffered in this society under successive governments. Both stories constitute an indictment of Argentina's history, focusing on the betrayal of its youth. Roffé has symbolically inscribed in both protagonists' accounts Argentine youth's unsuccessful efforts to rise against the regimes and institutions that betrayed and oppressed them.

La rompiente

After *Monte de Venus* had been censored by the military, a warning not to be taken lightly during those years, the dangers lurking behind official censorship weighed heavily on Roffé. Realizing that she could not write what she wanted, Roffé reflected on what being a writer really meant to her. She believes those years of reflection and private writing helped her find her own course and narrative voice. In the prologue to *La rompiente* (The breaker), 1986,[20] the writer discusses her literary activity during that time:

> The years between *Monte de Venus* and *La rompiente* were very rich for me as I studied and learned the writer's craft. This included my work as a journalist and essayist. I [also] wrote short stories and an interim novel, which I withdrew from the publishing house when they were getting it ready for publication. It was a narrative that still did not master an original narrative tone but, rather, was sustained by the hesitant ephemeral tone in fashion then. It was useful, nonetheless, as a private testimonial that got me closer to finding a style. *La rompiente* is a step further in the same direction, where I recuperate—paradoxically—the wish that sustained the writing of my first novel: the integration, by means of the written text, of a personal, alienated, and fragmented world.[21]

La rompiente represents Roffé's inner journey of self-discovery, a woman writer attempting to create from the depths of herself, in defiance of repression. To create from confinement and silence, Roffé breaks with constraining literary, political, and gender structures. It is

> a rupture with the critical realism that Roffé practiced in *Llamado al puf* and, especially, *Monte de Venus*; a rupture with the strict division of literature into genres; a rupture with the nationalist-authoritarian discourse used to justify the genocide and repression; a rupture with what is stereotyped as female; a rupture with the simplifying dualities—text/context; reality/fiction.[22]

La rompiente presents, in three parts, the personal story of the protagonist, which encloses the larger story of her generation and her country.

The narration underscores "an impediment, in an oblique, surreptitious, but also in an obsessive fashion: That of being able to speak and narrate, that of being able to break the silence."[23] "*La rompiente* is an inquiry into what is left unsaid, at the same time it proposes to investigate the ways of alluding to the forbidden, to cast away self-censorship and external censorship."[24]

Part 1, set during the years of silence, characterized by "estados de sitio, guerras sucias y lavados de alma" (states of siege, dirty wars, and soul-washings) (23) introduces the protagonist, who has no name. Years of silence in society at large are reflected in the protagonist's self-imposed silence and confinement, broken only by nightmares, letters, writing a journal, and unsuccessful attempts at writing a novel. As *La rompiente* opens, the protagonist, at the end of a trip (a common device used by Argentine women writers, meaning a desire to break away, literally and symbolically, from repressive reality) arrives at "the other coast." She has exiled herself to a foreign country, where "another language" is spoken. There she hopes to write her novel, a response to the question posed as she embarked on the journey: "¿[H]allaré, a dónde vaya el esplendor de una voz?" ([W]ill I find, wherever I may go, the splendor of a voice?) (124). "In order to be able to narrate, the protagonist has to undertake a journey that does not take her to 'una ciudad, sino a un estado mental'" (a city, but to a mental state) (17). From that privileged territory, she attempts to integrate the fragments of the broken mirror so that it will render a coherent image of herself.[25]

She tells her story to an interlocutor, who repeats it. Acting as a transcriber, the interlocutor narrates part 1 while talking to the protagonist, addressing her as "you":

> Yo, simplemente transcribo. . . . Rebobinemos: salió de la patria hace unos años. Ahora vive en un pueblito donde la exhuberante *ivy*—hago uso de sus palabras—se adhiere hasta los tuétanos. Insiste—según me ha confesado—en borronear una misma y única novela.
>
> (I, simply transcribe. . . . Let's rewind: You left the fatherland a few years ago. Now you live in a small town where the exuberant *ivy*—I use your words—clings to everything. You insist—according to what you have confessed to me—in sketching the same novel over and over.) (28)

To have the necessary information, the narrator reads the protagonist's diary and says,

Anoche leí su diario, ¿los apuntes marginales?—perdón—, lo que
Ud. denomina *líneas de fuerza*. La lectura y lo que alguna vez mencionó
con rubor en las mejillas: frustración, derrota, desesperanza, me
remitieron al tema de la tristeza.

(I read your diary last night, margin notes?—sorry—what you call
lines of strength. Reading them and [remembering] what you mentioned one day while blushing: frustration, failure, despair, made me
think of the theme of sadness.) (27; italics are Roffé's)

Roffé's use of the oral text, a conversation based on repetition and memo-
rization, is characteristic of women's writing; examples are Marta Traba's
Conversación al sur (Mothers and Shadows), 1981, and Alicia Steimberg's
Cuando digo Magdalena (When I say Magdalena), 1992. This device signifies a "rupture" with traditional narrative conventions. In the context of
La rompiente, it attempts to get around the censorship. A conversation—
an elaboration of Julia Grande's "Transcribed Recordings" in *Monte de
Venus*—bonds individuals and challenges external authority. Choosing the
oral text (and double-voiced discourse) over incriminating written material is also a technique of concealment, underscoring that terror and fear
are at its source. Masiello refers to

el doble discurso sostenido por toda mujer, en tanto que se siente
observada y víctima de una voz controladora externa, la doble voz de
La rompiente también deja vislumbrar el conflicto de todo sujeto social en busca de su autonomía y del placer.

(the double discourse sustained by every woman, to the extent that
she feels observed and victimized by an external, controlling voice. In
La rompiente, the double voice also allows us to perceive the conflict
of any social subject in search of her autonomy and pleasure.)[26]

At the end of part 1, the unidentified narrator asks the protagonist to
tell the plot of her novel. In part 2 the protagonist's forced silence is
broken, as she engages in oral strategies to narrate the story. The protagonist's narration changes to first person, and we are told fragments of
events that took place in her country of origin during her years of silence
prior to her protagonist's exile. The narrator of part 1 listens now as the
protagonist alternately reads, summarizes, and comments on "the novel":
"The novel of the second part, narrated, critiqued, commented on, is the
product of a repressive state, it is an attempt to narrate . . . between the
lines and based on an allegory . . . an experience of terror and silence."[27]

Part 2 reflects an era of terror during which all truth must be fragmented, hidden—rendered as a puzzle the clues of which have been scattered. Although these revised and altered fragments mark the character's attempts to escape the regime's vigilance, they also serve to subvert the taboos of the state. From the midst of the fragments emerges a kaleidoscope of characters, a group of gamblers who at times become literary figures, hiding under different names: the unnamed protagonist is "I," and also "Rahab"; the Professor is also "the former seminarian"; Boomer is "the critic" as well as "the critic called Boomer." The bonding of these individuals in a group structure represents a challenge to the efforts to divide and isolate them. The stories are in a constant process of change, like reflections in the mirrorlike surfaces of "the novel within the novel." The group of gamblers becomes one of the literati, and their story becomes a tale of passion and solitude as well as one of political persecution. The narration of "the novel" ends with the disappearance of the Professor and the terror unleashed in the lives of the other characters, who fear they will be the next targets. They burn all incriminating possessions, especially printed material, and go into hiding. The multifaceted, ambiguous story of the group suggests yet another tale—featuring a political and/or terrorist cell. According to Francine Masiello, these metamorphoses of the story into a political tale indicate that "the interplay of the texts, the interplay of words, and the interplay of the couple, yield to another, more important interplay: that of the disappearances and the terror implicit in surveillance."[28] Roffé uses these refracting plots and characters because she does not wish her text to participate in the restrictive values and patterns of authoritarian rule. Rather, she wants to open her text to multiple dimensions and meanings. María Teresa Gramuglio notes:

> In these metamorphoses, the text displays a narcissistic pleasure, similar to that of the protagonist as she stares at herself in the mirror: pleasure in mixing up the system of names, pleasure in disseminating the stories, in opening systems of counterpoint, in listening to its own echoes. Pleasure, in short, in repeating, inserting variations, the recurring matrix of a previous story.[29]

Part 3 of the narration uses the same point of view as part 1; however, to further blur the distinctions between fiction and reality, the fictional characters in part 2 (her novel) reappear in the narrator's "real" life. Supposedly the story of her "real" life, part 3 takes place during a state of siege (previous to the protagonist's exile narrated in part 1, when fear forced her to lock herself in her apartment and seek refuge in her story):

Creí que la reclusión era necesaria para contar una historia—escribe—; la historia se ha convertido en el pretexto ideal para mantener las puertas cerradas: hacerme insensible al mundo exterior—quizás de alguna forma lo he logrado.

(I thought reclusion was necessary in order to tell a story, she writes; the story has become the ideal pretext for keeping the doors closed, to make myself insensitive to the outside world. Maybe I have achieved that in some way.) (113)

During part 3 she does not speak but only writes. She reminisces about her personal life, about her grandmother, whom she resembles and who in agony also resorts to silence, and about a trip to Morocco, where she saw the house in which her grandmother was born. One day she realizes she is being watched more and more closely, so she decides to exile herself, taking the reader in a circle to the story narrated in part 1. In her exile the written text comes forth as a testimonial of a personal story and the collective memory. In addition to structural circularity, Roffé employs reflecting images to convey the effects of repression on the female character. The protagonist desperately seeks her reflected image, not only to protect her but to reaffirm an identity lost under repression.

During her confinement, the protagonist suffers "anhedonia: enfermedad cuyos síntomas son infelicidad y no encontrar placer en las cosas que otros disfrutan" (anhedonia: a disease whose symptoms are unhappiness and the impossibility of finding pleasure in the things that others enjoy) (22). Terms like "indolence," "tiredness," "exhaustion," and "asphyxiation" abound, creating an atmosphere of despair and conveying the feeling of self-devaluation experienced by the protagonist. Plagued by self-doubt and a negative self-image, the protagonist sees her lover's (Boomer's) missing hand as a sign of her own maimed self: "[E]n el muñón de Boomer vi mi propia invalidez" (I saw my own disability in Boomer's stump) (90). But Boomer reflects not only her disfigured self. He helps her to recover her wholeness. The protagonist's love affair with Boomer takes place at an ocean resort. During their lovemaking, the protagonist speaks of the sea: "Quiero ver el mar. El mar, por Dios, el mar" (I want to see the sea. The sea, by God, the sea) (57). She also wants "orgiásticas zambullidas" (orgiastic dives) (59), connecting the sea imagery with a recovery of her sexuality. Images of enclosure and mutilation are negated by the ocean, "the space of pleasure and enjoyment,"[30] of rebirth and affirmation of the female self. Although the protagonist's entrapment is a result of her marginality and meaninglessness decreed by the state, the allusions to water suggest: (1) refuge from the confinement of her flat where fear has pushed her, and (2) a return to the female body and its regenerating fluids, reasserting her female physical and spiritual identity.

Water evokes dreamlike states that protect her from external threats: "Soñé que descendía al mar. Las olas arremetían contra mí como si fuese una veleta. La furia del agua me levantaba" (I dreamed that I went down to the sea. The waves pounded against me as if I were a weathervane. I was raised by the water's fury) (59). In addition to protecting, water frees the protagonist. It is the medium that will allow her to write: "Ahora, salir de estas aguas estancadas y encontrar el curso de un torrente propio ¿me será asequible?" (Now, leaving these stagnant waters and finding the course of my own torrent, will I be able to attain it?) (58). The water imagery relates to the mirror, where the protagonist gazes at her naked body, recognizing it as she attempts to recuperate her lost sense of humanity and identity:

> Ahora ella se funde con la imagen del espejo. La calidez de su boca empaña la imagen. En el espejo quedan sus labios imprecisos, la marca de sus labios, un hálito que se va esfumando, una huella en la arena que un viento barre.

> (Now she merges with the image in the mirror. The warmth of her mouth blurs the image. Remaining on the mirror are her imprecise lips, the imprint of her lips, a breath that gradually disappears, an imprint on the sand swept by a wind.) (70)

The protagonist attempts to appropriate the imprint of her body on the mirror. According to Francine Masiello, "[C]ontemporary women writers redefine the corporeal self in its materiality and, from there, they begin to construct an alternative version of the female." They present "the female body . . . as an aggregate of fluids, organs, and tissue that undermines any sense of a unified self. It is this kind of reconsideration that allows a definition of the female drawn from the resources of women's creativity rather than formulating the feminine from alien masculinized concepts."[31] It is an attempt to redefine the female body in terms different from those emanating from the reductive official discourse. When the protagonist apprehends her body in its materiality, she becomes free from official readings of the body, which can deny and make it disappear. As the novel closes, the protagonist is in her room, and the night is pierced by the frightening sirens of police cars. At this point, her body is the source of her writing. Its fluids and secretions defy the closed order of authoritarian discourse:

[A]unque esconda en su interior un océano revuelto por la tempestad que se avecina. . . . Hoy el mar le parece una figura recurrente. Se ve fluctuando con la marea, haciendo lo indecible por deshacerse de todos los lazos: sentirse poseída de sí misma y desposeída del mundo. El futuro en blanco la acongoja en sobresaltos.

([A]lthough she might hide inside her an ocean troubled by an approaching storm. . . . Today the sea seems a recurring figure to her. She sees herself fluctuating with the tide, doing the indescribable to sever all ties: to feel herself possessed by her own self and dispossessed from the world. The blank future worries and startles her.) (123)

The narration surges, adopting the rhythm of her body flooded by menstrual blood. Thus, "Roffé searches for the metaphor of women's menstruation [used by women writers] to explain themselves, and to explain the yet unmarked spaces that open up to [their] writing."[32] The protagonist's writing, from within her confined, menstruating body, seeks to explain and to defy the external threat, until she seeks exile in a place described as a liquid source of regeneration: "una especie de boya encantada que la sacaría a flote del naufragio" (a sort of enchanted buoy that would raise her from the shipwreck) (18). The protagonist anchors her writing in the female body, a metaphor for her artistic production, as the water imagery prevalent throughout the novel turns into her menstrual blood described in the text's final sentence: "Ahora, sangra" (Now, she bleeds) (124).[33] *La rompiente* disrupts official discourse, shaping alternative voices, in a recovery of the female physical and spiritual self. Roffé has developed in her novels a fictional corpus, a woman-centered discourse, and a narrative that constitutes a testimonial against repression and for remembrance.

CONVERSATION WITH REINA ROFFÉ

Buenos Aires, 4 June 1987

M.F.: Could you talk about your life, about the events and people you consider to be the most important?

R.R.: I was the firstborn child, granddaughter, and niece in a big family on both sides, a middle-class family with artistic inclinations. I was named after my paternal grandmother who was, undoubtedly, a very important person in my life, as well as that of my aunts and uncles. Until my tenth birthday I was a happy child spoiled by the whole family. My aunts and uncles were young, single, and fun-loving. We were always celebrating something. The house where I spent my childhood, which belonged to my grandmother Reina, was where the family got together for celebrations, and I would always be a part of them. I followed my aunts' and uncles' love affairs with great expectations and curiosity. The discovery of their secrets, their love affairs, and uncovering the reasons for their happiness and sadness filled me with delight. The house was the center of my first discoveries about the adult world. I owe much to my aunts and uncles. They transmitted to me their love for literature and their fascination for poetry and music. Besides, they furnished me with immensely rich literary material. For me that house resembled a huge stage, where they acted out their stories without hiding anything from me. I was both a spectator and accomplice, as well as a great traitor who revealed some of the family secrets in my first novel *Llamado al puf.*

M.F.: When and how did you begin to write?

R.R.: When I was about ten I started putting sentences together. At first it was a game, a way of entertaining myself. From then on, I became a sullen and solitary child. I wanted "a room of my own" and my own secret, too. I started writing poems imitating Alfonsina Storni, who was greatly admired at home. After that I wrote short plays. At that time, I enjoyed reading plays very much because they seemed more direct, more real, than a novel. The characters speak directly without the odious intervention of the traditional narrator who conveys his thoughts throughout many pages or provides lengthy descriptions of settings, clothing, and characters. When I was in my teens, I became fascinated with short stories and started writing some. Later on, I tried writing longer works, and when I was seventeen I wrote my first novel, which I have already mentioned, *Llamado al puf.*

M.F.: Were there specific influences that made you start writing?

R.R.: Reading, and identifying with the worlds that books transmitted to me. I remember one particular afternoon at my grandmother's house. The family was gone, except for one of my aunts. She was teaching a piano lesson at the other end of the house. Someone had lent me Simone de Beauvoir's *The Broken Woman.* I grabbed a bottle of liquor, locked myself in one of the bedrooms and, while I sipped the liquor, I devoured the stories, which had a profound impact on me. Those hours of solitude were extremely rewarding. Although the stories were not mine, I experienced a total coexistence. I discovered that to write is, in some way, like being with other people, even on a desert island.

M.F.: Has a specific event in your life influenced you to take up writing?

R.R.: Maybe what I just told you. Although I don't know exactly why

I write, I do know that people write for many reasons. They write to get attention, to appease anguish, to find a place in life, because it gives them pleasure or displeasure, because of vanity, to destroy ghosts, to bring them back to life, because they don't get to talk enough, because they were failures in ballet class, out of boldness, not to die, to die in peace, to while away the time, to make something happen, for no reason at all.

M.F.: Who are your favorite authors?

R.R.: The ones that come to mind, in no particular order, are Virginia Woolf, Vladimir Nabokov, Katherine Mansfield, Iris Murdoch, Anthony Burgess, Flannery O'Connor, J. D. Salinger, Peter Handke, Marguerite Yourcenar, Marguerite Duras, Muriel Spark.

M.F.: And your favorite Latin American writers?

R.R. First of all Jorge Luis Borges, and also Felisberto Hernández and Juan Rulfo, among many others I don't recall right now.

M.F.: What writers have influenced your work?

R.R.: All the ones I've mentioned, no matter how different they may seem. Careful reading always leaves its marks.

M.F.: Do you belong to a specific literary generation in Argentina?

R.R.; In the early 1970s many new writers started publishing. Although some had already been published, most of them, including myself, appeared on the literary scene for the first time during the 1970s. To identify us as a group, the critics pointed out the theme of marginality as a common characteristic. While many of us dealt with the theme of being on the fringe of society, in my opinion the works also denote different interests and the use of different forms of expression regarding content and form. On the other hand, the theme of marginality that was tacked on us is not new. It had already been dealt with by other writers as a means to transcend immediate reality and to attack the establishment. If there is a trait that characterizes us, it is precisely the fact that we did not form a group that adhered to a common, prevalent aesthetic current. The work was mainly individual. I don't feel I belong to a defined generation, because the ages, discursive modes, and ideologies of the writers of the 1970s differ considerably. We didn't have literary magazines like *Martín Fierro* or *Contorno*, which had brought writers together in the past. Maybe we come closer to being a contemporaneous group, rather than a generation bound by a common social, political, and cultural background.

M.F.: Besides the writers you already mentioned, do you feel an affinity with any other Argentine writers?

R.R.: I would add Roberto Arlt, Julio Cortázar, Silvina Ocampo, José Blanco, and Manuel Puig.

M.F.: What are you reading now?

R.R.: I am reading again the works of Nabokov and Borges and reading *Mujeres* (Women) by Phillippe Soller.

M.F.: Is writing easy for you?

R.R.: Sometimes I start working from a clear theme, but often I take off from just a vague idea that I suspect holds some interest. I go to work, taking notes to flesh it out, associating it to other ideas; and if it persists it is surely the start of a short story or a novel. It's generally the fragment of a story that takes up several months of work, because writing is not easy for me. I'm extremely conscientious; I read and reread each fragment I write over again. I correct a lot and write several versions of the same text.

M.F.: Do you have a writing schedule or routine?

R.R.: I write in the mornings. I'm an early morning person. I need all my energy, the morning sunlight, and the first hours of daylight to write.

M.F.: Do you need to write in a particular environment?

R.R.: I prefer to be alone in a room of my own, that room of one's own that has always been hard for women to find.

M.F.: How do you choose a theme?

R.R.: I must confess that I don't work on the basis of great themes and that I'm not interested in narrating an extraordinary story. I'm bored by a defined and weighty plot, themes, heroes, and characters. I prefer to work with insignificant situations and antiheroes and focus beyond significant facts.

M.F.: Are your works autobiographical?

R.R.: There's always an autobiographical element, because writers start from their own experience. The content of our writing can't be separated from the subjective and social frame that originated it. But the autobiographical element in literature must transcend what is merely personal and social and comprise a larger field. It is the writer's task to present autobiographical material in a transcendent manner so that it produces a true coexistence with the reader.

M.F.: What has been the critical reaction to your works?

R.R.: Both good and bad. But that isn't important to me. What matters is the opinion of a few people whose opinions I value.

M.F.: Have your works been translated?

R.R.: David Unger translated "Revelations" and Carolyn Harris and Marilyn Chin translated an excerpt from *La rompiente* titled "High Tide."

M.F.: Is it hard to publish in Argentina?

R.R.: Yes, because publishers will only touch books that ensure a minimum sale of three thousand volumes. It's hard to find a publisher who will touch the book of a young writer who doesn't conform to the tendencies that sell in the current book market.

M.F.: Are you able to live off your works?

R.R.: No!

M.F.: Is it harder for a woman writer to publish, to be reviewed, and to receive prizes?

R.R.: Yes, because in Argentina, the literary production of women is still underrated. The majority of male writers ignore the current literature by women. They still think that literature written by women is trivial, too anecdotal, or sentimental, that it revolves around the home and a cloistered domestic life, that it is repetitive, interrogative, too detailed, and characterized by a tone of anger or resentment. However, although there is no understanding of the value of female literature as a new or alternative mode of discourse, there is the growing realization, among editors with a good business sense, that quantities of books and articles dealing with women's issues are being sold and generating international interest, and that this might lead to a lucrative business. So, it's easier now for women writers to win more recognition than in the past, but only because our work responds to the demand of the international market and not due to a true evaluation of contemporary female literary production.

M.F.: Who are your favorite contemporary Argentine women writers?

R.R.: The novelists Noemí Ulla, Hebe Uhart, Alicia Steimberg, Cecilia Absatz; the poets Liliana Ponce, Diana Belessi, Mirta Rosenberg, Mirta De Filpo; the playwrights Griselda Gambaro and Diana Raznovich.

M.F.: Do you think there is a female style of writing different from male writing?

R.R.: Let me preface my response by saying that female writing is not a contemporary phenomenon. Women have been writing for a long time. The division of literature into female and male makes me stop and think. It seems that faced with increasing female literary production, both in quantity and quality, male critics started promoting these labels. The term "female literature" had negative connotations and was used to refer to a minor body of literature. It was believed that the author, the authority, had to be male. But in answer to your question, I think there is a female discourse that is different from the male mode. Marta Traba wrote in an article that the female expressive system is conditioned by a particular perception, elaboration, and projection. Women talk from another perspective. We have a different perception of the world. When we express ourselves through our own voices, our sensitivity and imagination, censored or self-censored, criticized and critical, produces literary works with different effects and signifiers. My goal is to attain a literary discourse that is beyond the female or male modes and nearer to total transgression That is the real meaning of literature for me.

M.F.: What is the situation of women and women writers in Argentina now?

R.R.: I think that all Argentines are the victims of a profound individual and social crisis that stems from our history, not only the recent dictatorship but successive dictatorships. It is the product of an authoritarian ideology that predominated and still persists. Although we are living in democracy, Argentine authoritarianism is still obvious in the minds and behavior of everyday people. Women are not oblivious to this phenomenon. We are brought up according to an ideology that promotes fanaticism, patriarchy, and indifference as mechanisms to deny our circumstances. So it's common to encounter women who are misogynists or indifferent, but there are also many women who are concerned with social problems and women's issues, made apparent by the many women's organizations that deal with female problems. Concerning the situation of the women writers, I believe the quality of current female writing shows that we are acquiring visibility against all odds.

M.F.: Are you a feminist?

R.R.: Yes, I believe that feminism offers a very important framework for the analysis of women's issues. Feminism has given women the tools for understanding their situations, allowing them to act independently, to detect their true selves and face the consequences. It has been very useful for me. However, I'd like to be able to get on to another stage where we wouldn't have to place labels on ourselves or be labeled feminists just because we hold another worldview, dare to enact it, and demand to be respected for it.

M.F.: How do you include your feminist views in your works?

R.R.: I suppose my works include many views, among them my understanding of feminism and how I perceive the world from the vantage point of my femininity. But I don't write feminist theory. What I attempt to create is literature.

M.F.: Where were you during the years of the "dirty war" in Argentina?

R.R.: I stayed in Buenos Aires until 1981. I spent the worst years of the "dirty war" here. Then I left for the United States and returned to my country in 1984 when a democratic government was installed.

M.F.: Were you able to write and publish during those years?

R.R.: I was able to write, but it was very difficult for me to publish. My novel, *Monte de Venus*, was prohibited in 1976 and that really inhibited me. I chose not to publish, because it became a question of survival. I decided to wait for better times.

M.F.: Did your themes and language change as a result of censorship?

R.R.: Not really. The changes came as a result of my own development as a writer.

M.F.: What are you writing now?

R.R.: Short stories, and I'm taking notes for my next novel.

M.F.: Is there a change in direction in what you're writing now?

R.R.: I can't say. But I do want to fulfill a desire I've had since I wrote my first novel: to integrate, through my writing, an alienated and fragmented personal world, and transcend a cloistered existence. I think I'm slowly doing that.

Buenos Aires, 30 October 1993

M.F.: Can you tell me about the themes in your forthcoming novel *A la intemperie* (In the open)?

R.R.: A new theme appears in my narrative with *La rompiente*: "the journey," which is also developed in my next novel, completed at the beginning of this year but still unpublished, and provisionally titled *A la intemperie*.

M.F.: Does *A la intemperie* continue the story developed in your previous novel?

R.R.: Although both narrations are independent and function separately in what concerns their structure, they are linked by their thematic content. A content that is approached from different angles to explore the different alternatives posed by the journeys from one place to the other, the internal and external journeys, the exodus for political, economic, or personal reasons; and, especially, how these forms of "exile" affect the way we perceive and experience reality and question our sense of identity. *La rompiente* starts with the protagonist's journey to a foreign country and one question: "Wherever I may go, will I find the splendor of a voice?" The entire text is the answer. That journey abroad, where another language is spoken, connects with silence as a theme, alluding to the years of silence during the military dictatorship and also to the obstacle encountered by the woman (the protagonist) to speak, name, write from within herself. Not being able to speak freely in her country of origin, the need for another, more permissive frame of reference, a territory privileged by distance to finally have access to the word serves, in *La rompiente*, to integrate the parts of a fragmented story. *A la intemperie* starts with the return to the country of origin, and although in this case a question is not formulated, the text raises the utopian character of the journey's destination. It underscores the bewilderment when facing a time period that was not experienced (directly), but was experienced from outside; it inquires into whether it is possible to return, to recuperate the continuity of a space culturally and emotionally fractured by absence.

M.F.: Is there a female perspective to this novel, as was present in your previous works?

R.R.: While the theme of exile or journey is recurrent in literature, especially in Argentine literature of these past decades, my inquiry originates in the need to face it from the perspective of a woman protagonist, from a female identity, which is always implicitly questioned and now is forced to account for two worlds at the same time, faced with the effects that her uprooting has on her personality, her aesthetics, and even, her language. *La rompiente* and *A la intemperie* result from this inquiry.

BIBLIOGRAPHY

Primary Sources (listed chronologically)

Roffé, Reina. *Llamado al puf.* Buenos Aires: Editorial Pleamar, 1973.
———. *Monte de Venus.* Buenos Aires: Ediciones Corregidor, 1976.
———. *La rompiente.* Buenos Aires: Puntosur Editores, 1987.
———. *A la intemperie.* Forthcoming.

Short Fiction by Reina Roffé (listed chronologically)

Roffé, Reina. "Fuera de foco." In *Ultimos relatos,* edited by Miguel Briante, Germán L. García, Luis Gusman, J. C. Martini Real, M. Pichón Rivière, Ricardo Piglia, Rodolfo Rabanal, and Reina Roffé. Buenos Aires: Nemont Ediciones, 1977.
———. "Alta marea." *Puro cuento* 1 (November-December 1986): 12–13.
———. "Revelaciones." *Crisis* 52 (March 1987).

Works Available in Translation (listed chronologically)

Roffé, Reina. "Let's Hear What He Has To Say." Translated by H. Ernest Lewald. In *The Web: Stories by Argentine Women,* edited by H. Ernest Lewald, 165–70. Washington D.C.: Three Continents Press, 1983.
———. "High Tide." Translated by Carolyn Harris and Marilyn Chin. *The Iowa Review* 14 (1984): 54–57.
———. "Revelations." Translated by David Unger. *Present Tense* 12 (Spring 1985): 24–25.

————. "Flut." Translated by Wolfgang Eitel. In *Fallen die Perlen vom Mond?* edited by Mempo Giardinelli and Wolfgang Eitel. Munich: Piper Verlag, 1991.

————. "Eine Stadt in Grau und Beige." In *Erkundigungen: 21 Erzähler vom Rio de la Plata*, edited by Eduardo Belgrano Rawson, Tomás Eloy Martínez, Rodolfo Fogwill, J. C. Martini Real, Tununa Mercado, Ricardo Piglia, Juan José Saer, and Reina Roffé. Berlin: Verlag Volk, 1993.

Critical Works and Interviews by Reina Roffé (listed chronologically)

Roffé, Reina. "Juan Rulfo: autobiografía armada." 1st ed. *Latinoamericana* 1 (December 1972): 73–178; *Juan Rulfo: autobiografía armada.* 2d ed. Buenos Aires: Editorial Corregidor, 1973; *Juan Rulfo: autobiografía armada.* 3d ed. Barcelona: Montesinos, El Sur 1, 1992.

————. "Juan Rulfo: las mañas del zorro: entrevista con Juan Rulfo." *Clarín*, 25 July 1974.

————. "Soy un pensamiento pasajero en la mente de los que me quieren: entrevista con Adolfo Bioy Casares." *Siete días*, 29 July 1977.

————. "La historia que nadie conoce de Manucho Mujica Láinez." *Siete días*, 27 October 1977.

————. "Alicia Moreau de Justo: la política de lo femenino." *La Opinión*, 23 December 1979.

————. "Diversidad y dispersión en la narrativa argentina actual." In *El Cono Sur: dinámica y dimensiones de su literatura*, edited by Rose S. Minc, 146–52. Upper Montclair, N.J.: Montclair State College, 1985.

————. "Entrevista con Mempo Giardinelli." *Imagine* 2 (Winter 1985): 121–26.

————. *Espejo de escritores.* Hanover, N.H.: Ediciones del Norte, 1985.

————. "Omnipresencia de la censura en la Argentina." *Revista iberoamericana* 51 (July-December 1985): 909–15.

————. "Borges: reportaje a una voz: última ficción." *Tiempo Argentino*, 22 June 1986.

————. "Contra la Kultura: entrevista con Manuel Puig." *Tiempo Argentino*, 29 June 1986.

————. "Los textos: itinerario de una escritura." Foreword to *La rompiente*, by Reina Roffé, 9–11. Buenos Aires: Puntosur Editores, 1987.

————. "Qué escribimos las mujeres en la Argentina de hoy." In *Literatura argentina hoy: de la dictadura a la democracia*, edited by Karl Kohut and Andrea Pagni, 205–13. Frankfurt: Vervuert Verlag, 1989.

————. "Daniel Moyano: el fuego interrumpido." *Página 12*, 27 June 1993.

Videotaped Interviews by Reina Roffé (listed chronologically)

Borges, Jorge Luis. "El memorioso." Interview by Reina Roffé. Videotape *Espejo de escritores*. Hanover, N.H.: Ediciones del Norte 1983.

Puig, Manuel. "Del 'kitsch' a Lacan." Interview by Reina Roffé. Videotape *Espejo de escritores*. Hanover, N.H.: Ediciones del Norte, 1983.

Rulfo, Juan. "Inframundo." Interview by Reina Roffé. Videotape *Espejo de escritores*. Hanover, N.H.: Ediciones del Norte, 1983.

Cortázar, Julio."Modelo para desarmar." Interview by Saúl Sosnowski, introduction by Reina Roffé. Videotape *Espejo de escritores*. Hanover, N.H.: Ediciones del Norte, 1985.

Goytisolo, Juan. "La libertad de los parias." Interview by Randolph Pope, introduction by Reina Roffé. Videotape *Espejo de escritores*. Hanover, N.H.: Ediciones del Norte, 1985.

Onetti, Juan Carlos. "Un escritor." Interview by Jorge Ruffinelli, introduction by Reina Roffé. Videotape *Espejo de escritores*. Hanover, N.H.: Ediciones del Norte, 1985.

Rama, Angel. "Más allá de la ciudad letrada." Interview by Mario Szichman, introduction by Reina Roffé. Videotape *Espejo de escritores*. Hanover, N.H.: Ediciones del Norte, 1985.

Vargas Llosa, Mario. "Maestro de las voces." Interview by Miguel Oviedo, introduction by Reina Roffé. Videotape *Espejo de escritores*. Hanover, N.H.: Ediciones del Norte, 1985.

Secondary Sources

Avellaneda, Andrés. "Canon y escritura de mujer: un viaje al centro de la periferia." *Espacios*, 10 November 1991.

Company, Flavia. "Voces solistas." Review of *Juan Rulfo: autobiografía armada*, by Reina Roffé. *La Vanguardia*, 2 October 1992.

De Miguel, Ester. "Voces ambiguas y ambigua la trama." Review of *La rompiente*, by Reina Roffé. *La Nación*, 8 November 1987.

"Estantería." Review of *La rompiente*, by Reina Roffé. *Hoy en la noticia*, 6 December 1987.

Fares, Gustavo, and Eliana Hermann. "Reina Roffé." In *Escritoras argentinas contemporáneas*, 191–216. New York: Peter Lang, 1993.

Flori, Mónica. "Entrevista con Reina Roffé: sobre escritura femenina y su última novela *La rompiente*." *Alba de América* 6 (July 1988): 423–28.

Foster, David William. "The Demythification of Buenos Aires in Selected Argentine Novels of the Seventies." In *Alternate Voices in the*

Contemporary Latin American Narrative, 60–106. Columbia: University of Missouri Press, 1985.

―――."Los parámetros de la narrativa argentina durante el 'Proceso de Reorganización Nacional.'" In *Ficción y política: la narrativa argentina durante el proceso militar*, edited by Daniel Balderston et al., 96–108. Buenos Aires: Alianza Editorial, 1987.

Gimbernat González, Ester. "*La rompiente* (R. Roffé) o la integración en la escritura." In *Aventuras del descuerdo: novelistas argentinas de los 80*, 186–90. Buenos Aires: Danilo Albero Vergara, 1992.

Gramuglio, María Teresa. "Aproximaciones a *La rompiente*." Postliminal study of *La rompiente*, by Reina Roffé. Buenos Aires: Puntosur Editores, 1987.

Gudiño Kieffer, Eduardo. "Juventud sin rumbo." Review of *Monte de Venus*, by Reina Roffé. *Clarín*, 2 December 1976.

Kapschutschenki, Ludmila. "Primer Concurso Bienal Internacional de Novela Breve." *Hispania* 70 (September 1987): 555.

Kliagine, Dominique. "The Uprootedness of Exile." Review of *La rompiente*, by Reina Roffé." *Buenos Aires Herald*, 25 October 1987.

Luzzani, Thelma. "Las letras distintas." Review of *La rompiente*, by Reina Roffé. *Clarín*, 24 December 1987.

Magno, Laura. Review of *La rompiente*, by Reina Roffé. *El Porteño*, 10 November 1987.

Martini Real, J. C. "Prólogo." Foreword to *Llamado al puf*, by Reina Roffé, 15-20. Buenos Aires: Ediciones Pleamar, 1973.

―――. "Dejemos hablar al viento." Review of *La rompiente*, by Reina Roffé. *Humor*, 1–15 October 1986.

Masiello, Francine. "Contemporary Argentine Fiction: Liberal (Pre-)Texts in a Reign of Terror." *Latin American Research Review* 16 (1981): 219–24.

―――. "Cuerpo/presencia: mujer y estado social en la narrativa argentina durante el proceso militar." *Nuevo texto crítico* 2 (July-December 1989): 155–71.

―――. "Subversions of Authority: Feminist Literary Culture in the River Plate Region." *Chasqui: revista de literatura latinoamericana* 21 (May 1992): 39–47.

Meinhardt, Warren L. Review of *Juan Rulfo: autobiografía armada*, 3d ed., by Reina Roffé. *Explicación de textos literarios* 22 (1993–94): 99–100.

Mon, Carlos Roberto. Review of *La rompiente*, by Reina Roffé. *La Razón*, 30 December 1987.

Moyano, Daniel. "El difícil argumento de los cuentos de Rulfo." Review of *Juan Rulfo: autobiografía armada*, 3d ed., by Reina Roffé. *El Mundo*, 16 May 1992.

Muñoz, Amparito. "Datos para una ficha: reportaje a Reina Roffé." *Fin de siglo*, 2 August 1987, 87.

"Novela de Roffé." Review of *La rompiente*, by Reina Roffé. *Hoy en la noticia*, 6 December 1987.

Pinto, Antonio. "Reina Roffé." *Cultura* 17 (November-December 1986): 45.

"Reina Roffé segundo tiempo." *Panorama*, 10 October 1976, 122.

Richter Martínez, Marily. "Textualizaciones de la violencia: *Informe bajo llave* de Marta Lynch y *La rompiente* de Reina Roffé." Berlin: Freie Universität Berlin. Forthcoming.

Rosenvinge, Teresa. "Algo único." Review of *Juan Rulfo: autobiografía armada*, by Reina Roffé. *Diario 16*, 7 May 1992.

Saavedra, Hernán. "En busca del tiempo perdido." Review of *Llamado al puf*, by Reina Roffé. *Claudia*, 1 April 1973.

"Seducción del puf." Review of *Llamado al puf*, by Reina Roffé. *Confirmado*, 25 February 1973, 45.

Silvestre, Susana. Review of *La rompiente*, by Reina Roffé. *Acción*, 1 January 1988.

Szurmuk, Mónica. "La textualización de la represión en *La rompiente* de Reina Roffé." *Nuevo texto crítico* 3 (1990): 123–31.

Conclusion

The six contemporary women writers from Argentina presented in this book represent two generations—the fifties and the seventies—that are outstanding in the history of Argentine letters. It is apparent from the essays and conversations that their literature shares the bond of a common experiential, cultural, and sociopolitical background.

The main recurring traits in their work reflect contemporary Argentine society and contemporary Argentine writing. There were four primary concerns in the analysis of their works and in the questions posed to them during the interviews: (1) How do these writers reflect their sociopolitical reality, and the social and political aspects of their work? (2) How do these writers use the craft of fiction to liberate themselves from the repressive authoritarianism that they have experienced? (3) How is their rejection of authoritarianism tied to the emergence of a literature that strives to overcome a patriarchal, traditional literary canon and create a feminist literary text (apparent in the themes, strong female characters, and in the techniques and discourse)? (4) How does a weltanschauung bearing both a metaphysical and existential dimension emerge from their work?

The sociopolitical reality dealt with in these works covers Argentine history from the 1940s to the 1980s: two Perón eras (1946–55 and 1973–76) and the military dictatorships known as the Proceso (1976–83). Peronism is a recurrent theme in the works of these novelists. In Alicia Jurado's novels, it provides a background to the plots. She portrays a new society of the forties and fifties dominated by materialism and greed. She critiques Peronism not through direct testimonials but by focusing on changing values and their effects on the family structure and relationships. The result is a generation gap, as old, traditional values are replaced by the birth of a new society characterized by industrialization, a rising proletariat, and the migration of the rural population to the cities. This

247

new reality, cast as a vague and distant threat, is portrayed from the perspective of the genteel, upper-crust *porteño* characters. Her novels are typical of the fifties in dealing with the upper-middle class rather than the emergence of the masses in Argentine society, a characteristic of the Peronist era.

An oblique treatment of Peronism is also characteristic in Alicia Steimberg's *Músicos y relojeros* and Reina Roffé's *Llamado al puf,* but for different reasons. In these novels, we see the effects of Peronism from the limited perspective of child narrators. Their narrators are struck by the repercussions of economic depression and rampant inflation on families, friends, and neighbors. In Steimberg's account, the deteriorating standards of living are seen from the perspective of a child who cannot understand the political and economic developments taking place. Roffé allows an omniscient narrator to make devastating judgments on the bourgeoisie who cling to their lifestyle as they sink into the working class. Her narrator exposes a country that has become a pawn in a capitalist and imperialistic scheme.

Orphée deals directly with Peronism in *Uno,* a novel whose main theme is the influence of Peronism on Argentine society. The title *Uno* refers to the opposition to Perón by characters who represent a range of social classes. The work covers an important year in the struggle against Perón. It opens on 1 May 1954, the date of Perón's address at the traditional Labor Day rally in Plaza de Mayo, and closes on 16 June 1955. The ending portrays a failed coup against Perón on that date, symbolizing the decay of a divided society. Focusing on a short time span and emphasizing the political framework through the use of symbolic events, Orphée gives a picture of indifference, violence, and chaos. Orphée's *La última conquista de El Angel* offers a picture of the practice of torture during the height of the Peronist era (1953–55). The novel reflects the barbaric side of Peronism and offers insights into the origins of practices expanded during the Proceso.

We are offered another view of Peronism in Roffé's second novel, *Monte de Venus,* which shows the impact on the lives of high school students of Perón's return to Argentina and his rise to power in the 1970s. Argentine youth were frustrated by Peronism, an experience that shattered their hopes for the future.

Our last view of Peronism is again symbolic. In *Cama de ángeles,* Alina Diaconú blends the images of an unidentified couple waving from a balcony (the Peróns?) with a character's memory of her parents. The suggestion is that contemporary Argentines view themselves as orphaned children with a yearning for parental figures. Consequently, they support strongmen as their leaders.

We are offered a range of treatments of Peronism, from Jurado's vision of its impact on a wealthier social sector, to Steimberg and Roffé's portrayal of the erosion of middle-class values and the disillusionment of the younger generation, to Orphée's comprehensive treatment and Diaconú's metaphorical representation. It is interesting to note that all these novelists present characters who express feelings of disempowerment, of being driven by a blind force over which they have no control. These writers see Peronism as a consequence of the individualism and isolation characteristic of Argentine society both at the social and individual level. The society is prone to manipulation by unscrupulous leaders like Perón, because individuals are incapable of working together as a cohesive force for social stability. Roffé, the youngest writer, is the only novelist who attempts to cast Peronism in the light of an international political and economic system. She emphasizes Argentina's dependency in the international arena.

The Proceso was ushered in by Peronism between 1974 and 1976, after Perón's death. Although the writers could not refer to the Proceso during the 1970s and 1980s, they could use Peronist imagery to conceal their critique *(Cama de ángeles, Monte de Venus)*. Furthermore, using metaphor and symbolism to treat Perón and Evita as part of a mythopoetic element in Argentine culture and reality is a tendency in modern Argentine fiction. Examples are Luisa Valenzuela's *Como en la guerra* (As in war), 1977, and Mario Szichman's *A las 20:25, la señora entró en la inmortalidad (At 8:25, Evita Became Immortal)*, 1981.

Only two novels in our study, Absatz's *Los años pares* and Diaconú's *El penúltimo viaje*, deal directly with the Proceso. (Other novels, as we have seen, deal with it metaphorically.) They were both published in the eighties, after Argentina's return to democracy. Both portray female characters who are innocent bystanders victimized by military repression. These novels are not testimonials; however, they share as a central theme the female quest for identity within an authoritarian, patriarchal society. While violence spreads through Argentina and society disintegrates into chaos, female characters discover inner knowledge and strength by means of "real," symbolic journeys.

The Proceso generated three responses from writers: (1) silence (Steimberg and Roffé), the most common response in order to survive; (2) exile (Orphée); and (3) the development of a new type of novel, which I call the novel of censorship (Steimberg, Diaconú, and Roffé). I will restrict myself to the novel of censorship and how it links the sociopolitical and the creative response of these writers.

Writing under these circumstances causes a break in the literary tradition. The writer has to alter her style and discourse to hide a thematic content that may be read as an ideological interpretation of reality. What develops is a literature that coexists with and represents the other face of the official and authoritarian discourse. It is a marginal literature, "borderline," to use Julia Kristeva's term.[1] This literature is characterized by a deliberate distortion of reality with a profusion of fantasy and ambiguity, metaphor and symbolism, and a fragmentary discourse and structure.

An example of borderline literature is Steimberg's novel, *La loca 101*, published in 1973. After writing this novel, repression and censorship forced the writer to undergo a period of silence that lasted eight years. The novel's main theme is madness, reflecting the effects of repression on the population, especially on intellectuals targeted by the regime. As Steimberg expressed in the interview, she felt during that time that she was raving, and transposed her state of mind into a work of fiction. Madness is coupled with the theme of death, which in Steimberg's fiction develops from its autobiographical origin to encompass her view of society. It is also blended with imagery of institutionalized confinement and violence, all cloaked with and narrated from the point of view of madness. With madness as the narrative viewpoint, traditional discourse and logic are transgressed, and a fragmented narration and structure result. The critics of this novel have named this reorganization "a narrative puzzle," requiring the reader to decode the text in order to make sense of it. And to do that, we have to link the text to the historical moment, viewing it as a response to a reality that cannot be narrated by traditional techniques. The result is an ambiguous and multifaceted text cushioned in irony and humor to deflect attention from feelings of terror and alienation. The use of amnesia (an alternative to madness) in Steimberg's *Cuando digo Magdalena* is a device that, used as a narrative point of view, weakens the centers of power and control and dismantles an authoritarian narration and discursive text. It is replaced by a hesitant and fragmented voice narrating from the inner depths of a female protagonist.

The use of madness as a narrative technique and as a metaphor for the effects of repression is also constant in Diaconú's novels. As in Steimberg's *La loca 101*, Diaconú's characters narrate from the point of view of madness in *La Señora, Buenas noches, profesor*, and *Los ojos azules*, thus drawing their reader into conflicting narrations, a world where the borders between reality and illusion, sanity and insanity, are blurred. In Diaconú's works, Argentine reality is portrayed through the lack of freedom of her characters, who live in confined places. Because of fear, they have lost the will to live. The political reality is also present in the recurrent figure of the dictator cast in a world of madness and conjured in symbolic terms by characters who waver between reality and madness. We encounter this figure in the central characters' brief stay at a circus/hospital in *Cama de ángeles*, where they are confined and victimized by a mad doctor/dictator, who runs the place with impunity. In Diaconú's following novel, *Los ojos azules*, the female protagonist is confined at the same time in a psychiatric clinic and on a (hallucinated?) island ruled by despotic and hideous old men. They subject her to abuse and finally kill her, an oblique interpretation of life in contemporary Argentina. *Los devorados* disguises madness as obsessive addictions (alcohol, cocaine, nymphomania, carnivorous plants) that destroy people. The novel becomes a tale of abjection and human despair, a subversion of traditional fictional devices, metaphorically tearing apart the monologic dimensions of patriarchal discourse and censorship.

Diaconú's response to official repression is a narrative that blends several accounts of reality couched in insanity. The narrator manipulates several levels of a story that negate and distort one another to conceal the truth. As in Steimberg's novels, the result is a fragmented and fallible narration and narrative structure designed to blur the text and mask it—an alternative to silence.

Roffé's *La rompiente* is also representative of borderline fiction in its response to the political reality and its effects on the writer. It came out after *Monte de Venus* was prohibited and the novelist was forced to adopt an eleven-year silence. Although Diaconú and Steimberg developed the point of view of madness from which to write their novels of censorship, all three characteristics of the novel of the Proceso exist in *La rompiente*: silence, exile, and censorship. The novel strikes us as devoid of a traditional plot. No traditional points of reference are present. It is a novel without a story, and it does not project the unfolding of developments that lead to a plot.

When the novel opens, the reader gathers that the protagonist has been exiled and is arriving at her place of exile. But the reasons for her exile are never revealed, nor is her past. We are reading a novel that questions the basic tenets of how a work of fiction is crafted. There is a deconstruction of fiction, which is "reconstructed" in a very particular manner. The deconstruction of the fictional work responds to the historical events that silenced the writer, and were transfigured into a protagonist—a silenced writer—who in her exile searches for a voice. Traces of this historical context are scattered throughout the narrative, but are not placed in the story so as to constitute a plot. We learn that the female protagonist joined some kind of a group while she lived in a place where people were persecuted and muzzled by military repression. We also learn that, at some point, the protagonist was warned that she would become a target, so she chose exile. Prior to her exile, there was a period when the protagonist was locked in her room, writing a disjointed story about the Proceso, inscribed both in a novel and a diary, while refusing to speak to anybody, including her family. Once settled in exile, she meets the interlocutor, the recipient and narrator of parts of her story. This interlocutor shapes the account from fragments of the diary and parts of their interrupted conversations. A voice recites the story to the protagonist—an ambiguous, distorted, and fallible story that includes not only what was said at that point, but also previous conversations outside the primary narration, which are used as if they were reflecting surfaces.

María Teresa Gramuglio points out in her study of the novel that there is a first-person narrator who points to a previous text, an oral narration, and a second narrator whose function has been changed from that of listener to narrator. She contends, therefore, that the basis for the novel is simulation, because it is constructed on a dialogue that is not really a dialogue but a series of monologues, remembrances that repeat a former narrative. Nevertheless, the interlocutor, who is repeating what someone else told him/her, remits to us the written version of the previous oral and written materials, which become the body of the novel.[2] The result is a novel that is the sum of various mixed and ambiguous stories, which fail to lead to a logical conclusion. Perhaps the only conclusion is a new beginning, as the narrator emerges from silence to produce a story from the beginning of her exile, a story as disjointed and illogical as the years of defeat and death when no literature was possible. Therefore, Roffé's response is a new literature that has produced a transformed text with concealed meanings.

As we have seen, authoritarian repression in Argentina, a characteristic of a patriarchal society, has engendered a silent society and attempted to ban literature. Writers have responded by creating a new feminist literary novel that deviates from the traditional literary canon and subverts patriarchal literature. The four featured novelists of the 1970s created works that project female and feminist visions. These novelists are writing from within a society that upholds patriarchal idiosyncrasies, especially concerning women's roles and female sexual behavior. Insofar as life very often imitates art, these writers create new female characters who transgress traditional behavior and values. The characters project a new woman as role model and as the subject of literary works.

In the creation of these new female characters, certain traditional literary limitations are overcome. In mainstream literature, marriage is the goal for women, who wait in the background for their male hero (he is usually the subject of the work). Female characters are usually cloistered while they await the male hero, thus reflecting traditional social roles. Their life story must end in marriage or the dreaded alternatives: madness and suicide. But these novels transform women characters into protagonists and narrators. The object becomes an active subject, instead of being cast in the traditional role of the Other. These women are usually alone in life, single, and economically independent *(Té con canela, Monte de Venus, La rompiente, El penúltimo viaje)*. If they have been married, most end up divorced *(Su espíritu inocente, El árbol del placer, Los años pares, Los ojos azules)*, projecting the image of women who are alone and trying to find themselves. They embark on outward journeys symbolic of an inner quest *(Los ojos azules, El penúltimo viaje, Los años pares, La rompiente)*, rewriting the motif of the quest as a prerogative of the male hero.

The traditional meaning of madness, suicide, and enclosure is also altered by female writers. Although madness and suicide were traditional endings for novels seeking to punish a female character who deviated from societal norms, these novels *(La Señora, Los ojos azules, La loca 101)* use them to critique a patriarchal society. Confinement, a traditional symbol of female submissiveness, is utilized in these novels as a means of self-discovery. We encounter several protagonists who wish to escape their alienating modern circumstances in order to embark on an inner journey. To do that, they spend time alone in their apartments *(Té con canela)* or childhood homes *(Llamado al puf)*, or seek the solitude of a train journey *(El penúltimo viaje)* or a country estate *(Cuando digo Magdalena)* as a means to discover what really matters to them.

The sexual behavior in these works breaks from social codes and becomes a tool of self-discovery. As we saw before, marriage is not the main goal of these protagonists. They seek sexual relations, sometimes casual ones, without the traditional feeling of guilt *(Té con canela, Monte de Venus, Enamorada del muro)*. As these writers attempt to destroy social and cultural taboos, we see another recurrent trait in these works: implicit and explicit lesbianism *(Monte de Venus, Té con canela, Los ojos azules)*. Diaconú carries her attempts to obliterate gender roles and differences to the metaphoric level by using a transvestite, androgynous protagonist narrator *(Cama de ángeles)*.

These novels, then, use traditional motifs within a thematic quest for identity to define what being female means from a female perspective. To do so, male definitions about women must be overcome, a task these writers accomplish by manipulating plots and motifs, especially those concerning female behavior and sexual roles. Male discourse has been traditionally used to silence women, but these women writers have created a new discourse that transmits a feminist vision and a new plot focusing on women from their own perspective.

The silenced woman must regain her own voice to tell her story, the account of her search for self-definition. At the same time, she must come to terms with her own fragmentation, which has resulted from living in an authoritarian, patriarchal society and being perceived and narrated from a male perspective. To create this new feminist text, the writer follows a process defined by critic Sharon Keefe Ugalde:

> The process at work in women's writing is cyclical in nature: Subversiveness-destruction-deconstruction followed by reconstruction-creation. . . . The central target of the subversive phase is phallogocentrism, whose logic, dichotomies and sense of hierarchy predetermine female experience.[3]

The path to liberation outlined by Keefe Ugalde requires confronting both patriarchal thought and logic as well as the male-dominated language. A female vision and discourse overcome the dominant logic and language, and elucidate an authentic female identity and experience.

This process is apparent in Diaconú's *El penúltimo viaje*, a novel that symbolizes the collapse of authoritarian patriarchy through the protagonist's father, a powerful political figure who falls into disgrace in the Communist hierarchy in an Eastern European country and flees to the West with his children. Diaconú presents authoritarianism and the discourse used to project it as her central theme. She appropriates this world by the narration of its disintegration, projected through a feminist vision and discourse.

The father, a symbol of authoritarianism, has total control over others, especially his family. His discourse and authoritarian presence dominate the first part of the novel and the protagonist's childhood. As we read the narration of the protagonist's memories of her childhood, we hear only the voice of her father, which silences the rest of the characters—a metaphor for what happens to subjugated people, especially women. In an attempt to dispossess the patriarchal discourse of its authority, Diaconú points to the authoritarian and patriarchal nature of society. At the same time she uses a female narrator to recreate the world and the male authoritarian voice. As the novel unfolds and the family arrives in the West, the father figure crumbles. His speech becomes contradictory and stagnant; his power is destroyed. While the paternal figure fades, the voices of other characters, especially the females (the protagonist's mother, maternal grandmother, nannies, and female servants), become stronger. A transformation also takes place as the protagonist matures and comes to terms with her past while finding her own identity and voice. It becomes evident that the narrative voice that at first seemed patriarchal and hegemonic is actually the voice of the female narrator canceling out the former patriarchal language, which is inauthentic and stripped of power. Diaconú has thus dramatized the relationship between patriarchal power and language in order to annul it.

Diaconú uses the disintegration of the authoritative figure and voice to project the story of a female in search of self, narrated by a female. The quest and the novel are shaped by memories colored by emotion, thus preserving a traditional female perception of reality. Previously devalued, this perception proves to be an effective tool in projecting an authentic female vision—a vision based on an inner dialogue. This inner dialogue is characteristic of the emergence of a female voice, which wavers between a woman's own world vision and what an imposed, hegemonic concept and discourse dictate. Steimberg's *Cuando digo Magdalena* depicts the emergence of a female conscience (and voice), sentenced to obliterate her memories, rescuing the fragments of her identity and the past. The result is a dissident, female reading of history, surging forth from the protagonist's inner self.

To conclude, I would like to comment on the metaphysical and existential vision that these texts project. The metaphysical is conspicuously absent in many of these works, but it is alluded to in some, allowing us to determine the existence of a common view, a product of a shared cultural and social experience. The yearning for the Absolute (linked to political torture leading to self-destruction in *Uno* and *La última conquista de El Angel*) is present in Orphée's novels as her characters set out on a futile quest for God. What they find instead are absurd and cruel circumstances that mark their lives. They find it impossible to attain transcendence as they stumble around in an absurd world. Life is felt as a satanic experience in which (in the absence of God) the human being becomes the incarnation of evil, living to inflict pain and suffering on others.

In Diaconú's novels, the yearning for transcendence has been suppressed by the state and is incarnated in authoritarian political figures who have usurped God's place *(Los ojos azules, El penúltimo viaje)*. There is a ritualization of death, symbolized by a physical attempt by the living to claim a space (a ritual shrine) for their loved ones, signifying at the same time the death of spirituality and a yearning and lamentation for its loss. In some works by Diaconú as well as those of Steimberg, we find that the absence of God and religion has made the characters seek transcendence through sects *(Enamorada del muro)*, political parties *(El penúltimo viaje)*, psychotherapy, and other endeavors perceived as fads *(El árbol del placer* and *Cuando digo Magdalena)*.

A world characterized by the absence of God and spirituality projects a bleak existential vision. With the exception of the characters in Jurado's novels, who still embrace traditional values in a collapsing world, the characters of these writers are extremely alienated from themselves in a society that denies them their rightful place. They are outcasts consumed by feelings of anxiety, fear, and guilt, which they try to overcome by spending their lives in a journey to expiate these flaws. Although their feelings of alienation stem from characteristics that plague a contemporary world stripped of spiritual and transcendental values, they reflect the particular strains and upheavals of Argentine society, which has sought to annihilate its most creative elements.

In the preceding pages we have focused on the sociopolitical aspect, the creative process, the feminist literary text, and the metaphysical and existential vision. What strikes us is the strength and creative spirit of these writers, who have managed to produce rich literature from the attempted destruction of their society and cultural and literary traditions. Theirs is not testimonial literature per se; however, it will remain as witness to the times, as well as examples of artistic development ushering in a new genre of fiction. Their inspiration was crafted on the collapse of their society, on a literary canon, and on the ideals and values of their generation. Notwithstanding, Jurado, Orphée, Diaconú, Steimberg, Absatz, and Roffé represent the writers of their era who were able to spread their wings and rise like phoenixes from the ashes.

Notes

Preface

1. Ivette E. Miller and Charles M. Tatum, eds., *Latin American Women Writers: Yesterday and Today* (Pittsburgh, Pa.: The Review, 1977); Beth Miller, ed., *Women in Hispanic Literature: Icons and Fallen Idols* (Berkeley: University of California Press, 1983); Carmelo Virgillo and Naomi Lindstrom, eds., *Women as Myth and Metaphor in Latin American Literature* (Columbia: University of Missouri Press, 1985); Magdalena García Pinto, *Women Writers of Latin America: Intimate Stories*, trans. Trudy Balch and Magdalena García Pinto (Austin: University of Texas Press, 1991); Debra A. Castillo, *Talking Back: Toward a Latin American Feminist Literary Criticism* (Ithaca: Cornell University Press, 1992).

2. Doris Meyer and Marguerite Fernández Olmos, eds., *Contemporary Women Authors of Latin America*, 2 vols. (Brooklyn, N.Y.: Brooklyn College Press, 1983); H. Ernest Lewald, ed. and trans., *The Web: Stories by Argentine Women* (Washington, D.C.: Three Continents Press, 1983); Alberto Manguel, ed., *Other Fires: Short Fiction by Latin American Women* (New York: Clarkson N. Potter, 1986); Evelyn Picon Garfield, *Women's Voices from Latin America: Interviews with Six Contemporary Authors* (Detroit, Mich.: Wayne State University Press, 1987); Evelyn Picon Garfield, ed. and trans., *Women's Voices from Latin America: Selections from Twelve Contemporary Authors* (Detroit, Mich.: Wayne State University Press, 1988); Marjorie Agosín, ed., *Landscapes of a New Land: Short Fiction by Latin American Women* (New York: White Pine Press, 1989); Celia Correas de Zapata, ed., *Short Stories by Latin American Women: The Magic and the Real* (Houston: Arte Público Press, 1990); Kathleen Ross and Ivette E. Miller, eds., *Scents of Wood and Silence: Short Stories by Latin American Women Writers*, special issue of *Latin American Literary Review* 19 (January-June 1991); Marjorie Agosín, ed., *Secret Weavers: Stories of the Fantastic by Women of Argentina and Chile* (New York: White Pine Press, 1992).

3. Sharon Magnarelli, *Reflections/Refractions: Reading Luisa Valenzuela* (New York: Peter Lang, 1988); Sonia Riquelme Rojas and Edna Aguirre Rehbein, eds., *Critical Approaches to Isabel Allende's Novels* (New York: Peter Lang, 1991); Adriana Castillo de Berchenko and Pablo Berchenko, eds., *La narrativa de Isabel Allende: claves de una marginalidad* (Perpignan, France: Centre de Recherches Ibériques et Latinoaméricaines, Université de Perpignan, 1990).

257

Introduction

1. Modernism is a literary movement originating in Spanish America in the 1880s, influenced by French symbolism and Pan-Asianism. It revolutionized the language and form of poetry and also brought about a transformation in prose writing. The Nicaraguan poet Rubén Darío gave the movement definition and its name. Modernism was superseded in the 1920s by the avant-garde.

2. The Boedo and Florida groups took their names from the respective Buenos Aires locations where writers met. The Boedo group was a socialist realist school of writers who identified with the poor and distrusted elitist literature. Roberto Arlt associated with this group. The Florida group was an elitist one represented by Jorge Luis Borges. Its writers incorporated avant-garde literary techniques and were interested in the formal aspects of literature. Like Borges, they also cultivated the psychological, the metaphysical, and the fantastic.

3. "Documentos de los narradores del 70," *Clarín,* 23 December 1981 and *Convicción,* 15 January 1982, quoted in *Cuentos de la crisis,* ed. May Lorenzo Alcalá (Buenos Aires: Editorial Celtia, 1986), 19.

Chapter 1: Alicia Jurado

1. Elsa T. de Pucciarelli, "Alicia Jurado: 'Hechicera de la tribu,'" *Sur* 348 (September-October 1981): 43.

2. H. Ernest Lewald, *The Web: Stories by Argentine Women Writers* (Washington, D.C.: Three Continents Press, 1983), 5–6.

3. Martin S. Stabb, "Argentine Letters and the Peronato: An Overview," *Journal of Interamerican Studies and World Affairs* 13 (July-October 1971): 452.

4. Alicia Jurado, *El mundo de la palabra* (Buenos Aires: Emecé Editores, 1990), 57.

5. Ibid., 162.

6. Alicia Jurado, *La cárcel y los hierros* (Buenos Aires: Editorial Goncourt, 1961), 99. Hereafter page references will be indicated parenthetically within the text.

7. Marcos Victoria, "Novelistas premiados por la Sociedad Argentina de Escritores," review of *La cárcel y los hierros,* by Alicia Jurado, *El Hogar,* 5 August 1962, 62.

8. Alicia Jurado, *El mundo* (see n. 4 above), 162.

9. Ibid., 110.

10. Ibid., 112–13.

11. Alicia Jurado, *En soledad vivía* (Buenos Aires: Editorial Losada, 1967), 132. Hereafter page references will be indicated parenthetically within the text.

12. Alicia Jurado, *El mundo* (see n. 4 above), 200–201.

13. "Cuentos entre el amor y la mentira," review of *Los rostros del engaño,* by Alicia Jurado, *Clarín,* 3 April 1969.

14. Alicia Jurado, *Los rostros del engaño* (Buenos Aires: Editorial Losada, 1968), 19.

15. Alicia Jurado, *El cuarto mandamiento* (Buenos Aires: Emecé Editores, 1974). Hereafter page references will be indicated parenthetically within the text. (Although the novel refers to the Fourth Commandment as "Honor Your Father and Mother," this is actually the Fifth Commandment.)

16. Martín Alberto Noel, "*El cuarto mandamiento* por Alicia Jurado," review of *El cuarto mandamiento,* by Alicia Jurado, *La Prensa,* 29 December 1974.

17. Luis Pazos, review of *Los hechiceros de la tribu*, by Alicia Jurado, *Somos*, 23 January 1981.

18. Alicia Jurado, *Los hechiceros de la tribu* (Buenos Aires: Emecé Editores, 1980), 91. Hereafter page references will be indicated parenthetically within the text.

19. Pucciarelli, "Alicia Jurado" (see n. 1 above), 45.

Chapter 2: Elvira Orphée

1. Evelyn Picon Garfield, "'Desprendida a hachazos de la eternidad': lo primordial en la obra de Elvira Orphée," *Journal of Latin American Lore* 5 (1979): 6–7.

2. Evelyn Picon Garfield, *Women's Voices from Latin America: Interviews with Six Contemporary Authors* (Detroit, Mich.: Wayne State University Press, 1987), 101–2. (*Lunfardo* is slang developed and used in Buenos Aires.)

3. Diane S. Birkemoe, "Contemporary Women Novelists of Argentina (1945–67)" (Ph.D. diss., University of Illinois, 1968), 258.

4. Elvira Orphée, *Dos veranos* (Buenos Aires: Sudamericana, 1956), 9. Hereafter page references will be indicated parenthetically within the text.

5. Rosa Chacel, "Un libro ciertamente nuevo," review of *Dos veranos*, by Elvira Orphée, *Sur* 245 (March-April 1957): 11.

6. Birkemoe, "Contemporary Women Novelists" (see n. 3 above), 258.

7. Picon Garfield, *Women's Voices* (see n. 2 above), 107.

8. Elvira Orphée, *Uno* (Buenos Aires: Fabril Editora, 1966), 66. Hereafter page references will be indicated parenthetically within the text.

9. María Luisa Bastos, "Elvira Orphée: *Uno*," review of *Uno*, by Elvira Orphée, *Sur* 272 (September-October 1961): 107.

10. Birkemoe, "Contemporary Women Novelists" (see n. 3 above), 275.

11. Bradley M. Class, "Fictional Treatment of Politics by Argentine Female Novelists" (Ph.D. diss., University of New Mexico, 1974), 99–100.

12. María Luisa Bastos, "Conversación con Elvira Orphée," *Zona franca* 3 (July-August 1977): 26–27.

13. Picon Garfield, *Women's Voices* (see n. 2 above), 100.

14. Birkemoe, "Contemporary Women Novelists" (see n. 3 above), 274.

15. Gwendolyn Díaz, "Escritura y palabra: *Aire tan dulce* de Elvira Orphée," *Revista iberoamericana* 51 (July-December 1985): 647.

16. Elvira Orphée, *Aire tan dulce,* 2d ed. (Caracas: Monte Avila, 1977), 67. Hereafter page references will be indicated parenthetically within the text.

17. Díaz, "Escritura" (see n. 15 above), 647.

18. Edgardo Moctezuma, "Para mirar tan lejos antes de entrar: Los usos del poder en *Aire tan dulce* de Elvira Orphée," *Revista iberoamericana* 45 (October-December 1983): 935.

19. Ibid., 941.

20. Elvira Orphée, *En el fondo* (Buenos Aires: Emecé Editores, 1969), 57. Hereafter page references will be indicated parenthetically within the text.

21. Picon Garfield, "'Desprendida a hachazos de la eternidad'" (see n. 1 above), 4.

22. Ibid., 22. Italics are Picon Garfield's.

23. María Luisa Bastos, "Tortura y discurso autoritario: *La última conquista de El*

Angel, de Elvira Orphée," in *The Contemporary Latin American Short Story,* ed. Rose S. Minc (New York: Senda Nueva de Ediciones, 1979), 113.

24. Elvira Orphée, *La última conquista de El angel,* 1st ed. (Caracas: Monte Avila Editores, 1977), 9. Hereafter page references will be indicated parenthetically within the text. Orphée writes in the prologue that the stories were written between 1961 and 1974; however, she states in an interview that "[her] book began in 1970, and the stories continued in heartbreaking succession until 1975." See García Pinto, *Women Writers* (see above, preface, n. 1), 157.

25. According to Orphée, Santiago Nudelman's *La era del terror y la tortura* (The era of terror and torture) "enumerated facts, prisoners' depositions, testimony given by people who saw a stained piece of clothing or who heard cries." See García Pinto, *Women Writers* (see above, preface, n. 1), 157.

26. García Pinto, *Women Writers* (see above, preface, n. 1), 157.

27. Ibid., 158.

28. Orphée, *La última conquista de El Angel,* 9. Orphée poses the following questions in the prologue that shed light on her intentions:

> ¿[C]ambiará alguna vez el orden sobrenatural?; ¿la tortura del hombre por el hombre no será sin principio ni fin y estará ligada a la condición humana?; ¿en este drama de transgresión, no serán los actores simultáneamente víctimas y victimarios?; ¿qué organización de poder o de revolución ha evitado la tortura?

> ([W]ill the supernatural order eventually change? Torture by human beings of other human beings—might it not be without a beginning or an end? might it be tied to the human condition? In this drama of transgression, aren't the actors victims and perpetrators at the same time? What organization based on power or revolution has avoided torture?)

29. Bastos, "Tortura y discurso autoritario" (see above, n. 23), 112. Italics are Bastos's.

30. Ibid., 113. María Luisa Bastos has pointed out the detective-story structure of each story. The stories' structures are also a parody of the torturers' sadomasochistic eroticism expressed in torturing, as the sessions follow a pattern similar to lovemaking. The erotic connotations are made explicit by the torturers' comments and their attack on the victims' sexual organs. The stories' structures and the ritualized content parody a religious ceremony (Catholic Mass) as well. The religious aspect is underscored by the heavy use of Christian imagery related to Christ's Passion.

31. Bell Gale Chevigny, "Ambushing the Will to Ignorance: Elvira Orphée's *La última conquista de El Angel* and Marta Traba's *Conversación al sur,*" in *El Cono Sur: dinámica y dimensiones de su literatura,* ed. Rose S. Minc (Upper Montclair, N.J.: Montclair State College, 1985), 103.

32. Picon Garfield, *Women's Voices* (see above, n. 2), 107.

33. Fernando Reati, *Nombrar lo innombrable: violencia política y novela argentina, 1975–1985* (Buenos Aires: Editorial Legasa, 1992), 104. Reati uses the example of the dehumanization of the victims versus the heightening of the torturers' human traits to align the readers' sympathies with the latter.

34. Ibid., 103.

35. Frank Graziano, *Divine Violence: Spectacle, Psychosexuality, and Radical Christianity in the Argentine "Dirty War"* (Boulder, Colo.: Westview Press, 1992), 137.

36. Reati, *Nombrar* (see above, n. 33), 102.

37. Chevigny, "Ambushing" (see above, n. 31), 103.

38. The *picana* is an electrified prod applied to the most sensitive parts of the body during torture. It was routinely used in interrogations during the periods depicted. Graziano, *Divine Violence* (see n. 35 above), 153–71, studies the eroticism of torture and the role of the *picana* and its phallic symbolism.

39. Picon Garfield, "Desprendida a hachazos de la eternidad," 13.

40. Picon Garfield, *Women's Voices from Latin America*, 113.

41. Other contemporary Argentine writers dealing with political themes are Luisa Valenzuela, *Aquí pasan cosas raras (Strange Things Happen Around Here)*, 1979; Ricardo Piglia, *Respiración artificial* (Artificial breathing), 1980; Marta Traba, *Conversación al sur (Mothers and Shadows)*, 1981; Osvaldo Soriano, *Cuarteles de invierno* (Winter barracks), 1981, and *No habrá más penas ni olvido* (There will be no more grief nor forgetting), 1983; Humberto Constantini, *De dioses, hombrecitos y policías (The Gods, the Little Guys and the Police)*, 1979, and *La larga noche de Francisco Sanctis (The Long Night of Francisco Sanctis)*, 1984; and Manuel Puig, *El beso de la mujer araña (Kiss of the Spider Woman)*, 1985.

42. At the time of the interview I had access to only the first edition of the novel.

43. Moctezuma, "Para mirar" (see n. 18 above), 929–42.

44. Ibid., 939–40.

45. The references to clocks and time allude to commemorations of Eva Perón's death on 26 July 1952 at 8:25 P.M. The hands of the clock on the Ministry of Labor Building remained fixed at 8:25 P.M., and the regular 8:30 P.M. radio newscasts were advanced by five minutes during the fortnight of mourning to facilitate the daily commemoration. The train reference underscores Perón's efforts to emulate Benito Mussolini. Mussolini credited himself with making trains run on time in Italy during his dictatorship, which for the fascists became a symbol of the effectiveness of his rule.

Chapter 3: Alina Diaconú

1. Osvaldo Gallone, "La atracción de la ambigüedad," review of *Los ojos azules*, by Alina Diaconú, *El periodista de Buenos Aires*, 8–14 May 1987, 31.

2. Elias Miguel Muñoz, *El discurso utópico de la sexualidad en Manuel Puig* (Madrid: Editorial Pliegos, 1987), 17. Italics are mine.

3. Osvaldo Seiguerman, review of *Cama de ángeles*, by Alina Diaconú, *La Opinión*, 15 June 1978.

4. Fernando Reati notes that Argentine writers use a variety of styles, such as "satire, the grotesque, humor, the picaresque, the mystery novel, memoirs, [and] historical revisionism" (56) instead of depicting extreme violence in their plots. Among the best-known writers cultivating strategies to represent an otherwise unrepresentable reality are Ricardo Piglia, *Respiración artificial* (Artificial breathing), 1980, Marta Traba, *Conversación al sur (Mothers and Shadows)*, 1981, Osvaldo Soriano, *Cuarteles de invierno* (Winter barracks), 1982, Jorge Asís, *Flores robadas en los jardines de Quilmes* (Flowers stolen in the Quilmes Gardens), 1982, and Luisa Valenzuela, *Cola de lagartija (The Lizard's Tail)*, 1983. See Fernando Reati, *Nombrar* (see above, chap. 2, n. 33), 54–65.

5. Francine Masiello, "La Argentina durante el Proceso: Las múltiples resistencias de la cultura," in *Ficción y política: la narrativa argentina durante el proceso militar*, ed. Daniel Balderston et al. (Buenos Aires: Alianza Editorial, 1987), 13.

6. Francine Masiello, "Texto, ley, transgresión: especulación sobre la novela feminista de vanguardia," *Revista iberoamericana* 51 (July–December 1985): 809.

7. Ibid.

8. Alina Diaconú, *La Señora* (Buenos Aires: Rodolfo Alonso Editor, 1975), 12. Hereafter page references will be indicated parenthetically within the text. The theme of the mother-daughter relationship in Diaconú's work was the focus of a preliminary study in my article, "Madres e hijas y creatividad femenina en *La Señora* de Alina Diaconú," *Confluencia* 8 (Spring 1993): 37–47.

9. Ester Gimbernat González, *Aventuras del desacuerdo: novelistas argentinas de los 80* (Buenos Aires: Danilo Albero Vergara, 1992), 163–64.

10. María Adela Renard, "Juego de opuestos," review of *Buenas noches, profesor,* by Alina Diaconú, *La Prensa,* 6 November 1983.

11. Alina Diaconú, *Buenas noches, profesor* (Buenos Aires: Corregidor, 1978), 229. Hereafter page references will be indicated parenthetically within the text.

12. Reati analyzes Enrique Molina's *Con el trapo en la boca* (With the rag in the mouth), 1983, a work narrated by a voice of a gender opposite the author's, in this case a male writer using a female narrative voice. According to Reati, women writers use a transgression of the author's gender in the narrative voice as a traditional strategy in their quest to find a female voice and to dismantle male authoritarian discourse. Nevertheless, it is clear that Diaconú, while subverting a gendered discourse, also underscores a narration that surges forth from the Other, the unknown constituting a threat to the status quo. See Reati, *Nombrar* (see above, chap. 2, n. 33), 211–19.

13. According to Gimbernat González, *Enamorada del muro* presents the same conformist endings as *La Señora* and *Buenas noches, profesor:* "[A]gain fever and solitude make Bruma seek refuge in her house, after the first confrontation with an alien and hostile world." See Gimbernat González, *Aventuras* (see above, n. 9), 163–64.

14. Alina Diaconú, *Enamorada del muro* (Buenos Aires: Corregidor, 1981), 67. Hereafter page references will be indicated parenthetically within the text.

15. Julia Kristeva, *Pouvoirs de l'horreur: essai sur l'abjection* (Paris: Editions du Seuil, 1980), 9.

16. Alina Diaconú, *Cama de ángeles* (Buenos Aires: Emecé Editores, 1983), 245. Hereafter page references will be indicated parenthetically within the text.

17. Elías Miguel Muñoz, "La búsqueda de un sexo 'verdadero': *Cama de ángeles* de Alina Diaconú," *Chasqui: revista de literatura latinoamericana* 21 (May 1992): 50.

18. Gimbernat González, *Aventuras* (see above, n. 9), 167.

19. Gallone, "La atracción" (see above, n. 1), 31.

20. Diaconú has stated that the three novels *Enamorada del muro, Cama de ángeles,* and *Los ojos azules* constitute a trilogy. (Opening statement delivered at symposium of the Instituto Literario y Cultural Hispánico, Montevideo, Uruguay, 9 August 1993).

21. Alina Diaconú, *Los ojos azules* (Buenos Aires: Editorial Fraterna, 1986), 95. Hereafter page references will be indicated parenthetically within the text.

22. Kristeva, *Pouvoirs* (see above, n. 15), 9.

23. Alina Diaconú, *El penúltimo viaje* (Buenos Aires: Javier Vergara Editor, 1989), 109. Hereafter page references will be indicated parenthetically within the text.

24. Roberto Delgado, "Viaje en tren desvelado por los recuerdos," review of *El penúltimo viaje,* by Alina Diaconú, *La Gaceta,* 15 October 1989.

25. Alberto Laiseca, "Introducción a la guerra de todos contra todos," review of *El penúltimo viaje,* by Alina Diaconú, *Nuevo Sur,* 4 June 1989.

26. Jorge Marbán, "Estructura y simbolismo en *El penúltimo viaje* de Alina Diaconú," *Confluencia* 7 (Spring 1992): 132.

27. Gimbernat González, *Aventuras* (see above, n. 9), 113.

28. Ibid., 116.

29. Marbán, "Estructura" (see above, n. 26), 135.

30. María Rosa Lojo, review of *Los devorados*, by Alina Diaconú, *Cultura*, 15 December 1992, 80.

31. María Esther De Miguel, "Atrapante novela," review of *Los devorados*, by Alina Diaconú, *La Nación*, 3 January 1993.

32. Carlos O. Antognazzi, "Trama sensual y compleja," review of *Los devorados*, por Alina Diaconú, *El Litoral*, 13 March 1993.

33. Lojo, review (see above, n. 30), 80.

34. Ibid.

35. Antognazzi, "Trama" (see above, n. 32).

36. Diaconú, opening statement (see above, n. 20).

37. Alina Diaconú, *Los devorados* (Buenos Aires: Editorial Atlántida, 1992), 28. Hereafter page references will be indicated parenthetically within the text.

38. Jean-François Lyotard, *The Post-Modern Condition: A Report on Knowledge*, trans. Geoff Bennington and Brian Massuri (Minneapolis: University of Minnesota Press, 1984), quoted in Francine Masiello, "La Argentina durante el Proceso" (see above, n. 5), 23.

39. Ibid.

40. Beatriz Sarlo, "Política, ideología y figuración literaria," in Balderston et al., *Ficción y política* (see above, n. 5), 43–46

41. Reati, *Nombrar* (see above, chap. 2, n. 33), 62.

42. Zulma N. Martínez, "La mujer, la creatividad y el eterno presente," *Revista iberoamericana* 51 (July-December 1985): 805.

43. At the time of the interview, I was particularly drawn to the psychological and existential aspects of Alina Diaconú's novels. As her latest novels were published, however, the important role of the social and historical aspects became clear to me.

Chapter 4: Alicia Steimberg

1. Alicia Steimberg, "La autobiografía, ese género inexistente" (paper delivered at symposium on Latin American Women Writers, San Miguel de Allende, Mexico, 23 June 1978), 1.

2. Miguel Russo, "Alicia Steimberg recuerda su larga trayectoria literaria y prepara un libro acerca de la ficción," *La Maga*, 8 July 1992.

3. Steimberg, "La autobiografía" (see above, n. 1), 2. Italics are Steimberg's.

4. Luis Gregorich, "La autora," *La Opinión*, 17 May 1978.

5. Ibid.

6. Alicia Steimberg, *Músicos y relojeros* (Buenos Aires: Centro Editor de América Latina, 1971), 50. Italics are mine. Hereafter page references will be indicated parenthetically within the text.

7. In a conversation with Steimberg on 8 April 1987 in Buenos Aires, Argentina, she emphasized the importance of her grandmother during her childhood and that the grandmother's stories about her own life were always injected with humor.

8. Ernesto Sábato, *La cultura en la encrucijada nacional* (Buenos Aires: Sudamericana Editorial, 1982), 108.

9. Gregorich, "La autora" (see above, n. 4).

10. Russo, "Alicia Steimberg recuerda" (see above, n. 2).

11. "Voz libre en la cultura," review of *La loca 101*, by Alicia Steimberg, *Voz libre*, 11 November 1973.

12. Mabel Moraña, *Memorias de la generación fantasma* (Montevideo: Monte Sexto, 1988), 134.

13. Marta Morello-Frosch, "La ficción de la historia en la narrativa argentina," in *The Historical Novel in Latin America*, ed. Daniel Balderston (Gaithersburg, Md.: Ediciones Hispamérica, 1986), 207.

14. Fernando Reati analyzes several Argentine novels of the Proceso that portray enclosed spaces and situations of confinement and asphyxiation as a metaphor for repression. See Fernando Reati, "Literatura argentina de la 'guerra sucia': el paradigma del espacio invadido," *Texto crítico* 14 (December 1988): 32.

15. Ibid., 35.

16. Examples of works evoking feelings of despair and failure cushioned in humor are Osvaldo Soriano's novels, *No habrá más penas ni olvido* (There will be no more grief nor forgetting), 1982, and *Cuarteles de invierno* (Winter barracks), 1983.

17. Alicia Steimberg, *Su espíritu inocente* (Buenos Aires: Editorial Pomaire, 1981), cover. Hereafter page references will be indicated parenthetically within the text.

18. Alicia Steimberg, *Como todas las mañanas* (Buenos Aires: Editorial Celtia, 1983), 11. Italics are Steimberg's. Hereafter page references will be indicated parenthetically within the text.

19. María Esther De Miguel, "Ni dormida ni despierta," review of *Como todas las mañanas*, by Alicia Steimberg, *El Cronista Comercial*, 27 April 1983.

20. Ibid.

21. Alicia Steimberg, *El árbol del placer* (Buenos Aires: Emecé Editores, 1986), 29. Hereafter page references will be indicated parenthetically within the text.

22. Gimbernat González points out that the "rhetoric of sickness" can be interpreted as an individual's physical response to an outside threat. See Gimbernat González, *Aventuras* (see above, chap. 3, n. 9), 289.

23. Ibid., 291.

24. Susan Rubin Suleiman, *Subversive Intent: Gender, Politics, and the Avant-Garde* (Cambridge: Harvard University Press, 1990), 36.

25. Andrés Avellaneda selects Ricardo Piglia's *Respiración artificial* (Artificial breathing), 1980, as the most outstanding example of the metaphorical use of the detective novel. Piglia uses "the structure of the [detective] inquiry as the format where the obtainment of knowledge and the pursuit of meaning coincide posed as a mystery to solve." See "Literatura argentina: Los años de la amputación," in *El Cono Sur: dinámica y dimensiones de su literatura*, ed. Rose S. Minc (Upper Montclair, N.J.: Montclair State College, 1985), 78.

26. Tununa Mercado, "Romper la amnesia," review of *Cuando digo Magdalena*, by Alicia Steimberg, *Carnets* 3, 24 October 1992.

27. Alicia Steimberg, *Cuando digo Magdalena* (Buenos Aires: Editorial Planeta), 200. Hereafter page references will be indicated parenthetically within the text.

28. Traditional logocentrism is stripped of its position of authority in light of deconstructivism and modern physics, which vindicate a female concept of time evident in women's fiction. See Martínez, "La mujer" (see above, chap. 3, n. 42), 799–806.

29. The term "musician" used in Steimberg's novel means temple cantor, and "watchmaker" refers to a watch repairman.

30. Informal form of address used in Argentina, consisting of the familiar personal pronoun *vos* (that is why it is called *voseo*) in place of *tú* (the standard singular familiar personal pronoun meaning "you") and the corresponding modified verb endings.

31. Steimberg uses *Amatista* as a pun. Its prefix *ama* is the third-person singular form of the Spanish verb "to love" and the suffix *-ista* refers to a person performing an activity.

Chapter 5: Cecilia Absatz

1. "Cecilia Absatz," *Babel* 1 (January 1989): 34.

2. Cecilia Absatz, *Feiguele y otras mujeres* (Buenos Aires: Ediciones De La Flor, 1976), 7. Hereafter page references will be indicated parenthetically within the text.

3. "Natu Poblet sale a comer con Cecilia Absatz," *First* 69 (June 1992): 54.

4. Ibid.

5. Cecilia Absatz, *Los años pares* (Buenos Aires: Editorial Legasa, 1985), back cover. Hereafter page references will be indicated parenthetically within the text.

6. Cecilia Absatz, "Las flores rojas de los semáforos," *Puro cuento* 17 (July-August 1989): 42–43.

7. Ibid.

8. Francisco Herrera, "La literatura erótica femenina tras los pasos de su propia mitología," *La Prensa*, 6 March 1990.

9. Ibid.

10. Mirta Reyes, "La literatura de la democracia," n. p., n. d., 18.

11. Juan Carlos Kreimer, "Mate con Ginseng," review of *Té con canela*, by Cecilia Absatz, *Humor*, 2 December 1982, 118.

12. "Cecilia Absatz: una escritora en busca del libro que sólo cuente lo esencial," *La Nación*, 6 April 1986.

13. Ibid.

14. Sandra M. Gilbert and Susan Gubar, *The Madwoman in the Attic: The Woman Writer and the Nineteenth-Century Literary Imagination* (New Haven: Yale University Press, 1979), 76.

15. Elaine Showalter, *A Literature of Their Own: Women Novelists from Brontë to Lessing* (Princeton: Princeton University Press, 1977), 13.

16. Sharon Keefe Ugalde, "Process, Identity and Learning to Read: Female Writing and Feminist Criticism in Latin America Today," *Latin American Research Review* 24 (1989): 226–27.

17. Alina Diaconú's *El penúltimo viaje* and Alicia Steimberg's *Cuando digo Magdalena* can also be considered revised bildungsromane; however, they fall under a category different from Absatz's novel, for they are failed versions of the genre. Their protagonists' quests end up, respectively, in physical elimination and the inability to transcend amnesia.

18. Elizabeth Abel, Marianne Hirsch, and Elizabeth Langland, eds., *The Voyage in Fictions of Female Development* (Hanover, N.H.: University Press of New England, 1983), 12–13.

19. Cecilia Absatz, *Té con canela* (Buenos Aires: Editorial Sudamericana, 1982), 13. Hereafter page references will be indicated parenthetically within the text.

20. Ester Gimbernat González analyzes the influence of the outsider who takes the protagonist on a journey in *Los años pares*, in Silvia Plager's *Prohibido despertar* (To wake up is forbidden), 1984, and in Perla Chirom's *Nostalgia del último domingo de verano* (Nostalgia for the last Sunday of summer), 1988. See Gimbernat González, *Aventuras* (see above, chap. 3, n. 9), 93.

21. "Cecilia Absatz: una escritora en busca del libro" (see n. 12 above).

22. *Capicúa* refers to a number that is the same whether it is read forward or backwards. It has the connotation of being a good-luck omen.

Chapter 6. Reina Roffé

1. Hernán Saavedra, "En busca del tiempo perdido," review of *Llamado al puf*, by Reina Roffé, *Claudia*, 1 April 1973.

2. J. C. Martini Real, "Prólogo," in Reina Roffé, *Llamado al puf* (Buenos Aires: Ediciones Pleamar, 1973), 17.

3. Francine Masiello, "Contemporary Argentine Fiction: Liberal (Pre-)Texts in a Reign of Terror," *Latin American Research Review* 16 (1981): 223.

4. Ibid., 219.

5. Francine Masiello has studied the subversion of traditionally patriarchal spaces and contexts in works by Marta Traba, Silvia Molloy, and Cristina Pieri Rossi. See "Subversions of Authority: Feminist Literary Culture in the River Plate Region," *Chasqui: revista de literatura latinoamericana* 21 (May 1992): 39–47.

6. Reina Roffé, *Llamado al puf* (Buenos Aires: Ediciones Pleamar, 1973), 45. Hereafter page references will be indicated parenthetically within the text.

7. Reina Roffé, "Los textos: itinerario de una escritura," in *La rompiente* (Buenos Aires: Puntosur Editores, 1987), 9.

8. Ibid., 10.

9. Daniel Balderston, "El significado latente en *Respiración artificial* de Ricardo Piglia y *En el corazón de junio* de Luis Gusmán," in Balderston et al., *Ficción y política*, (see above, chap. 3, n. 5), 107–8.

10. Pierre Macherey, *A Theory of Literary Production* (London: Routledge and Kegan Paul, l978), 85, quoted in ibid., 111, 118. Italics are Macherey's.

11. Ibid., 86–87.

12. Mónica Szurmuk, "La textualización de la represión en *La rompiente* de Reina Roffé," *Nuevo texto crítico* 3 (1990): 124.

13. "Reina Roffé segundo tiempo," *Panorama*, 10 October 1976, 122.

14. Ibid.

15. David William Foster, *Alternate Voices in the Contemporary Latin American Narrative* (Columbia: University of Missouri Press, 1985), 78.

16. Reina Roffé, *Monte de Venus* (Buenos Aires: Ediciones Corregidor, 1976), 129. Hereafter page references will be indicated parenthetically within the text.

17. Foster, *Alternate Voices* (see n. 15 above), 78–79.

18. Ibid., 81.

19. Eduardo Gudiño Kieffer, "Juventud sin rumbo," review of *Monte de Venus*, by Reina Roffé, *Clarín*, 2 December 1976. The boldface is Gudiño Kieffer's.

20. The title's "rompiente" can stand for both meanings of the word according to the text: (l) a female who breaks something; (2) a wave that breaks into foam.

21. Reina Roffé, "Los textos" (see n. 7 above), 11. Hereafter page references will be indicated parenthetically within the text.

22. Szurmuk, "La textualización" (see above, n. 12), 124.

23. María Teresa Gramuglio, "Aproximaciones a *La rompiente*," in Reina Roffé, *La rompiente* (see above, n. 7), 127.

24. Francine Masiello, "Cuerpo/presencia: Mujer y estado social en la narrativa argentina durante el proceso militar," *Nuevo texto crítico* 4 (July-December 1989): 167.

25. Esther Gimbernat González, "*La rompiente* (R. Roffé) o la integración en la escritura," in Gimbernat González, *Aventuras* (see above, chap. 3, n. 9), 186–87.

26. Masiello, "Cuerpo/presencia" (see n. 24 above), 167.

27. Szurmuk "La textualización" (see above, n. 12), 126.

28. Masiello, "Cuerpo/presencia" (see above, n. 24), 168.

29. Gramuglio, "Aproximaciones" (see above, n. 7), 130–31.

30. I have been inspired in my interpretation by Szurmuk's study of water imagery as a place for freedom and creativity for the protagonist. See Szurmuk, "La textualización" (see above, n. 12), 127.

31. Masiello, "Subversions of Authority" (see above, n. 5), 41.

32. Masiello, "Cuerpo/presencia" (see above, n. 24), 169.

33. The convergence of water imagery and the female bodily fluids to create a space of defiance of authoritarianism and a medium conveying a marginal, female voice is studied by Masiello and Szurmuk. See Masiello "Cuerpo/ presencia" (see above, n. 24), 169, and Szurmuk, "La textualización" (see above, n. 12), 127–28.

Conclusion

1. Kristeva, *Pouvoirs* (see above, chap. 3, n. 15), 9.

2. Gramuglio, "Aproximaciones a *La rompiente*," in Reina Roffé, *La rompiente* (see chap. 6, n. 7), 129.

3. Sharon Keefe Ugalde, "Process, Identity and Learning to Read: Female Writing and Feminist Criticism in Latin America Today," *Latin American Research Review* 24 (1989): 224.

Bibliography

Abel, Elizabeth, Marianne Hirsch, and Elizabeth Langland, eds. *The Voyage in Fictions of Female Development*. Hanover, N.H.: University Press of New England, 1983.

Agosín, Marjorie. *The Mothers of Plaza de Mayo*. Translated from the Spanish by Janice Malloy. Trenton, N.J.: Red Sea Press, 1990.

———, ed. *Landscapes of a New Land: Short Fiction by Latin American Women*. New York: White Pine Press, 1989.

———. *Secret Weavers: Stories of the Fantastic by Women of Argentina and Chile*. New York: White Pine Press, 1992.

Andersen, Martin Edwin. *Dossier Secreto: Argentina's Desaparecidos and the Myth of the "Dirty War."* Boulder, Colo.: Westview Press, 1993.

Ara, Guillermo. *Los argentinos y la literatura nacional.* Buenos Aires: Editorial Muermil, 1966.

Arancibia, Juana A., ed. *Evaluación de la literatura femenina latinoamericana del siglo XX*. San José: Editorial Universitaria Centroamericana, 1985.

Arancibia, Juana A., and Zulema Mirkin, eds. *Teatro argentino durante el Proceso (1976–1983): ensayos críticos-entrevistas.* Colección Estudios Hispánicos, no. 2. Buenos Aires: Editorial Vinciguerra, 1993.

Argentine Bibliography: A Union Bibliography of Argentine Holdings in the Libraries of the University of Buenos Aires. Boston: G. K. Hall, 1980.

Avellaneda, Andrés. "Canon y escritura de mujer: un viaje al centro de la periferia." *Espacios*, 10 November 1991.

———. "Literatura argentina: los años de la amputación." In *El Cono Sur: dinámica y dimensiones de su literatura*, edited by Rose S. Minc, 75–81. Upper Montclair, N.J.: Montclair State College, 1985.

———. "Realismo, antirrealismo, territorios canónicos: Argentina literaria después de los militares." In *Fascismo y experiencia literaria: reflexiones para una recanonización*, edited by Hernán Vidal, 578–88. Monographic Series of the Society for the Study of Contemporary Hispanic and Lusophone Revolutionary Literatures, no. 2. Minneapolis: Institute for the Study of Ideologies and Literature, 1985.

Bailey, Kay. "El uso de márgenes en *Cama de ángeles* de Alina Diaconú." Forthcoming.

————. "Exceso y repulsión en las novelas de Alina Diaconú." In *Utopías, ojos azules, bocas suicidas: la narrativa de Alina Diaconú*, edited by Ester Gimbernat González and Cynthia Tompkins, 67–81. Buenos Aires: Editorial Fraterna, 1993.

Balderston, Daniel. "El significado latente en *Respiración artificial* de Ricardo Piglia y *En el corazón de junio* de Luis Gusman." Translated from the English by Eduardo Paz Leston. In *Ficción y política: la narrativa argentina durante el proceso militar*, edited by Daniel Balderston, David William Foster, Tulio Halperin Donghi, Francine Masiello, Marta Morello-Frosch, and Beatriz Sarlo, 109–21. Buenos Aires: Alianza Editorial, 1987.

————. "'La verdad de la historia': History and Fiction in Ricardo Piglia's *Respiración artificial*." In *El Cono Sur: dinámica y dimensiones de su literatura*, edited by Rose S. Minc, 82–86. Upper Montclair, N.J.: Montclair State College, 1985.

————, ed. *The Historical Novel in Latin America*. Gaithersburg, Md.: Ediciones Hispamérica, 1986.

Balderston, Daniel, David William Foster, Tulio Halperin Donghi, Francine Masiello, Marta Morello-Frosch, and Beatriz Sarlo, eds. *Ficción y política: la narrativa argentina durante el proceso militar.* Buenos Aires: Alianza Editorial, 1987.

Bastos, María Luisa. "Tortura y discurso autoritario: *La última conquista de El Angel*, de Elvira Orphée." In *The Contemporary Latin American Short Story*, edited by Rose S. Minc, 112–19. New York: Senda Nueva de Ediciones, 1979.

Bayer, Osvaldo. "Pequeño recordatorio para un país sin memoria." In *Represión y reconstrucción de una cultura: el caso argentino*, compiled by Saúl Sosnowski, 203–28. Buenos Aires: Editorial de la Universidad de Buenos Aires, 1988.

Bilbija, Ksenija. "Hacia una búsqueda del idioma materno: *El penúltimo viaje* de Alina Diaconú." In *Utopías, ojos azules, bocas suicidas: la narrativa de Alina Diaconú*, edited by Ester Gimbernat González and Cynthia Tompkins, 23–34. Buenos Aires: Editorial Fraterna, 1993.

Birkemoe, Diane S. "Elvira Orphée." In "Contemporary Women Novelists of Argentina (1945–1967)," 258–312. Ph.D. diss., University of Illinois, 1968.

Bonet, Carmelo M. "Buenos Aires, su gente, sus barrios, sus novelistas." *Ficción* 40 (November-December 1962): 43–56.

Borello, Rodolfo A. "Autores, situación del libro y entorno material de la literatura argentina del siglo XX." *Cuadernos hispanoamericanos* 322–23 (1977): 35–52.

Borinsky, Alicia. "Ficciones de intimidad." In *Utopías, ojos azules, bocas suicidas: la narrativa de Alina Diaconú*, edited by Ester Gimbernat González and Cynthia Tompkins, 85–91. Buenos Aires: Editorial Fraterna, 1993.

Bousquet, Jean-Pierre. *Las locas de la Plaza de Mayo*. Translated from the French by Jacques Despres. Buenos Aires: El Cid Editor, 1983.

Bremer, Thomas. "Buenos Aires et Montevideo: sociologie de la 'ville racontée' jusqu'à l'apparition du roman social urbain." *Cahiers du monde hispanique et luso-brésilien* 42 (1984): 123–40.

Brinkman, Jorge. "Panorama de la novelística argentina." *Cuadernos del sur* 19–20 (February-March 1966): 147–56.

Caro Hollander, Nancy. "Women: The Forgotten Half of Argentine History." In *Female and Male in Latin America: Essays*, edited by Ann Pescatello, 141–58. Pittsburgh, Pa.: University of Pittsburgh Press, 1973.

Castillo, Debra A. *Talking Back: Toward a Latin American Feminist Literary Criticism.* Ithaca: Cornell University Press, 1992.

Castillo de Berchenko, Adriana, and Pablo Berchenko, eds. *La narrativa de Isabel Allende: claves de una marginalidad.* Perpignan, France: Centre de Recherches Ibériques et Latinoaméricaines, Université de Perpignan, 1990.

Castro-Larén, Sara, Sylvia Molly, and Beatriz Sarlo, eds. *Women's Writing in Latin America.* Boulder, Colo.: Westview Press, 1991.

Cesareo, Mario. "Cuerpo humano e historia en la novela del Proceso." In *Fascismo y experiencia literaria: reflexiones para una recanonización,* edited by Hernán Vidal, 501–33. Monographic Series of the Society for the Study of Contemporary Hispanic and Lusophone Revolutionary Literatures, no. 2. Minneapolis: Institute for the Study of Ideologies and Literature, 1985.

Chaney, Elsa M. *Supermadre: Women in Politics in Latin America.* Austin: University of Texas Press, 1979.

Chevigny, Bell Gale. "Ambushing the Will to Ignorance: Elvira Orphée's *La última conquista de El Angel* and Marta Traba's *Conversación al sur.*" In *El Cono Sur: dinámica y dimensiones de su literatura,* edited by Rose S. Minc, 98–104. Upper Montclair, N.J.: Montclair State College, 1985.

Ciria, Alberto. "La doctrina peronista y sus fuentes." *Mundo nuevo* 47 (May 1970): 10–29.

Class, Bradley Mellon. "Fictional Treatment of Politics by Argentine Female Novelists." Ph.D. diss., University of New Mexico, 1974.

C.O.N.A.D.E.P. (Comisión Nacional sobre la Desaparición de Personas). *Nunca más.* 13th ed. Buenos Aires: Editorial Universitaria de Buenos Aires, 1986.

Correas de Zapata, Celia, ed. *Short Stories by Latin American Women: The Magic and the Real.* Houston: Arte Público Press, 1990.

Cortázar, Julio. "The Fellowship of Exile." *Review* 30 (September-December 1981): 14–16.

Corvalán, Graciela. *Latin American Women Writers in English Translation: A Bibliography.* Los Angeles: Latin American Studies Center, California State University, 1980.

De Diego, Celia. "La generación argentina de 1945." *Comentario* 5 (January-March 1958): 29–44.

Dellepiane, Angela B. "Diez años de la novela argentina (Booms, best-sellers y premios)." *Problemas de la literatura: revista latinoamericana de teoría y crítica literaria* 1 (1972): 57–74.

———. "El aporte femenino a la narrativa última argentina." In *La escritora hispánica,* edited by Nora Erro-Orthmann and Juan Cruz Mendizábal, 61–71. Miami: Ediciones Universal, 1990.

———. "La novela argentina desde 1950 a 1965." *Revista iberoamericana* 34 (1968): 237–82.

Díaz, Gwendolyn. "Escritura y palabra: *Aire tan dulce,* de Elvira Orphée." *Revista iberoamericana* 51 (July-December 1985): 641–48.

Erro-Orthmann, Nora, and Juan Cruz Mendizábal, eds. *La escritora hispánica.* Miami: Ediciones Universal, 1990.

Fares, Gustavo. "This Text Which Is Not One: Escritoras argentinas contemporáneas." *Hispanic Journal* 12 (Fall 1991): 277–89.

Fares, Gustavo, and Eliana Hermann, eds. "Alicia Jurado." In *Escritoras argentinas contemporáneas*, 95–112. New York: Peter Lang, 1993.

———. "Alina Diaconú." In *Escritoras argentinas contemporáneas*, 57–60. New York: Peter Lang, 1993.

———. "Elvira Orphée." In *Escritoras argentinas contemporáneas*, 137–52. New York: Peter Lang, 1993.

———. *Escritoras argentinas contemporáneas.* New York: Peter Lang, 1993.

———. "Reina Roffé." In *Escritoras argentinas contemporáneas*, 191–216. New York: Peter Lang, 1993.

Feijoó, María del Carmen. "The Challenge of Constructing Civilian Peace: Women and Democracy in Argentina." In *The Women's Movement in Latin America: Feminism and the Transition to Democracy*, edited by Jane S. Jaquette, 72–94. Boston: Unwin Hyman, 1989.

Feinmann, José Pablo. "Política y verdad." In *Represión y reconstrucción de una cultura: el caso argentino*, compiled by Saúl Sosnowski, 79–94. Buenos Aires: Editorial Universitaria de Buenos Aires, 1988.

Flores, Angel, ed. *Spanish American Authors: The Twentieth Century.* New York: H. W. Wilson Company, 1992.

Flori, Mónica. "Alicia Jurado." In *Spanish American Authors: The Twentieth Century*, edited by Angel Flores, 449–51. New York: H. W. Wilson Company, 1992.

———. "Autoritarismo, exilio y recreación feminista en *El penúltimo viaje* de Alina Diaconú." *Alba de América* 10 (July 1992): 183–94.

———. "Cecilia Absatz and Alicia Steimberg: Two Contemporary Argentine Women Writers." *Chasqui: revista de literatura latinoamericana* 17 (November 1988): 83–92.

———. "La articulización de lo inexpresable: metaforización del cuerpo femenino en *Los ojos azules* de Alina Diaconú." *Alba de América* 12 (July 1994).

———."La técnica de la inversión en las novelas de Alina Diaconú." In *Utopías, ojos azules, bocas suicidas: la narrativa de Alina Diaconú*, edited by Ester Gimbernat González and Cynthia Tompkins, 55–63. Buenos Aires: Editorial Fraterna, 1993. First published in *Selecta* 2 (1990): 92–96.

———. "Madres e hijas y creatividad femenina en *La Señora* de Alina Diaconú." *Confluencia* 8 (Spring 1993): 37–47.

Forn, Juan. *Buenos Aires: una antología de nueva ficción argentina.* Barcelona: Editorial Anagrama, 1992.

Foster, David William. *Alternate Voices in the Contemporary Latin American Narrative.* Columbia: University of Missouri Press, 1985.

———. *Argentine Literature: A Research Guide.* 2d ed. New York: Garland, 1982.

———. *Contemporary Argentine Cinema.* Columbia: University of Missouri Press, 1993.

———. *Currents in the Contemporary Argentine Novel.* Columbia: University of Missouri Press, 1975.

———. "The Demythification of Buenos Aires in Selected Argentine Novels of the Seventies." In *Alternate Voices in the Contemporary Latin American Narrative*, 60–106. Columbia: University of Missouri Press, 1985.

———. "La nueva narrativa argentina vista por la nueva crítica." *Nueva narrativa hispanoamericana* 4 (1974): 227–50.

———. "Los parámetros de la narrativa argentina durante el 'Proceso de Reorganización Nacional.'" In *Ficción y política: la narrativa argentina durante el proceso militar*, edited by Daniel Balderston, David William Foster, Tulio Halperin Donghi, Francine Masiello, Marta Morello-Frosch, and Beatriz Sarlo, 96–108. Buenos Aires: Alianza Editorial, 1987.

Foster, David William, and Virginia Ramos Foster. *Research Guide to Argentine Literature*. Metuchen, N.J.: Scarecrow Press, 1970.

Fox-Lockert, Lucia. *Women Novelists from Spain and Spanish America*. Metuchen, N.J.: Scarecrow Press, 1979.

Franco, Jean. "Apuntes sobre la crítica feminista y la literatura hispanoamericana." *Hispamérica* 45 (December 1986): 31–43.

García Pinto, Magdalena. "Elvira Orphée." In *Women Writers of Latin America: Intimate Stories*, translated from the Spanish by Trudy Balch and Magdalena García Pinto, 145–61. Austin: University of Texas Press, 1991.

———. *Women Writers of Latin America: Intimate Stories*. Translated from the Spanish by Trudy Balch and Magdalena García Pinto. Austin: University of Texas Press, 1991.

Garzón Valdés, Ernesto, Manfred Mols, and Arnold Spitta, eds. *La nueva democracia argentina, 1983–86*. Buenos Aires: Editorial Sudamericana, 1987.

Gazarian Gautier, Marie-Lise. *Interviews with Latin American Writers*. Elmwood Park, Ill.: Dalkey Archive Press, 1989.

Geoghegan, Abel Rodolfo. *Bibliografía de bibliografías argentinas, 1807–1970*. Buenos Aires: Casa Pardo, 1970.

Ghiano, Juan Carlos. "La generación argentina de 1945." *Comentario* 18 (1958): 29–44.

Giardinelli, Mempo, ed. "Mujeres y escritura." *Proceedings of the Primeras Jornadas Sobre Mujeres y Escritura*. Buenos Aires: Editorial Puro Cuento, 1989.

Giardinelli, Mempo, and Graciela Gliemmo, eds. *La Venus de papel*. Buenos Aires: Beas Ediciones, 1993.

Gilbert, Sandra M., and Susan Gubar. *The Madwoman in the Attic: The Woman Writer and the Nineteenth-Century Literary Imagination*. New Haven: Yale University Presses, 1979.

Gimbernat González, Ester. *Aventuras del desacuerdo: novelistas argentinas de los 80*. Buenos Aires: Danilo AlberoVergara, 1992.

———. "*El árbol del placer* (A. Steimberg): Retóricas de la enfermedad." In *Aventuras del desacuerdo: novelistas argentinas de los 80*, 289–94. Buenos Aires: Danilo Albero Vergara, 1992.

———. "*El penúltimo viaje* (A. Diaconú): La memoria de la fisura." In *Aventuras del desacuerdo: novelistas argentinas de los 80*, 11–16. Buenos Aires: Danilo Albero Vergara, 1992.

———. "En los nones de *Los años pares* (C. Absatz)." In *Aventuras del desacuerdo: novelistas argentinas de los 80*, 94–98. Buenos Aires: Danilo AlberoVergara, 1992.

———. "*La rompiente* (R. Roffé) o la integración en la escritura." In *Aventuras del desacuerdo: novelistas argentinas de los 80*, 186–90. Buenos Aires: Danilo Albero Vergara, 1992.

———. "*Los ojos azules* (A. Diaconú): La descompaginación de los roles." In *Aventuras del desacuerdo: novelistas argentinas de los 80*, 32–38. Buenos Aires: Danilo Albero Vergara, 1992.

———. "Para eso está hecha la noche (A. Diaconú): *Cama de ángeles*." In *Aventuras del desacuerdo: novelistas argentinas de los 80*, 163–74. Buenos Aires: Danilo Albero Vergara, 1992.

———. "Utopías, ojos azules y bocas suicidas: un diálogo posible entre las novelas de Alina Diaconú." In *Utopías, ojos azules, bocas suicidas: la narrativa de Alina Diaconú*, edited by Ester Gimbernat González and Cynthia Tompkins, 37–52. Buenos Aires: Editorial Fraterna, 1993.

Gimbernat González, Ester, and Cynthia Tompkins, eds. *Utopías, ojos azules, bocas suicidas: la narrativa de Alina Diaconú*. Buenos Aires: Editorial Fraterna, 1993.

Goldar, Ernesto. *El peronismo en la literatura argentina*. Buenos Aires: Freeland, 1971.

González, Patricia Elena, and Eliana Ortega, eds. *La sartén por el mango: encuentro de escritoras latinoamericanas*. Río Piedras: Ediciones Huracán, 1985.

Gramuglio, María Teresa. "Aproximaciones a *La rompiente*." Postliminal study of *La rompiente*, by Reina Roffé. Buenos Aires: Ediciones Puntosur, 1987.

Graziano, Frank. *Divine Violence: Spectacle, Psychosexuality, and Radical Christianity in the Argentine "Dirty War."* Boulder, Colo.: Westview Press, 1992.

Gregorich, Luis. "La nueva generación de izquierda y el peronismo." *Cuaderno crítico* 2 (1965): 1–13.

———. "Literatura: una descripción del campo: Narrativa, periodismo, ideología." In *Represión y reconstrucción de una cultura: el caso argentino*, compiled by Saúl Sosnowski, 109–24. Buenos Aires: Editorial Universitaria de Buenos Aires, 1988.

Gudiño Kieffer, Eduardo. "Letter from Buenos Aires." *Review* 15 (1975): 85–88.

Guerra-Cunningham, Lucía. "Rite of Passage: Latin American Women Writers Today." In *Splintering Darkness: Latin American Women Writers in Search of Themselves*, edited by Lucía Guerra-Cunningham, 5–16. Pittsburgh, Pa.: Latin American Literary Review Press, 1990.

———, ed. *Mujer y sociedad en América Latina*. Irvine: University of California, 1980.

———. *Splintering Darkness: Latin American Women Writers in Search of Themselves*. Pittsburgh, Pa.: Latin American Literary Review Press, 1990.

Halperin Donghi, Tulio. "El presente transforma el pasado: el impacto del reciente terror en la imagen de la historia argentina." In *Ficción y política: la narrativa argentina durante el proceso militar*, edited by Daniel Balderston, David William Foster, Tulio Halperin Donghi, Francine Masiello, Marta Morello-Frosch, and Beatriz Sarlo, 71–95. Buenos Aires: Alianza Editorial, 1987.

———. "Estilos nacionales de institucionalización de la cultura e impacto de la represión: Argentina y Chile." In *Represión y reconstrucción de una cultura: el caso argentino*, compiled by Saúl Sosnowski, 27–48. Buenos Aires: Editorial Universitaria de Buenos Aires, 1988.

Hecker, Liliana. "Los intelectuales ante la instancia del exilio: militancia y creación." In *Represión y reconstrucción de una cultura: el caso argentino*, compiled by Saúl

Sosnowski, 195–202. Buenos Aires: Editorial Universitaria de Buenos Aires, 1988.

Hicks, D. Emily. *Border Writing: The Multidimensional Text.* Minneapolis: University of Minnesota Press, 1991.

Jaquette, Jane S., ed. *The Women's Movement in Latin America: Feminism and the Transition to Democracy.* Boston: Unwin Hyman, 1989.

Jitrik, Noé. *El escritor argentino: dependencia o libertad.* Buenos Aires: Ediciones del Candil, 1967.

———. *Ensayos y estudios de literatura argentina.* Buenos Aires: Editorial Galerna, 1970.

———*La nueva promoción.* Buenos Aires: Ediciones Biblioteca San Martín, 1959.

———. "Miradas desde el borde: el exilio y la literatura argentina." In *Represión y reconstrucción de una cultura: el caso argentino,* compiled by Saúl Sosnowski, 133–48. Buenos Aires: Editorial Universitaria de Buenos Aires, 1988.

Jofre Barroso, Haydée M. "Un casi reportaje al escritor argentino." *Mundo nuevo* 51–52 (September-October 1970): 45–52.

Keefe Ugalde, Sharon. "Process, Identity and Learning to Read: Female Writing and Feminist Criticism in Latin America Today." *Latin American Research Review* 24 (1989): 223–32.

King, John, and Nissa Torrents, eds. *The Garden of the Forking Paths: Argentine Cinema.* London: British Film Institute, 1988.

Kirkpatrick, Jeane. *Leader and Vanguard in Mass Society: A Study of Peronist Argentina.* Cambridge: MIT Press, 1971.

Kolodny, Annette. "Some Notes on Defining Feminist Literary Criticism." *Critical Inquiry* 2 (Autumn 1983): 75–92.

Koppelman Cornillon, Susan, ed. *Images of Women in Fiction: Feminist Perspectives.* Bowling Green, Ohio: Bowling Green University Popular Press, 1973.

Kovadloff, Santiago. "Por un futuro imperfecto." In *Represión y reconstrucción de una cultura: el caso argentino,* compiled by Saúl Sosnowski, 229–32. Buenos Aires: Editorial Universitaria de Buenos Aires, 1988.

Kristeva, Julia. *Pouvoirs de l'horreur: essai sur l'abjection.* Paris: Editions du Seuil, 1980.

Lafforgue, Jorge. "La narrativa argentina (Estos diez años: 1975–1984)." In *Represión y reconstrucción de una cultura: el caso argentino,* compiled by Saúl Sosnowski, 149–66. Buenos Aires: Editorial Universitaria de Buenos Aires, 1988.

———, ed. *Nueva novela latinoamericana.* 2 vols. Buenos Aires: Editorial Paidós, 1972.

Lagmanovich, David. "La narrativa argentina de 1960 a 1970." *Nueva narrativa hispanoamericana* 2 (January 1972): 99–117.

Lauter, Estella. *Women as Mythmakers: Poetry and Visual Arts by Twentieth-Century Women.* Bloomington: Indiana University Press, 1984.

Lewald, H. Ernest. *Argentina: análisis y autoanálisis.* Buenos Aires: Editorial Sudamericana, 1969.

———. "The Literary and Social Scene in the River Plate." *World Literature Today* 39 (1975): 61–65.

————. "Two Generations of River Plate Women Writers." *Latin American Research Review* 15 (1980): 231–36.

————, ed. *The Web: Stories by Argentine Women*. Washington D.C.: Three Continents Press, 1983.

Libertella, Héctor. "Algo sobre la novísima literatura argentina." *Vórtice* 1 (1974): 10–16.

Lichtblau, Myron I. "La representación novelística de la época de Perón." *Armas y letras* 4 (1961): 77–85.

Lindstrom, Naomi. "Changing Research Approaches to the Analysis of Innovative Argentine Texts." *Review of Bibliography* 35, no. 3 (1985): 314–24.

————. "Feminist Criticism of Latin American Literature: Bibliographic Notes." *Latin American Research Review* 15 (1980): 151–59.

————. *Jewish Issues in Argentine Literature: From Gernuchoff to Szichman*. Columbia: University of Missouri Press, 1989.

————. *Literary Expressionism in Argentina*. Tempe: Center for Latin American Studies, Arizona State University, 1977.

Lipp, Solomon. "Jewish Themes and Authors in Contemporary Argentine Fiction." In *El Cono Sur: dinámica y dimensiones de su literatura*, edited by Rose S. Minc, 49–55. Upper Montclair, N.J.: Montclair State College, 1985.

López Morales, Berta. "Language of the Body in Women's Texts." In *Splintering Darkness: Latin American Women Writers in Search of Themselves*, edited by Lucía Guerra-Cunningham, 123–30. Pittsburgh, Pa.: Latin American Literary Review Press, 1990.

Lorenzo Alcalá, May, ed. *Cuentos de la crisis*. Buenos Aires: Editorial Celtia, 1986.

Magnarelli, Sharon. *The Lost Rib: Female Characters in the Spanish-American Novel*. Lewisburg, Pa.: Bucknell University Press, 1985.

————. *Reflections/Refractions: Reading Luisa Valenzuela*. New York: Peter Lang, 1988.

Manguel, Alberto, ed. *Other Fires: Short Fiction by Latin American Women*. New York: Clarkson N. Potter Publishers, 1986.

Manzor-Coats, Liliana. "The Reconstructed Subject: Women's Testimonials as Voices of Resistance." In *Splintering Darkness: Latin American Women Writers in Search of Themselves*, edited by Lucía Guerra-Cunningham, 157–71. Pittsburgh, Pa.: Latin American Review Press, 1990.

Marbán, Jorge. "Estructura y simbolismo en *El penúltimo viaje* de Alina Diaconú." *Confluencia* 7 (Spring 1992): 131–35.

————. "Visión de lo cotidiano y perspectiva existencial en la cuentística de Alina Diaconú." In *Utopías, ojos azules, bocas suicidas: la narrativa de Alina Diaconú*, edited by Ester Gimbernat González and Cynthia Tompkins, 23–34. Buenos Aires: Editorial Fraterna, 1993..

Marengo de Caminotti, Delia. "La mujer: personaje en la novela." *Revista de la Universidad Nacional de Córdoba* 10 (March-June 1969): 339–61.

Martínez, Tomas Eloy. "El lenguaje de la inexistencia." In *Represión y reconstrucción de una cultura: el caso argentino*, compiled by Saúl Sosnowski, 187–94. Buenos Aires: Editorial Universitaria de Buenos Aires, 1988.

Martínez, Zulma N. "La mujer, la creatividad y el eterno presente." *Revista ibero-americana* 51 (July-December 1985): 799–806.

Martini Real, J. C. "Especificidad, alusiones y saber de una escritura." In *Represión y reconstrucción de una cultura: el caso argentino,* compiled by Saúl Sosnowski, 125–32. Buenos Aires: Editorial Universitaria de Buenos Aires, 1988.

———"Prologo." Foreword to *Llamado al puf,* by Reina Roffé. Buenos Aires: Ediciones Pleamar, 1973.

Masiello, Francine. *Between Civilization and Barbarism: Women, Nation, and Literary Culture in Modern Argentina.* Lincoln: University of Nebraska Press, 1992.

———. "Contemporary Argentine Fiction: Liberal (Pre-)Texts in a Reign of Terror." *Latin American Literary Review* 16 (1981): 218–24.

———. "Cuerpo/presencia: mujer y estado social en la narrativa argentina durante el proceso militar." *Nuevo texto crítico* 4 (July-December 1989): 155–71.

———. "*En breve cárcel:* la producción del sujeto." In *El Cono Sur: dinámica y dimensiones de su literatura,* edited by Rose S. Minc, 220–29. Upper Montclair, N.J.: Montclair State University, 1985.

———. "La Argentina durante el Proceso: las múltiples resistencias de la cultura." Translated from the English by Eduardo Paz Leston. In *Ficción y política: la narrativa argentina durante el proceso militar,* edited by Daniel Balderston, David William Foster, Tulio Halperin Donghi, Francine Masiello, Marta Morello-Frosch, and Beatriz Sarlo, 11–29. Buenos Aires: Alianza Editorial, 1987.

———. "Subversions of Authority: Feminist Literary Culture in the River Plate Region." *Chasqui: revista de literatura latinoamericana* 21 (May 1992): 39–47.

——— "Texto, ley, transgresión: especulación sobre de la novela (feminista) de vanguardia." *Revista iberoamericana* 51 (July-December 1985): 807–22.

———. "Women, State, and Family in Latin American Literature of the 1920s." In *Women, Culture, and Politics in Latin America,* 27–47. Seminar on Feminism and Culture in Latin America. Berkeley and Los Angeles: University of California Press, 1990.

Meyer, Doris. *Victoria Ocampo: Against the Wind and the Tide.* New York: George Braziller, 1979.

Meyer, Doris, and Marguerite Fernández Olmos, eds. *Contemporary Women Authors of Latin America.* 2 vols. Brooklyn, N.Y.: Brooklyn College Press, 1983.

Miller, Beth. *Mujeres en la literatura.* Mexico: Fleischer Editora, 1978.

———, ed. *Women in Hispanic Literature: Icons and Fallen Idols.* Berkeley: University of California Press, 1983.

Miller, Ivette E., and Charles M. Tatum, eds. *Latin American Women Writers: Yesterday and Today.* Pittsburgh, Pa.: The Review, 1977.

Minc, Rose S., ed. *The Contemporary Latin American Short Story.* New York: Senda Nueva de Ediciones, 1979.

———, ed. *El Cono Sur: dinámica y dimensiones de su literatura.* Upper Montclair, N.J.: Montclair State College, 1985.

———. *Número especial dedicado a las escritoras de la América Hispana.* Special issue of *Revista iberoamericana* 51 (July-December 1985).

Moctezuma, Edgardo. "Para mirar tan lejos antes de entrar: los usos del poder en *Aire tan dulce*, de Elvira Orphée." *Revista iberoamericana* 45 (October-December 1983): 929–42.

Mora, Gabriela, and Karen S. Van Hooft, eds. *Theory and Practice of Feminist Literary Criticism*. Ypsilanti, Mich.: Bilingual Press/Editorial Bilingüe, 1982.

Moraña, Mabel. *Memorias de la generación fantasma*. Montevideo: Monte Sexto, 1988.

Morello-Frosch, Marta. "Biografías fictivas: formas de resistencia y reflexión en la narrativa argentina reciente." In *Ficción y política: la narrativa argentina durante el proceso*, edited by Daniel Balderston, David William Foster, Tulio Halperin Donghi, Francine Masiello, Marta Morello-Frosch, and Beatriz Sarlo, 60–70. Buenos Aires: Alianza Editorial, 1987.

———. "La ficción de la historia en la narrativa argentina reciente." In *The Historical Novel in Latin America*, edited by Daniel Balderston, 201–8. Gaithersburg, Md.: Ediciones Hispamérica, 1986.

———. "Significación e historia en *Respiración artificial* de Ricardo Piglia." In *Fascismo y experiencia literaria: reflexiones para una recanonización*, edited by Hernán Vidal, 489–500. Monographic Series of the Society for the Study of Hispanic and Lusophone Revolutionary Literatures, no. 2. Minneapolis: Institute for the Study of Ideologies and Literature, 1985.

Muñoz, Elías Miguel. *El discurso utópico de la sexualidad en Manuel Puig*. Madrid: Editorial Pliegos, 1987.

———. "La búsqueda de un sexo 'verdadero': *Cama de ángeles* de Alina Diaconú." In *Utopías, ojos azules, bocas suicidas: la narrativa de Alina Diaconú*, edited by Ester Gimbernat González and Cynthia Tompkins, 95–104. Buenos Aires: Editorial Fraterna, 1993. First published in *Chasqui: revista de literatura latinoamericana* 21 (May 1992): 49–54.

Nash, June, and Helen Icken Safa, eds. *Sex and Class in Latin America: Women's Perspectives on Politics, Economics and Family in the Third World*. Brooklyn, N.Y.: Praeger, 1976.

Nash, June, Helen Icken Safa, and contributors. *Women and Change in Latin America*. South Hadley, Mass.: Bergin and Garvey, 1989.

Newman, Kathleen. *La violencia del discurso: el Estado autoritario y la novela política argentina*. Translated from the English by Beba Eguía. Buenos Aires: Catálogos Editora, 1991.

———. "The Modernization of Femininity: Argentina, 1916–26." In *Women, Culture, and Politics in Latin America*, 74–104. Seminar on Feminism and Culture in Latin America. Berkeley and Los Angeles: University of California Press, 1990.

Orgambide, Pedro F., and Roberto Yahni. *Enciclopedia de la literatura argentina*. Buenos Aires: Editorial Sudamericana, 1970.

Pagés Larraya, Antonio. "Buenos Aires en la novela." *Revista de la Universidad de Buenos Aires* 4 (January 1946): 253–75.

Paz, Octavio, ed. "Literatura argentina actual: Un panorama." *Vuelta sudamericana* 1 (March 1987): 5–66.

Pellerin, Gilles, and Oscar Hermes Villordo, eds. *Rencontres: Encuentros: Ecrivains et artistes de l'Argentine et du Québec/Escritores y artistas de Argentina y de Quebec*. Québec: Editions Sans Nom, 1989.

Peltzer, Federico J. "Panorama de la literatura argentina contemporánea." *Señales* 121 (1960): 5–11.

———. "Panorama de la última novelística argentina." *Cuadernos de idioma* 2 (1967): 53–96.

Pendle, George. *Argentina*. New York: Macmillan, 1957.

Pescatello, Ann. *Power and Pawn: The Female in Iberian Families, Societies and Cultures*. Westport, Conn.: Greenwood Press, 1976.

———, ed. *Female and Male in Latin America: Essays*. Pittsburgh, Pa.: University of Pittsburgh Press, 1973.

Pezzoni, Enrique. "La realidad argentina y sus actuales intérpretes." *Razón y fábula* 12 (1969): 112–18.

———. "Transgresión y normalización en la narrativa argentina contemporánea." *Revista de occidente* 100 (1971): 172–91.

Picon Garfield, Evelyn. "'Desprendida a hachazos de la eternidad': lo primordial en la obra de Elvira Orphée." *Journal of Latin American Lore* 5 (1979): 3–23.

———. "Elvira Orphée." In *Women's Voices from Latin America: Interviews with Six Contemporary Authors*, 97–113. Detroit, Mich.: Wayne State University Press, 1987.

———. *Women's Voices from Latin America: Interviews with Six Contemporary Authors*. Detroit, Mich.: Wayne State University Press, 1987.

———, ed. *Women's Voices from Latin America: Selections from Twelve Contemporary Authors*. Detroit, Mich.: Wayne State University Press, 1988.

Plotnik, Viviana. "Alegoría y Proceso de Reorganización Nacional: Propuesta de una categoría de mediación socio-histórica para el análisis discursivo." In *Fascismo y experiencia literaria: reflexiones para una recanonización*, edited by Hernán Vidal, 532–77. Monographic Series of the Society for the Study of Hispanic and Lusophone Revolutionary Literatures, no. 2. Minneapolis: Institute for the Study of Ideologies and Literature, 1985.

Poletti, Syria. "Apuntes para la valorización de las novelistas argentinas actuales." *Davar* 101 (1965): 64–68.

Portantiero, Juan Carlos. *Realismo y realidad en la narrativa argentina*. Buenos Aires: Editorial Procyon, 1961.

Portnoy, Alicia. *The Little School: Tales of Disappearance and Survival in Argentina*. San Francisco: Cleis Press, 1986.

———, ed. *You Can't Drown the Fire: Latin American Women Writing in Exile*. Pittsburgh, Pa.: Cleis Press, 1988.

Pratt, Annis, Barbara White, Andrea Loewenstein, and Mary Wyer. *Archetypal Patterns in Women's Fiction*. Bloomington: Indiana University Press, 1981.

Prieto, Adolfo. "Los años sesenta." *Revista iberoamericana* 125 (October-December 1983): 889–901.

Rama, Angel. "Literature and Exile." *Review* 30 (September-December 1981): 10–13.

Reati, Fernando. "Literatura argentina de la 'guerra sucia': el paradigma de espacio invadido." *Texto crítico* 14 (December 1988): 26–36.

———. *Nombrar lo innombrable: violencia política y novela argentina, 1975–1985*. Buenos Aires: Editorial Legasa, 1992.

Richter Martínez, Marily. "Textualizaciones de la violencia: *Informe bajo llave* de Marta Lynch y *La rompiente* de Reina Roffé." Berlin: Freie Universität Berlin. Forthcoming.

Riquelme Rojas, Sonia, and Edna Aguirre Rehbein, eds. *Critical Approaches to Isabel Allende's Novels*. New York: Peter Lang, 1991.

Rodríguez Monegal, Emir. *El juicio de los parricidas: la nueva generación argentina y sus maestros*. Buenos Aires: Editorial Deucalión, 1956.

———. *Jorge Luis Borges: A Literary Biography*. 1st paperback ed. New York: Paragon House, 1977.

Roffé, Reina. "Diversidad y dispersión en la narrativa argentina actual." In *El Cono Sur: dinámica y dimensiones de su literatura*, edited by Rose S. Minc, 146–52. Upper Montclair, N.J.: Montclair State College, 1985.

———. "Los textos: itinerario de una escritura." Foreword to *La rompiente*, by Reina Roffé. Buenos Aires: Puntosur Editores, 1987.

———."Omnipresencia de la censura en la Argentina." *Revista iberoamericana* 51 (July-December 1985): 909–15.

Ross, Kathleen, and Ivette E. Miller, eds. *Scents of Wood and Silence: Short Stories by Latin American Women Writers*. Special issue of *Latin American Literary Review* 19 (January-June 1991).

Rozitchner, León. "Exilio: guerra y democracia: una secuencia ejemplar." In *Represión y reconstrucción de una cultura: el caso argentino*, compiled by Saúl Sosnowski, 167–86. Buenos Aires: Editorial Universitaria de Buenos Aires, 1988.

Sábato, Ernesto. *La cultura en la encrucijada nacional*. Buenos Aires: Editorial Sudamericana, 1982.

Sarlo, Beatriz. "El campo intelectual: un espacio doblemente fracturado." In *Represión y reconstrucción de una cultura: el caso argentino*, compiled by Saúl Sosnowski, 96–107. Buenos Aires: Editorial Universitaria de Buenos Aires, 1988.

———. "Política, ideología y figuración literaria." In *Ficción y política: la narrativa argentina durante el proceso militar*, edited by Daniel Balderston, David William Foster, Tulio Halperin Donghi, Francine Masiello, Marta Morello-Frosch, and Beatriz Sarlo, 30–59. Buenos Aires: Alianza Editorial, 1987.

Scobie, James. *Argentina: A City, a Nation*. New York: Oxford University Press, 1964.

Senkman, Leonardo. "De la legitimación del israelita argentino a la asunción de la identidad de algunos escritores judeoargentinos." In *El Cono Sur: dinámica y dimensiones de su literatura*, edited by Rose S. Minc, 56–71. Upper Montclair, N.J.: Montclair State College, 1985.

———. *La identidad judía en la literatura argentina*. Buenos Aires: Editorial Pardes, 1983.

Showalter, Elaine. *A Literature of Their Own: Women Novelists from Brontë to Lessing*. Princeton: Princeton University Press, 1977.

———. *The New Feminist Criticism: Essays on Women, Literature and Theory*. New York: Pantheon, 1985.

Shumway, Nicolas. "Apuntes sobre el revisionismo crítico en la Argentina." In *El Cono Sur: dinámica y dimensiones de su literatura*, edited by Rose S. Minc, 153–57. Upper Montclair, N.J.: Montclair State College, 1985.

Simpson, John, and Jana Benett. *The Disappeared and the Mothers of the Plaza.* New York: St. Martin's Press, 1985.

Solari Irigoyen, Hipólito. "Antidemocracia y democracia en la Argentina." In *Represión y reconstrucción de una cultura: el caso argentino,* compiled by Saúl Sosnowski, 19–26. Buenos Aires: Editorial Universitaria de Buenos Aires, 1988.

Sontag, Susan. *Illness as Metaphor.* New York: Farrar, Straus and Giroux, 1977.

Sosnowski, Saúl. "Alicia Steimberg: Enhebrando pequeñas historias." *Essays on Foreign Languages and Literatures* 17 (1987): 104–10.

———. "La dispersión de las palabras: novelas y novelistas argentinos de la década del setenta." *Revista iberoamericana* 49 (October-December 1983): 955–63.

———, comp. *Represión y reconstrucción de una cultura: el caso argentino.* Buenos Aires: Editorial Universitaria de Buenos Aires, 1988.

———, ed. *La orilla inminente: escritores judíos argentinos.* Buenos Aires: Editorial Legasa, 1987.

Stabb, Martin S. "Argentine Letters and the Peronato: An Overview." *Journal of Interamerican Studies* 13 (July-October 1971): 434–55.

Suleiman, Susan Rubin. *Subversive Intent. Gender, Politics, and the Avant-Garde.* Cambridge: Harvard University Press, 1990.

Szurmuk, Mónica. "La textualización de la represión en *La rompiente* de Reina Roffé." *Nuevo texto crítico* 3 (1990): 123–31.

Taylor, Julie M. *Eva Perón: The Myths of a Woman.* Chicago: University of Chicago Press, 1979.

Timmerman, Jacobo. *Prisoner Without a Name, Cell Without a Number.* New York: Knopf, 1981.

Tjarks, Alicia V. de. "Participación de la mujer en el proceso histórico latinoamericano." *Revista de la Universidad Nacional de Córdoba* 10 (March-June 1969): 153–82.

Tompkins, Cynthia. "La posmodernidad de *Cama de ángeles.*" In *Utopías, ojos azules, bocas suicidas: la narrativa de Alina Diaconú,* edited by Ester Gimbernat González and Cynthia Tompkins, 107–20. Buenos Aires: Editorial Fraterna, 1993.

Verbitzky, Bernardo. *Literatura y conciencia nacional.* Buenos Aires: Editorial Paidós, 1975.

———. "Proposiciones para un mejor planteo de nuestra literatura." *Ficción* 12 (1958): ·3–20.

Verdugo, Iber H. "Testimonio y denuncia en la literatura argentina." *Aportes* 8 (1968): 39–87.

Vidal, Hernán. "Hacia un modelo general de la sensibilidad social literaturizable bajo el fascismo." In *Fascismo y experiencia literaria: reflexiones para una recanonización,* edited by Hernán Vidal, 1–63. Monographic Series of the Society for the Study of Contemporary Hispanic and Lusophone Literatures, no. 2. Minneapolis: Institute for the Study of Ideologies and Literature, 1985.

———, ed. *Fascismo y experiencia literaria: reflexiones para una recanonización.* Monographic Series of the Society for the Study of Contemporary Hispanic and Lusophone Revolutionary Literatures, no. 2. Minneapolis: Institute for the Study of Ideologies and Literature, 1985.

Vigillo, Carmelo, and Naomi Lindstrom, eds. *Woman as Myth and Metaphor in Latin American Literature*. Columbia: University of Missouri Press, 1985.

Viñas, David. "Después de Cortázar: historia y privatización." *Cuadernos hispanoamericanos* 78 (June 1969): 734–39.

———. *Literatura argentina y realidad política*. Buenos Aires: Editorial Jorge Alvarez, 1964.

Viñas, Ismael. "Algunas reflexiones en torno a las perspectivas de nuestra literatura." *Ficción* 15 (September-October 1958): 6–21.

Women, Culture, and Politics in Latin America. Seminar on Feminism and Culture in Latin America. Berkeley and Los Angeles: University of California Press, 1990.

Index

283